Feel free to put your initials on
this card to show that you
have read this book.

The Library Store   #47-0103

LIVING WITH GUNS

LIVING
WITH
GUNS

A LIBERAL'S CASE

for the

SECOND AMENDMENT

Craig R. Whitney

PUBLICAFFAIRS
New York

Copyright © 2012 by Craig R. Whitney.

Published in the United States by PublicAffairs™, a Member of the Perseus
Books Group
All rights reserved.

Printed in the United States of America.

No part of this book may be reproduced in any manner whatsoever without written permission except in the case of brief quotations embodied in
critical articles and reviews. For information, address PublicAffairs, 250
West 57th Street, 15th Floor, New York, NY 10107.

PublicAffairs books are available at special discounts for bulk purchases in
the U.S. by corporations, institutions, and other organizations. For more
information, please contact the Special Markets Department at the
Perseus Books Group, 2300 Chestnut Street, Suite 200, Philadelphia, PA
19103, call (800) 810-4145, ext. 5000, or e-mail
special.markets@perseusbooks.com.

Book Design by Timm Bryson

Library of Congress Cataloging-in-Publication Data
Whitney, Craig R., 1943–
    Living with guns : a liberal's case for the Second Amendment / Craig Whitney.
        p. cm.
    Includes bibliographical references and index.
    ISBN 978-1-61039-169-6 (hardback) — ISBN 978-1-61039-170-2 (e-book)
1. Firearms—Law and legislation—United States. 2. Gun control—United States.
3. United States. Constitution. 2nd Amendment. I. Title.

KF3941.W4425 2012
323.4'3—dc23

                                                                    2012028556

First Edition

10 9 8 7 6 5 4 3 2 1

CONTENTS

CHAPTER SEVEN

THE THINKING BEHIND GUN RIGHTS

191

CHAPTER EIGHT

WHAT CAN BE DONE

209

A well regulated Militia, being necessary to the security of a free State, the right of the people to keep and bear Arms, shall not be infringed.

SECOND AMENDMENT TO THE
CONSTITUTION OF THE UNITED STATES,
RATIFIED AS PART OF THE BILL OF RIGHTS, 1791

To trust arms in the hands of the people at large has, in Europe, been believed, and so far as I am informed universally, to be an experiment fraught only with danger. Here by a long trial it has been proved to be perfectly harmless; neither public nor private evils having ever flowed from this source, except in instances of too little moment to deserve any serious regard.... The difficulty here has been to persuade the citizens to keep arms, not to prevent them from being employed for violent purposes.

TIMOTHY DWIGHT IV, *TRAVELS IN
NEW-ENGLAND AND NEW-YORK*, 1823

Undoubtedly some think that the Second Amendment is outmoded in a society where our standing army is the pride of our Nation, where well-trained police forces provide personal security, and where gun violence is a serious problem. That is perhaps debatable, but what is not debatable is that it is not the role of this Court to pronounce the Second Amendment extinct.

JUSTICE ANTONIN SCALIA,
US SUPREME COURT, MAJORITY OPINION IN
DISTRICT OF COLUMBIA V. HELLER, 2008

From 1993 to 1997, there were 180,533 firearm-related deaths in the United States, an average of over 36,000 per year. Fifty-one percent were suicides, 44 percent were homicides, 1 percent were legal interventions, 3 percent were unintentional accidents, and 1 percent were of undetermined causes.... In my view, there simply is no untouchable constitutional right guaranteed by the Second Amendment to keep loaded handguns in the house in crime-ridden urban areas.

JUSTICE STEPHEN G. BREYER,
US SUPREME COURT, DISSENTING OPINION IN
DISTRICT OF COLUMBIA V. HELLER, 2008

INTRODUCTION

Mention the Second Amendment, and all too often, people reach for their revolvers. Discussion degenerates into a hysteria that may win elections for hard-liners and fund lobbying campaigns but changes nothing. *Living with Guns* is my attempt to defuse that hysteria.

Americans on both sides of the debate about guns can and must find common ground. We can only begin to claim it by reexamining the right to bear arms, what it means, why it was enshrined in the Bill of Rights, and how it came to be misunderstood. The bottom line is that our national affinity for firearms isn't going away, no matter what anti-gun advocates would like to think. True believers in gun rights may not have all the answers, but they are certainly right about one thing: We *can* live with guns. We have no other choice, with so many of them around.

Do Americans have an individual constitutional right to own and use guns? *Living with Guns* maintains that the Second Amendment recognizes that they do have that individual right. A conservative majority of the Supreme Court has said they do, too, in two 5–4 rulings in 2008 and 2010 against handgun bans in Washington, DC, and Chicago. The Court went further, finding that the Second Amendment gave Americans that right primarily for self-defense. Many state legislatures around the country say Americans have an individual right to firearms; all states but Illinois, plus the District of Columbia and some cities, like New York, allow carrying of handguns in most places. "Stand-your-ground" or "castle-doctrine" laws in many states make it easier to legally justify killing in self-defense. Yet the constitutional right to bear arms does not make people who carry guns a law unto themselves.

George Zimmerman, the neighborhood-watch-patrol volunteer who shot a seventeen-year-old black teenager in February 2012 as he was walking back to his father's girlfriend's home in a gated community in Sanford, Florida, told police that he used the 9-mm semi-automatic pistol, which he had a license to carry, in self-defense. The boy attacked him and was pounding his head into the ground face-first, putting him in mortal fear for his life, he claimed.

But standing police instructions to Zimmerman and all other neighborhood volunteers in Sanford are that volunteers have no business carrying guns when they are on patrol. Zimmerman reported the teenager, walking through the rain with his hoodie up, as a suspicious possible intruder, and then acknowledged to a police dispatcher that he had left his car to follow the boy after he started running. "OK, we don't need you to do that," the dispatcher told Zimmerman, who replied, "OK."

If George Zimmerman had followed these instructions and stayed in his vehicle, Trayvon Martin would still be alive today, and Zimmerman would not have been charged with second-degree murder, facing a possible sentence of life in prison if convicted. He had, of course, a constitutional right to bear arms—a uniquely American right, but one that is subject to reasonable regulation in the interest of public safety. It is also a right that, from its origins in colonial days, has always been connected with civic duty.

There are 300 million guns in America today, about 100 million of them handguns, and probably at least 60 million gun owners. Yet, to listen to the National Rifle Association and the Republican Party in the 2012 election campaign, you would think Second Amendment rights were hanging by a thread. Mitt Romney warned that the Supreme Court could reverse itself if President Barack Obama were reelected and got a chance to pack the Court with liberal justices who would rule in favor of strict gun control. In contrast, he promised, he would be a president who would protect Second Amendment rights and stand up for hunters and "those who seek to protect their homes and families." Obama had said little about gun rights in four years in the White House, but conservatives and the NRA worked themselves into a lather over Attorney General Eric Holder, accusing him of being a lifelong "anti-gun extremist" and of using concerns about Mexican drug cartels smuggling guns across the border as a pretext for imposing new restrictions on American gun owners. The frenzy built in 2011 after a botched federal sting operation called "Fast and Furious" that allowed some gun dealers to sell arms to suspected smugglers in hopes of tracing them to the cartels in Mexico. Instead, the authorities lost track of them, and two of the weapons turned up at the scene of the killing of a border patrol agent in a shootout near the border in Arizona in late 2010. Holder told a congressional hearing he could not explain how it happened, and the Justice Department started requiring licensed firearms dealers in the four Southwest border states to report all multiple rifle purchases—law-abiding gun users and straw men for smugglers alike.

After the 2012 election, the gun wars that have been going on since the 1960s seem likely to continue, unless something happens to change the way both liberals and conservatives, supporters of gun rights and proponents of gun control, look at each other's positions on this issue.

Living with Guns offers a different way of looking at the Second Amendment, one that might make it easier for both sides to find common ground, if our political leaders would stop listening to lobbyists who pander to fears—whether fear of guns or fear of losing the right the Second Amendment protects—and start trying instead to find realistic solutions to the real gun problems we have.

Motivated by curiosity about how the Second Amendment came to be appended to the Constitution, in 2009 I began conducting extensive historical research. It came as a surprise even to me, as a conservative liberal (if there is such a thing), when I came to the conclusion that the Second Amendment did, indeed, recognize an individual right to own and use firearms for self-defense, hunting, or any other lawful purpose that Americans have been exercising since Jamestown and Plymouth Rock. But I also found that with the right came a civic duty, which was then to use those firearms in the common defense when called upon. Notably absent in the current stalemated debate about the Second Amendment is any sense of obligation, of civic duty, connected with the right to bear arms today— yet surely there is such a duty, to exercise the right responsibly and not recklessly. Keeping guns out of the hands of as many law-abiding citizens as possible is not the right way to encourage fulfillment of that duty, any more than arming as many of them as possible is the right way to control violent crime.

I am no lawyer or scholar of constitutional law; I am no Supreme Court justice. I have no gun in this fight. I grew up with friends in a (then-) small town in central Massachusetts who enjoyed hunting and fishing and had guns, but my family did not live in the country and could not afford rifles. I acquired some familiarity with arms when I served in the US Navy during the Vietnam War, and I carried a .45 pistol for a year while stationed in Saigon. I would be the last person to argue that this made me, a navy public affairs officer, an expert on small arms. Later, when I was a foreign correspondent for the *New York Times* in Saigon, Germany, Moscow, Paris, and London, the way Americans so furiously raged with each other about guns baffled me as much as it baffled people in the countries I covered. I have never felt the need for a firearm to defend myself or my family during the twenty years, off and on, that I have lived in New York City as a reporter and editor.

But if I did, I would have almost no chance of getting a permit to carry a handgun on the street, and little chance of getting one to have only in my apartment. Why not? Because I wouldn't be able to demonstrate to the police that I have a need for it, and they have almost complete discretion in deciding who gets a permit. I don't run a risky business like transporting diamonds through the streets—I'm not in the jewelry business and I'm not a Brink's guard.

This is a strange state of affairs for a constitutional amendment that is part of the Bill of Rights. Consider that I don't have to demonstrate a need for my First Amendment right of free speech. I don't have to demonstrate a need for my Fifth Amendment right not to be compelled to incriminate myself, or for my Sixth Amendment right to a speedy trial. Why should I have to demonstrate a need for my Second Amendment right, the right of the people to keep and use arms?

Liberals would counter that it's just too dangerous for so many people to have guns, and that really only the police should have them. Supporters of strict gun control (like New York City's mayor Michael Bloomberg) argue that times have changed since the Bill of Rights was ratified in 1791, and that in a country where 30,000 people a year are killed by gunfire (over half of them suicides), the right of the general public to live in safety is paramount. Others, long supported by the few Supreme Court rulings on the Second Amendment before 2008, would argue that it did not give anyone the constitutional right to keep and bear arms except in some sort of connection with volunteer military service in the "militia," whose preservation by the states was the amendment's original purpose, designed to thwart any attempted imposition of federal tyranny by a standing army.

Conservatives and supporters of gun rights take a very different view. Today, after decades of turbulent change, a revolution in race relations, urban riots, and court rulings circumscribing the powers of the police, they believe that law-abiding Americans are entitled to guns to protect themselves against violent crime, and that they have a duty only to themselves and their families. The assassinations of President John F. Kennedy, his brother Robert Kennedy, and Martin Luther King Jr., and repeated mass shootings have not convinced them otherwise. With "concealed carrying" allowed in all or parts of every state but Illinois, conservatives in both the House and Senate in Washington have been pushing hard for a national law to allow people to take concealed weapons with them across state lines, as long as they observe local regulations. The House passed such a bill in November 2011. If such a law were passed and signed by the president, it would still bar concealed carrying in places where local laws don't allow it, such as Illinois, the District of Columbia, and New York City, and in places where guns are forbidden, such as airports and schools, but who knows how many people might forget these distinctions or think they no longer applied?

Liberals can point out that violent crime has been receding nationwide, steadily and dramatically, over the past decade and more (rejecting conservative claims that it is actually all those state laws permitting people to carry pistols that have deterred much crime). Liberals argue that only tighter restrictions that prevent as many people as possible from owning guns—law-abiding people as well as criminals—can stop the almost daily shootings in our city streets, and our periodic mass murders.

An effective ban on possession of handguns was the way both the District of Columbia and the city of Chicago tried to deal with their gun violence problems—until the 5–4 conservative majority opinion in *District of Columbia et al. v. Heller* in 2008, written by Justice Antonin Scalia, overturned the ban. The Second Amendment right is an individual right, the Court ruled, and you don't have to be part of any militia to exercise it. Gun control is not unconstitutional, but banning a complete class of guns commonly used for self-defense is. Gun rights could clash with the right to public safety, the Court said: "Nothing in our opinion should be taken to cast doubt on longstanding prohibitions on the possession of firearms by felons and the mentally ill, or laws forbidding the carrying of firearms in sensitive places such as schools and government buildings, or laws imposing conditions and qualifications on the commercial sale of arms."

Liberals and others dismayed by the *Heller* decision feared that it would set off a tsunami of challenges to gun regulations nationwide. The very day it came down, on June 29, 2008, Otis McDonald, a retired African American man who wanted a pistol to defend himself in the crime-ridden Chicago inner-city neighborhood he lived in, and others filed a challenge to a handgun ban in Chicago that was very similar in its effect to the one in Washington. The case, *McDonald et al. v. City of Chicago, Illinois, et al.,* got to the Supreme Court after three federal appeals judges in Chicago upheld the ban on the basis of previous Supreme Court precedents they felt only the high court could overrule. And on June 28, 2010, the Supreme Court effectively agreed with McDonald and his supporters that the individual right to keep and bear arms was a right that all law-abiding American citizens have wherever in the United States they may live.

As Scalia wrote in *Heller,* the Constitution is not a document whose pieces we can just cut or chop off to suit changing conditions. Americans all have the same rights, though people in downtown New York City or Los Angeles may not all have the same attitudes about guns as people in Wyoming, Montana, or Maine (or even as people in upstate New York and the California Sierra Nevada). People who use shotguns and rifles for hunting or target practice look on firearms differently than people who fear for their safety or property and want pistols to ensure that they can deter criminals, or as a last resort to defend themselves. Firearms regulations cannot, need not, and should not be the same in the fields and forests of rural America as they are in violence-ridden inner cities awash in illegal guns.

But regulations also do not have to be deeply intrusive to be effective. Accomplishing the goal of keeping guns out of the hands of people who everybody agrees should not have them—not devising regulations that make it difficult for *anybody* to get hold of guns— should be the central purpose of firearms regulations. The regulations on the books to screen out unqualified buyers that Scalia pointed to are full of loopholes and not enforced in private gun sales—only in sales by federally licensed firearms dealers, which may be only about half of all gun sales. These rules should be tightened up and rigorously applied in sales of all kinds.

And, because it is true, as the NRA says, that "guns don't kill people—people do," the authorities need to work with neighborhoods and groups most prone to violent behavior to alter that behavior—to teach that, almost always, guns are not the solution to any dispute. Lawmakers should realize that despite what the NRA keeps screaming at them, it is not unconstitutional for Americans to expect to live in public safety, protected from gun violence.

Intelligent regulation designed to provide that protection can and should be focused more on human behavior and human needs than on the weapons themselves. Such regulation can be worked out, if gun owners collectively recognize the civic *responsibility* that, from the earliest colonial days, was always inseparable from the civic *right* to keep and bear arms.

What we can't do is remain stalemated. Those on the left can't continue to hold out hope for a gun-free America that won't ever come to be, and those on the right can't blind themselves to the responsibility that must be attached to gun ownership. If we continue to hang on to these illusions, the debate will never end. And if nothing at all is done, as seemed likely even after the deeply troubled James F. Holmes shot twelve people to death and wounded fifty-eight at the multiplex in Aurora, Colorado, in July 2012, it's always just going to be a matter of time until the next mass shooting.

CHAPTER ONE

THE GUN BATTLES OF OUR DAY

That's how cultural war works.
CHARLTON HESTON

America grew up with guns, my generation learned when we were kids in the 1950s. The West was won with guns, John Wayne and James Arness told us on screens big and small. *G Men, The Untouchables,* and *Bonnie and Clyde,* all seem pretty tame today, with movies that show bullets tearing into flesh and gore spurting out, or brains slowly sliding down blood-spattered walls after a shot to the head, in one film after another, not to speak of video games where you can inflict terminal injury yourself, at least on digital adversaries.

Entertainment aside, Americans identify themselves in part by metaphors and symbols based on firearms, and myths whose power derives from their basis in truth—the shot heard 'round the world, the Minutemen who won (or at least started) the Revolutionary War, Wild Bill Hickok and the gunslingers who tamed the West. Even our language smells of gunpowder. "She's a real pistol." "I've got him in my sights." "Half-cocked." "Loaded for bear." "Stick to your guns." "Under the gun." "Gun-shy." "Trigger-happy." "Lock, stock, and barrel." If it hadn't been for a .38 pistol that little Louis Armstrong found in his mother's trunk one Christmas week in New Orleans, we wouldn't have "Satchmo"—he was arrested for illegal possession of a firearm after firing off six blank shots one night during street celebrations and sentenced to the Colored Waifs' Home for Boys. There he learned to play the cornet, and changed the course of American music.[1]

In those days, a hundred years ago, gun rights were not the controversial subject they later became. Guns were in common use then, not just in New Orleans but all over America. Regulations abounded—state and local regulations, for safety and order—as they had since colonial days. The national problem of organized crime that arose in the wake of Prohibition prompted the first federal gun-control laws, but there was little public objection to keeping the mob from getting its hands on machine guns, which had not been used in militia service in the early days of the republic and therefore were considered not to be protected by the Second Amendment. The guns that were owned by civilians were, by and large, long guns, meaning rifles and shotguns, and they were used mainly for hunting. In the 1930s, long guns outnumbered handguns seven to one.[2]

Whether the global bloodletting of World War II had an effect on American thinking about arms for self-defense is unclear—though gun-rights activists nowadays often use the anti-Semitic laws passed by the Nazis to disarm Jews as an example of what could happen to Americans if their gun rights were taken away. It was not abuse of power by the federal government, however, but social stresses and strains that emerged in the turbulent 1960s that changed the way many Americans think about firearms.

The 1960s were the turning point for the cultural war over guns as we know it. By that decade, rising crime, increasing racial tensions in large cities, and a loss of public confidence in the ability or the willingness of the police to provide protection had led millions of Americans to buy weapons for personal protection, and the firearms industry met the increased demand. In 1951, domestically produced and imported handguns totaled 380,462. By 1965, that figure had more than doubled, to 973,823, and two years later it had risen to 1.6 million. Nearly half of those guns were cheap imports, "Saturday night specials." In 1968 alone, handgun imports rose to 1,155,368 (many if not most of those weapons were bought that year by Samuel Cummings, an international arms dealer, in anticipation that Congress would move to restrict them and that demand for already imported ones would soar), and total sales of handguns were about 2.5 million.

By 1969, a national commission estimated that there were 24 million handguns in private hands. And in those turbulent years of race riots and rising crime, more guns decidedly meant more homicides. In Detroit, for example, guns were involved in 39 percent of the 140 homicides in 1965; in 1968, a year after one of the most violent race riots in American history, the city had 389 murders, and guns were used in 72 percent of them.[3]

Congress was reluctant to pass gun laws that would be taken as a threat to the lawful use of weapons by ordinary Americans. The assassination of President John F. Kennedy in Dallas in 1963 did little to shake this reluctance, though it vividly dramatized the availability of dangerous firearms. Lee Harvey Oswald had mail-ordered the 6.5-mm Carcano rifle with telescopic sight that he used to kill the president, but though Congress was pressed in the aftermath of the assassination to ban mail-order sales of shotguns and rifles, the legislators would not do it.

Congress refused again after the assassination of Dr. Martin
Luther King Jr. in 1968. King himself was a polarizing figure in the
mid-1960s, when American society was in the throes of the greatest
racial, political, and social turmoil since the Great Depression. His
calls for nonviolent civil disobedience mobilized African Americans
all over the South to resist the many discriminatory laws that enforced segregation. Yet those years also inspired white fear. King's
calls for nonviolence contrasted with deeply unsettling racial trau-
mas like the riots in the Watts African American ghetto in Los Angeles in 1965 that killed thirty-seven people and did $40 million
worth of damage. Meanwhile, King's leadership in the civil rights
movement was under challenge by such apostles of violence as Malcolm X, who spoke out in Cleveland in 1964 with the message that
"it's time for Negroes to defend themselves. Article number two of
the constitutional amendments provides you and me the right to
own a rifle or a shotgun."[4] Activists such as Huey Newton and Bobby
Seale in Oakland, California, took the right seriously and required
recruits to their Black Panthers to be armed and to know how to use
firearms because "the gun is the only thing that will free us." In their
black uniforms, they carried their weapons openly, because California law required permits only for concealed carrying.

By early 1967, the Panthers were beginning to cow the Oakland
police, and on May 2 of that year, thirty of them, including six
women, showed up at the state capitol, openly carrying pistols and
shotguns—loaded, as the law then allowed in public places, as long
as they were not used to threaten anyone. They had chosen that day
because the legislature was debating a proposal backed by Don Mulford, a Republican assemblyman from the county that includes Oakland, to make it illegal to openly carry loaded guns within city limits.
Bobby Seale mounted the capitol steps to proclaim that it was time
"for black people to arm themselves" against what he called the terror

white America was inflicting on blacks everywhere. As Adam Winkler notes in his book *Gunfight: The Battle over the Right to Bear Arms in America,* "The Sacramento 'Invasion,' as the papers called it, was a huge success for the Panthers—and a historic event that came to define the bold, assertive protest mentality of late 1960s radicals. Their visit to the capitol made headlines across the country and television news broadcast film of the event over and over. . . . Whites were horrified and began to call for the government to take more aggressive action to stop the Panthers."[5] And the California legislature passed the Mulford Act, which provided a five-year jail term for anyone, white or black, caught carrying a loaded gun on a public street anytime after the moment Governor Ronald Reagan signed it on July 28, 1967—just after the deadliest race riot in American history in Detroit, where police and the National Guard came under fusillades of gunfire. The California law was not aimed at blacks, both Reagan and Mulford insisted. Nevertheless, it clearly was, and even though it also limited whites' gun rights, for a while the fear of violence—reinforced by the summer of racial violence made worse by the availability of Saturday night specials—began to carry the day.

King's assassination by a bullet fired from a .30-caliber rifle in April 1968 caused more deadly riots, in Washington and elsewhere, and by June of the same year, after Sirhan B. Sirhan shot Senator Robert F. Kennedy to death with a .22-caliber Iver Johnson Cadet 55-A revolver in the Ambassador Hotel ballroom in Los Angeles, public opinion, or at least the lawmakers' assessment of it, had shifted.

To many ordinary Americans, gun violence seemed to be running out of control. With so many assassinations, the riots, and racial unrest at a boiling point, the United States looked much like a Third World republic. Something had to be done. On June 6, the day of Kennedy's assassination, President Lyndon B. Johnson pleaded to

Congress "in the name of sanity, in the name of safety and in the name of an aroused nation to give America the gun-control law it needs," or at least one that could get through Congress. The following day, Congress responded by passing the Omnibus Crime Control and Safe Streets Act, which barred licensed dealers from filling mail orders for handguns (though Sirhan had not bought his gun by mail) and made it illegal for them to sell one to anyone under twenty-one.

The White House continued to press for stricter measures and was even able to get five Hollywood gunslingers, Charlton Heston, Kirk Douglas, Gregory Peck, James Stewart, and Hugh O'Brian, to endorse some of them. O'Brian read out the tough guys' plea on television, on *The Joey Bishop Show,* on June 18. "President John F. Kennedy was murdered by a rifle. Martin Luther King was murdered by a rifle. Medgar Evers was murdered by a rifle," viewers heard; the bill would not "deprive the sportsman of his hunting gun" or deny to "any responsible citizen his Constitutional right to own a firearm."[6] And all five—including Charlton Heston—subscribed to these words: "Our gun control laws are so lax that anyone can buy a weapon—the mentally ill, the criminal, the boy too young to bear the responsibility of owning a deadly weapon. Sixty-five hundred people are murdered every year with firearms in the United States. This is an outrage and when it is compared with the far, far lower rates in other free countries, it is intolerable. . . . The carnage will not stop until there is effective control over the sale of rifles and shotguns."[7]

And in October, Johnson was able to sign into law the Gun Control Act of 1968, mandating the federal licensing of individuals and companies selling firearms and establishing categories of people to whom licensed dealers could not sell firearms or ammunition. Guns and ammo could no longer be sold to convicted criminals, fugitives, users of illegal drugs, the mentally disturbed, illegal aliens, people subject to restraining orders, or people discharged less than honorably from the armed forces. The law established a minimum age of eighteen for ownership of long guns and confirmed that handgun buyers had to be at least twenty-one. It banned the importation of surplus military firearms, and made the Bureau of Alcohol, Tobacco and Firearms (ATF) responsible for enforcement.

Still, the 1968 act was hardly draconian. Anyone barred from buying a gun could still get one just by lying to the dealer, who was not obligated to do anything more than take the customer's word that he or she was not a criminal or a drug addict—though an illegal purchaser, if caught with a weapon, could then be prosecuted.

Nevertheless, a backlash was soon to come. If, as in the case of the Mulford Act, racism inspired gun laws that made it hard for blacks to arm themselves, whites soon discovered that those same laws applied just as much to them, and they began to fear losing their own gun rights. The backlash got a big boost in 1969 when the National Commission on the Causes and Prevention of Violence, established by President Johnson, made startling recommendations in its report, calling for the federal government and the states to confiscate 90 percent of the 24 million handguns then owned by private citizens and to prosecute anybody who refused an order to turn them in. The commission, with Milton S. Eisenhower in the chair, counted 8,000 firearms homicides annually at that time and recommended federal standards that would restrict ownership of handguns to people who could demonstrate "reasonable need" for them. "Serious efforts at state and local regulation have consistently been frustrated by the flow of firearms from one state to another," the report said, concluding:

> Our studies have convinced us that the heart of any effective national firearms policy for the United States must be to reduce the

availability of the firearm that contributes the most to violence. This means restrictive licensing of the handgun. . . . The challenge for this commission—and for the nation as a whole—is to find ways to cope with illegitimate uses of guns without at the same time placing undue restrictions on legitimate uses. We believe this is possible if both the advocates and the opponents of gun control legislation will put aside their suspicions and preconceptions, accept the fact of a common danger without exaggerating its dimensions and act for the common good.[8]

Nearly half a century later, it is easy to forget just how profoundly shaken the country was by the turbulence of the late 1960s and hard to understand what could have led the Eisenhower commission to such a radical conclusion. But things seemed to be spiraling out of control. There were: young people protesting against the Vietnam War. National guardsmen shooting to kill at Kent State. Race riots. A wave of violent big-city crime in the 1960s continued rising into the 1970s, not always connected with racial tensions, by any means. In New York City, the *New York Times* columnist David Brooks has recently recalled, "people in all classes lived in fear," with daily muggings, murders, and wasted neighborhoods that were no-go zones even for the police. "The crime wave killed off the hippie movement," Brooks wrote. "The hippies celebrated disorder, mayhem, and the whole Dionysian personal agenda. By the 1970s, the menacing results of that agenda were all around. . . . The crime wave eroded the sense of solidarity that existed after World War II. The rich isolated themselves. The middle classes moved to the suburbs."[9]

But by the time the Eisenhower commission submitted its recommendations, Richard M. Nixon was president. If confiscating handguns from law-abiding citizens who wanted to protect themselves wasn't the "undue restriction" the commission report said it wanted to try to avoid, such people asked themselves, then what was? Nixon's administration had no interest in implementing such measures, and no wonder—the "silent majority" was now mobilized and alarmed. All it wanted was protection. If government could not protect Americans from violence, government should not confiscate arms people could use to protect themselves from it. Handgun sales went soaring.

Congress, responsive to the backlash, soon began watering down various provisions of the 1968 Gun Control Act, exempting shotgun and high-powered rifle ammunition from regulation in late 1969, for example, because hunters were balking at regulation of guns used mainly for recreation. In the early 1970s, the ATF came to be seen as a meddlesome enforcer of laws that did little to keep things like Saturday night specials from proliferating but made it hard for people who lived in rural areas to acquire and keep guns. The NRA leadership that had supported the 1968 laws was overthrown and replaced by leaders who, starting in the mid-1970s, began calling for their repeal.

Little support for stronger gun controls was evident over the next few years, even after two attempts on President Gerald R. Ford's life in 1975, both by women armed with handguns. In 1976, in what supporters of gun rights came to regard as a major turning point, voters in Massachusetts—the only state (along with the District of Columbia) that had gone for George McGovern against Nixon in the 1972 presidential election—rejected a ban on handguns with a robust majority of 69 percent.

Eight years after the Gun Control Act, few on either side of the debate were satisfied with its effects. For all the changes it had made, what the 1968 act clearly did not do was reduce violent crime or deaths and injuries from firearms. By 1976, homicides involving firearms totaled nearly 12,000 a year, according to Federal Bureau of

Investigation figures, with suicides and accidents bringing the total number of annual deaths by firearms to about 25,000. After there were 235 murders, a record number, in the District of Columbia in 1974, 155 of them committed with handguns, the District Council began considering legislation to try to control this kind of violence and in 1976 adopted a complete ban on handguns in homes. People could have rifles or shotguns, but they had to keep them disassembled. As Winkler writes, "even if you owned a shotgun, you couldn't use it against a burglar coming through the window."[10]

Yet the DC lawmakers were under no illusion about how effective a ban in the district alone would be. The District of Columbia is a small and porous place where burglars would have no problem bringing in firearms, legally or illegally, from neighboring Virginia, where gun laws were more relaxed, or from Maryland. If local policy makers deluded themselves into thinking their ban might inspire a wave of similar legislation nationwide, as they apparently did, they were way behind the curve of public opinion everywhere except Illinois, where Chicago's gun violence problem was as bad as Washington's and a handgun ban was enacted in 1982.

The NRA emerged from all this turmoil, under its new leadership, as an organization fired up to do everything in its power to keep government from curbing the right to keep and bear arms. The NRA president, Woodson D. Scott, called on members in 1980 to support the repeal of the Gun Control Act as "a legislative monstrosity saddled upon the people in a period of emotionalism" in 1968.[11] The new leadership members made defense of the Second Amendment as absolute and paramount as they thought the amendment made the right to keep and bear arms, and they increased the size and funding of the NRA's lobbying arm, the Institute for Legislative Action, to fight any further legislative attempts to limit it.

Similar to "Pain Killer" lobbying in Congress makes it so hard to pass reform

NRA membership grew, its coffers swelled, and for Congress, its lobbying arm became truly a national force to be reckoned with.

When the presidential election of 1980 came around, the Republican candidate's ideas were closely in sync with the NRA's. As governor of California, Ronald Reagan had come a long way from where he had been when he had signed the Mulford Act. He was a lifelong member of the NRA and had written in 1975, in a magazine called *Guns and Ammo,* "The Second Amendment is clear, or ought to be. It appears to leave little if any leeway for the gun control advocate. . . . There are some in America today who have come to depend absolutely on government for their security. And when government fails they seek to rectify that failure in the form of granting government more power. So, as government has failed to control crime and violence with the means given it by the Constitution, they seek to give it more power at the expense of the Constitution."[12] The Republican Party, in tune with its nominee's thinking, dropped its support for any kind of gun-control legislation, and a conservative tide swept Reagan into the White House.

Reagan did not change his position even after a mentally disturbed young man, John W. Hinckley, tried to shoot him to death on March 30, 1981. Hinckley used a .22 pistol, a Saturday night special he bought for $29 in a Dallas pawnshop, to try to kill the president as he was leaving the Capital Hilton Hotel. Reagan was badly wounded; the bullet entered his body under his armpit, puncturing his lung and causing him to lose a catastrophic amount of blood. But, though it was a bullet designed to explode inside its target, it did not go off inside his body. The presidential press secretary, James Brady, was not so lucky. The bullet that struck him penetrated his skull and exploded in his brain, not killing him but leaving him permanently disabled; a policeman and a Secret Service officer were also injured, less seriously.

The usual people made the usual calls for tighter gun-control laws after that, but without Reagan's support, most of them went nowhere. Instead, in 1986, Congress passed and he signed a law known as the Firearms Owners' Protection Act, which loosened restrictions on sales of weapons and ammunition by federally licensed gun dealers that had been imposed in 1968 and made it possible for unlicensed private individuals to sell firearms, as a hobby, at gun shows. Dealers could now sell ammunition, though not firearms, by mail.

But James Brady and his wife, Sarah, did not follow Reagan's lead on gun control after the assassination attempt. While the Firearms Owners' Protection Act was still being debated, Sarah Brady had an experience—another life-changing experience—that turned her into an "implacable foe of easy access to handguns," as Wayne King of the *New York Times* described it in a profile written later: Her five-year-old son, Scott, crawled into a pickup truck that belonged to a family friend and picked up what he thought was a toy on the front seat, and then pointed it at his mother—a loaded .22 pistol like the one that had left his father an invalid. She became chairwoman of an organization called Handgun Control, Inc., in 1989, and two years later was the head of the Center to Prevent Handgun Violence.

Eventually, Reagan himself came around. Ten years after the attempt on his life, Reagan wrote an op-ed article in support of the Brady bill, published in the *New York Times* on March 29, 1991:

> This nightmare might never have happened if legislation that is before Congress now—the Brady bill—had been law back in 1981.... Critics claim that "waiting period" legislation in the states that have it doesn't work, that criminals just go to nearby states that lack such laws to buy their weapons. True enough, and all the more reason to have a Federal law that fills the gaps.... California, which has a

15-day waiting period that I supported and signed into law while Governor, stopped nearly 1,800 prohibited handgun sales in 1989. New Jersey has had a permit-to-purchase system for more than two decades. During that time, according to the state police, more than 10,000 convicted felons have been caught trying to buy handguns. Every year, an average of 9,200 Americans are murdered by handguns, according to Department of Justice statistics. This does not include suicides or the tens of thousands of robberies, rapes and assaults committed with handguns. This level of violence must be stopped. Sarah and Jim Brady are working hard to do that, and I say more power to them. If the passage of the Brady bill were to result in a reduction of only 10 or 15 percent of those numbers (and it could be a good deal greater), it would be well worth making it the law of the land.

(Sarah Brady had not been successful in persuading Congress under Reagan's successor, George H. W. Bush, to enact a national five-day waiting period for handgun sales, because of strong opposition from the NRA.)[13] Some in the firearms industry proposed instead something that was not then yet technically feasible—computerized, instantaneous background checks. "In the computer age, there is no reason why a person's criminal and mental health record cannot be electronically checked at the point of sale," a booklet put out by the gun maker Sturm, Ruger & Company, Inc., in 1989 said. "There should also be adequate safeguards so that a person improperly denied a purchase can appeal the decision to an impartial fact-finder."

When the Bradys' bill finally did become law, in 1993 with President Bill Clinton's signature, it bore their name—the Brady Handgun Violence Prevention Act, which went into effect in 1994. Its most salient feature was the waiting period for handguns, but it did not cover private sales between individuals. That September, Congress passed the Violent Crime Control and Law Enforcement Act, the so-called Assault Weapons Ban. That was a misnomer even when it was enacted for ten years, because it "grandfathered" millions of the "banned" weapons already in circulation, as well as magazines holding more than ten rounds that had been made or imported before the ban on them went into effect. The law named nineteen types of semiautomatic firearms that closely resemble fully automatic assault weapons used by the military or law-enforcement authorities. Some of them look black and menacing, like the AK-47s the Vietcong used in Vietnam or the M-16s that GIs used to shoot back at them, but not being fully automatic, most of the banned weapons were little different in firepower from rifles used to hunt deer or bear or from ordinary semiautomatic pistols. Still, "assault" handguns with extended magazines inserted forward of the grip also had features enabling shooters to fire repeatedly with greater speed and accuracy that made them more deadly in self-defense situations—or in assaults. Including variations as identified by the ATF, there were 118 guns covered by the law that could not be manufactured, sold, or bought by ordinary citizens in the United States—unless they had bought such weapons before the ban began, that is. The ban also covered military features like flash suppressors, folding stocks, and silencers.

Before 1994, "assault" weapons were not weapons of choice for criminals, statistics show. "Assault" weapons accounted for only 8 percent of guns traced from crimes, and at that, they were mainly handguns, according to one study done for the Justice Department. However, large-capacity magazines had been used in up to 26 percent of all handguns that were used in crimes and also figured disproportionately "in guns used in murders of police and mass public shootings."[14] Other studies, such as one in Wisconsin that showed that "assault" guns had been involved in just as many homicides in

Milwaukee in the three years after the ban went into effect as in the three years before it,[15] did not show any conclusive effect on violent crime. In 2004, Congress and the George W. Bush administration, under pressure from the NRA, allowed the ban on "assault weapons" and high-capacity magazines for handguns to lapse. All of them have been freely available to qualified buyers since then.[16]

Even before 2004, in spite of its support by Reagan himself, the Brady law did not stand unaltered. The Supreme Court ruled in 1997 (5–3, in an opinion by Justice Scalia in *Printz v. United States*) that some of it was unconstitutional—the requirement that local law-enforcement authorities carry out background checks during the five-day waiting period to weed out criminals, drug addicts, the mentally ill, the violence-prone, and others not legally allowed to buy firearms. The high court said that requiring state and local authorities to do this amounted to impressing them into federal service. They could still perform the checks if they wanted to, and the waiting period itself was not invalidated, but in any case, in 1998 was replaced with a digitized clearance system, the National Instant Check System (NICS), run by the FBI.[17]

The NICS remains in effect today. As the FBI's website explained it in 2011:

> NICS is used by Federal Firearms Licensees (FFLs) to instantly determine whether a prospective buyer is eligible to buy firearms or explosives. Before ringing up the sale, cashiers call in a check to the FBI or to other designated agencies to ensure that each customer does not have a criminal record or isn't otherwise ineligible to make a purchase. More than 100 million such checks have been made in the last decade, leading to more than 700,000 denials.
>
> NICS is located at the FBI's Criminal Justice Information Services Division in Clarksburg, West Virginia. It provides full service

to FFLs in 30 states, five U.S. territories, and the District of Columbia. Upon completion of the required Bureau of Alcohol, Tobacco, Firearms and Explosives (ATF) Form 4473, FFLs contact the NICS Section via a toll-free telephone number or electronically on the Internet through the NICS E-Check System to request a background check with the descriptive information provided on the ATF Form 4473. NICS is customarily available 17 hours a day, seven days a week, including holidays (except for Christmas).

But the NICS applies only to sales by federally licensed dealers, leaving private sales, 40 percent of the total, not subject to any kind of background check. To further protect Second Amendment rights, Congress also imposed fundamental limits on the federal government's powers of enforcement. At the insistence of gun-rights advocates, section 103(i) categorically forbids the use of NICS data to create any kind of gun registration system: "No department, agency, officer, or employee of the United States may (1) require that any record or portion thereof generated by the system established under this section be recorded at or transferred to a facility owned, managed, or controlled by the United States or any State or political subdivision thereof; or (2) use the system established under this section to establish any system for the registration of firearms, firearm owners, or firearm transactions or dispositions," except for those in the categories barred from weapons purchases.

In 1997, the year before the NICS was established, Charlton Heston had become first vice president of the NRA. That year, in a speech to the conservative Free Congress Foundation, he sounded a very different tune than he had in his 1968 television endorsement of tougher gun-control laws:

I am not really here to talk about the Second Amendment or the NRA, but the gun issue clearly brings into focus the war that's going on. Rank and file Americans wake up every morning, increasingly bewildered and confused at why their views make them lesser citizens . . . Heaven help the God-fearing, law-abiding, Caucasian, middle class, Protestant, or—even worse—Evangelical Christian, Midwest, or Southern, or—even worse—rural, apparently straight, or—even worse—admittedly heterosexual, gun-owning or—even worse—NRA card–carrying, average working stiff, or—even worse—male working stiff, because not only don't you count, you're a downright obstacle to social progress . . . and frankly mister, you need to wake up, wise up and learn a little something about your new America . . . in fact, why don't you just sit down and shut up?

That's why you don't raise your hand. That's how cultural war works. And you are losing. . . .

The Constitution was handed down to guide us by a bunch of those wise old dead guys who invented this country. Now, some flinch when I say that. Why? It's true . . . they were white guys. So were most of the guys who died in Lincoln's name opposing slavery in the 1860s. So why should I be ashamed of white guys? Why is "Hispanic pride" or "black pride" a good thing, while "white pride" conjures up shaved heads and white hoods? Why was the Million Man March on Washington celebrated in the media as progress, while the Promise Keepers March on Washington was greeted with suspicion and ridicule? I'll tell you why: Cultural warfare.

Now, Chuck Heston can get away with saying I'm proud of those wise old dead white guys because Jesse Jackson and Louis Farrakhan know I fought in their cultural war. I was one of the first white soldiers in the civil rights movement in 1961, long before it

So much anger

was fashionable in Hollywood, believe me, or in Washington for that matter. In 1963 I marched on Washington with Dr. Martin Luther King to uphold the Bill of Rights. I'm very proud of that. As vice-president of the NRA I am doing the same thing.[18]

By this time, the United States had become a divided country. It was populated by two cultures with very different attitudes about a lot of things, and hardly just firearms. The urban, liberal "educated elite" that had embraced the far-reaching social changes of the 1960s and accepted racial integration thought and felt very differently about taxes, wealth, the power of government, and how to fight crime in the streets than alienated political and social conservatives, who yearned for a restoration of the traditional values of the past.

So what is the national conversation about guns today? On one side, it's "Mr. and Mrs. America, turn 'em all in," as Senator Dianne Feinstein once put it when she acknowledged that she didn't have the votes in the Senate to simply seize all "assault weapons"; on the other side, Heston's sepulchral "From my cold, dead hands." Gun confiscation is a shibboleth that brings together everybody on the gun-rights side, just as it is a chimera dreamed of by all on the gun-control side.

What is absolutely clear is that it could never happen in twenty-first-century America. A Gallup poll published in October 2011 showed that only 20 percent of the men and 31 percent of the women polled (1,005 adults in all fifty states, with a margin of error of plus or minus 4 percent) favored a ban on handguns—26 percent overall, down from 60 percent in 1959, when Gallup first started asking the question.[19] But whatever public opinion may be, outlawing handguns, or making them almost impossible for anyone to acquire, is not a reasonable approach to gun regulation. Gun-control laws that restrict the gun-owning rights of all citizens—criminals and law-abiding citizens alike—just encourage paranoia among the law-abiding part of the population that values the right to have guns. And the paranoia is constantly fanned by groups like the NRA that bank on beliefs trumping facts in most political arguments.

When President Obama took office in 2008, word went out from the NRA and other gun-rights groups that his secret agenda was to take guns and ammunition away from everybody who owned them, and to make them impossible to get for anybody who didn't.

The facts didn't support this claim. Although, as an Illinois state legislator, Obama had supported the handgun ban there, like many other Democrats, gun control was never central to his presidential agenda. He did not campaign for gun regulations in 2008, when his party's platform recognized the right to bear arms as "an important part of the American tradition" and promised to "preserve Americans' Second Amendment right to own and use firearms." It even hedged on gun control: "We believe that the right to own firearms is subject to reasonable regulation, but we know that what works in Chicago may not work in Cheyenne." In a primary debate in Philadelphia that February, Obama was asked if he supported the District of Columbia handgun ban then being challenged in the Supreme Court. He answered: "As a general principle, I believe that the Constitution confers an individual right to bear arms. But just because you have an individual right does not mean that the state or local government can't constrain the exercise of that right, in the same way that we have a right to private property but local governments can establish zoning ordinances that determine how you can use it."

Q: But do you still favor the registration and licensing of guns?
A: I think we can provide common-sense approaches to the issue of illegal guns that are ending up on the streets. We can make

sure that criminals don't have guns in their hands. We can make certain that those who are mentally deranged are not getting ahold of handguns. We can trace guns that have been used in crimes to unscrupulous gun dealers that may be selling to straw purchasers and dumping them on the streets.

To people concerned about their gun rights, that reassurance was belied by an off-the-cuff remark Obama made in San Francisco two months later, saying that it wasn't surprising that frustrated working-class voters "cling to guns or religion or antipathy to people who aren't like them or anti-immigrant sentiment or anti-trade sentiment as a way to explain their frustrations."

After Obama took office, his attorney general said a month after the inauguration that the administration wanted to reinstitute the ban on "assault" weapons, but it was just talk—followed by no action whatsoever. An Arizona man, Christopher Broughton, brought one (perfectly lawfully), an AR-15, to a protest in Phoenix while Obama was making a speech there that August because, he said, "In Arizona I still have some freedoms," adding that though he agreed with a local preacher who had said he prayed for Obama's death, he would leave the timing of the demise up to God.[20]

Obama continued his silence on gun control even after President Felipe Calderón of Mexico pleaded before a joint session of Congress in May 2010 for a resumption of the ban on military-style weapons because he said so many of them were smuggled across the border by drug cartels. Obama signed laws allowing guns to be carried (in locked containers) in checked baggage on Amtrak trains, and allowing people carrying loaded weapons legally to bring their guns with them into national parks where state law permits. Although the federal law does not allow *firing* a gun in a national park, for protection against bears, fellow visitors, or any other reason,

Obama's signature bitterly disappointed many of his supporters, but not only them. "To me, it seems to be a conflict with the purpose of the national park system," said Theodore Roosevelt IV, a Republican like his great-grandfather and namesake, who as president signed legislation in the early twentieth century that helped make the national park system what it is today. "You don't need to bring a gun into a national park," he believes.[21]

Like "birthers," some gun-rights enthusiasts didn't let facts get in the way of their convictions. Right after Obama was elected, gun sales soared—because, such people thought, he might ban them—and in his first year in office the number of federal background checks for prospective buyers rose to 14 million, peaking in November 2009 (from 11.2 million in 2007).[22] These checks do not correlate one-to-one with gun purchases, but still. At the end of 2011, the number rose well beyond 14 million, with gun-rights supporters gloating that Santa Claus was toting guns down the chimney at a record rate for Christmas. More than 2 million of those background checks were made for buyers in Kentucky alone, and more than 1 million just in Texas.

Obama declared in 2011 that "like the majority of Americans, I believe that the Second Amendment guarantees an individual right to bear arms. And the courts have settled that as the law of the land. In this country, we have a strong tradition of gun ownership that's handed from generation to generation. Hunting and shooting are part of our national heritage. And, in fact, my administration has not curtailed the rights of gun owners—it has expanded them, including allowing people to carry their guns in national parks and wildlife refuges." He added: "I know that every time we try to talk about guns, it can reinforce stark divides. People shout at one another, which makes it impossible to listen. We mire ourselves in stalemate, which makes it impossible to get to where we need to go as a country."[23]

All eyewash, according to the NRA. As its executive vice president, Wayne LaPierre, put it in *American Rifleman*, the group's official journal, in its February 2012 issue, "Obama and company are engaged in a conspiracy of public deception intended to:

1. Lull gun owners into a false sense of security to decimate the ranks of groups like the NRA and neutralize gun owners as a political force in elections, and thereby;
2. Win re-election to a second term in the White House, at which point they will be immune from elections and free to consolidate and misuse their ever-increasing power to;
3. Excise the Second Amendment from our Bill of Rights forever through legislation, litigation, regulation, executive orders, judicial fiat, international treaties and every lever of unchecked power that they can wrest from all three branches of government.

LaPierre kept telling NRA members like me in appeal after appeal that donating money would help the NRA ensure Democratic defeat in the November 2012 elections and "make sure Barack Obama is a one-term president," with no chance to pack the Supreme Court with anti-gun justices and destroy my Second Amendment right. "It's not just *firearm* freedom that's endangered," LaPierre thundered—"*all* of our freedoms are on the line."

I wondered, could I possibly be the only member of the NRA who is a Democrat? I seemed to have joined a Republican super–political action committee. To be sure, the possibility that a reelected President Obama could appoint to the Supreme Court justices who do not view gun rights the way the conservative majority did in *Heller* and *McDonald* is not totally far-fetched; after all, at her Senate confirmation hearings in 2009, Sonia Sotomayor told Senator Patrick Leahy that she accepted that the Second Amendment was an individual right. "I understand how important the right to keep and bear arms is to many people; one of my godchildren is a member of the NRA," she said then. But in 2010, sitting on the bench as a justice, she joined Justice Breyer's strong dissent to the *McDonald* opinion— "In sum, the Framers did not write the Second Amendment in order to protect a private right of armed self-defense. There has been, and is, no consensus that the right is, or was, 'fundamental.' No broader constitutional interest or principle supports legal treatment of that right as fundamental," the Breyer dissent proclaimed.

I think that it's clear that when it comes to guns and politics, the cultural war Charlton Heston was playing to in that 1997 speech is still very much with us, and passions run as high as they did when the first amendments to the Constitution were being debated— often with echoes of the rhetoric of those days, as will be seen. In 2009, when a panel of three federal judges in Chicago ruled against the *McDonald* challenge to the handgun ban there, Hal Turner, a conservative radio shock jock from New Jersey, wrote in a blog that "these judges deserve to be killed. Their blood will replenish the tree of liberty; a small price to pay to assure freedom for millions." Turner was arrested and charged with making a threat to murder the three judges. Legally, it could not be held to be a threat unless there was some real prospect that he or his followers could carry it out, and it took the federal government three trials, held in Brooklyn instead of Chicago, to convict Turner; the first two ended with hung juries. He was sentenced to thirty-three months in prison.

People in different regions of the country have different ideas about guns—and about many other things besides—but is that any reason to replace civic discourse with the ideological rants that pass for discussion of gun rights in America today? College-educated Americans who live in big cities or affluent suburbs in the twenty-first century are far removed from their ancestors on the frontier who had to depend on their own facility with firearms for protection against attack. Nowadays, many of them like to think they live in a civilized society where people should not need guns to protect themselves and can rely on the law and the police to keep them safe. But not all Americans think this way. "Country people are take-care-of-yourself people," David Thweatt, the school superintendent in Harrold, a town in north-central Texas, told a *New York Times* reporter in 2008, explaining why the school board there had decided to let some teachers carry concealed weapons. "They are not under the illusion that the police are there to protect them."

Indeed, thirty states have passed "castle-doctrine" laws that remove a long-standing common-law requirement that NRA and other such lobbyists viewed as an obstacle to the right to fire a gun in self-defense against an intruder in your own home who threatens you with deadly violence. English law, and American law in most states until recently, permitted using a weapon in self-defense only as a last resort—you had to try to get away from the threat and avoid armed confrontation if possible. Castle-doctrine laws say you have no such obligation.

And twenty-one of those states have gone further and passed "stand-your-ground" laws, "shoot-first" laws as their critics dub them, that make it legally justifiable to shoot in self-defense even outside your home—and even if you haven't done your best to thwart an attacker with other means, or tried to get away.[24] Florida passed one of the first combined castle-doctrine and shoot-first laws in 2005, and it allows deadly force to be used by law-abiding people outside the home not only in self-defense but "to prevent the imminent commission of a forcible felony."[25] Only the police should have this much power, which is an outright invitation to vigilantism.[26] Neighborhood watch groups have proliferated in many places besides Florida, but even there they are not supposed to take weapons with them on patrol.

The Florida law, which also protects people who shoot in self-defense from being sued for it, came under fire in early 2012 because of the death of Trayvon Martin on February 26 in a shooting by a neighborhood watch patrol volunteer in a gated community in Sanford. The seventeen-year-old had been visiting his father and was walking back to the father's girlfriend's home in The Retreat at Twin Lakes from a 7-Eleven store. George Zimmerman, the white-Hispanic watch patrol volunteer, had followed him in his vehicle on patrol and then gotten out of the car, despite police instructions to stay inside and leave the rest to them. Zimmerman, who had a license to carry a pistol, knew that he should not have had it with him while on neighborhood watch, according to the Sanford police. Zimmerman told them that he got out of the car to find a street sign so he could report his exact location. The teenager then attacked him from behind and went for the gun, Zimmerman claimed, so he had to use deadly force or face serious injury or death.

A nationwide uproar ensued after police said that without a witness to what had happened, the stand-your-ground law gave them no grounds to charge or arrest Zimmerman, reinflaming the debate about guns and gun laws, with polarizing overtones and charges of racism. Both federal and state investigations were launched, and nearly a month after the shooting, President Obama, criticized by some African American groups and liberals for not speaking out earlier, said, "Every parent in America should be able to understand why it is absolutely imperative that we investigate every aspect of this and that everybody pulls together—federal, state, and local—to figure out exactly how this tragedy happened. . . . If I had a son, he'd look like Trayvon."[27] Finally, on April 11, a Florida state attorney charged Zimmerman with second-degree murder, punishable by life in prison, and took him into custody. He was later released on $150,000 bail, later increased to $1 million.

A jury will presumably decide what really happened that rainy night. But it was obvious that Florida's shoot-first law had serious flaws, and Governor Rick Scott appointed a task force to take another look at it and other state gun laws in the wake of the tragedy. At times, the way the NRA urges ordinary Americans to arm themselves and urges legislators to pass laws allowing them to blast away when threatened makes you wonder, again, whether these legislators and lobbyists are aware that criminals can take advantage of these same laws and make it more difficult for police to prosecute them. It also makes you wonder if either lawmakers or the gun lobby are aware that crime rates today are much lower, not higher, than they were in the 1960s (they would only argue that the declining crime rate is a result of more people carrying guns these days, often deterring criminals from assault). Still, urban liberals who think that only "gun nuts" or bigots want to carry guns are mistaken. The Second Amendment is a right of all Americans, and the desire to carry a gun does not always make the person who carries more likely or eager to use it, as many on the left seem to think.

Gun owners often carry pistols because they want to feel more secure, to be prepared to deal with threats to their own or their loved ones' safety, but the effect is not always what they expected. Ralph Blumenthal, a reporter for the *New York Times* who was based in Texas, took the ten-hour training course required for a concealed-carry permit and, in an article about the experience, wrote, "In the end, and to my surprise, I learned about more than shooting. I learned about not shooting." Blumenthal's story quoted an instructor, Sam Pruett, telling the class, "Shooting is always the last resort." And even then, as another gun expert, Clint Smith of Thunder Ranch in Lakeview, Oregon, once put it, "Every bullet has a lawyer attached to it." "It was never permissible to wave a weapon in warning, if, say, someone cut you off on the highway," Blumenthal wrote, characterizing Pruett's message to the group, "and the only permissible blood-alcohol level for anyone carrying a gun is zero." When force became unavoidable, the instructor said, it had to be minimal. "'The object is to stop, to control or neutralize,' he said. 'The objective is not to kill.'"[28]

Justin Whitney, my nephew, an information security engineer who works for a major bank in Phoenix, bought his first gun while living in a dodgy neighborhood in Worcester, Massachusetts, where he felt he and his girlfriend at the time could be vulnerable to assault if someone broke into their apartment. "I had had only negative interactions with the police as a kid," he explained. With the police unable to prevent regular break-ins on the street they lived in, he believed it would be foolish to depend entirely on the forces of order for protection against even worse crimes, such as murder or rape. "I thought I couldn't live with myself if somebody broke in and I had to watch something horrible happen to her without trying to do something, or die trying."

He did feel a sense of reassurance, but far from making him feel invulnerable and more aggressive, carrying a gun made his reactions in potentially threatening situations more cautious than they had been before he got a pistol. "When somebody comes over and challenges me, I imagine, what if he's drunk or on drugs or is carrying a weapon himself?" he told me. Carrying made him think hard about all kinds of unforeseeable consequences. When he broke up with his girlfriend later, he gave his guns to another friend to keep for him until things settled down. "When I'm carrying and I go to a restaurant and find that it has posted a sign saying 'No weapons,' I have to go back to the car to lock up the gun, but somebody might have seen me doing that and then know I'm unarmed, or could steal the car to get the weapon. You can never be perfectly safe."

Terence Nelan, a website designer who now lives in New Hampshire, had the same unexpected cautious feeling after he got a gun for the first time, while living in Connecticut: "I found that if you're carrying, you tend to want to avoid a confrontation. It's difficult to know if you'll make the right decision under pressure, so you don't want to get into a situation where you can't predict how things are going to unfold—it's best just to avoid a situation like that."

While self-protection is certainly a major reason for wanting to own a handgun, recreation is another. Shooting is sport, difficult as that may be for liberals who abhor both guns and hunting to understand. I went one October with Whitney and some of his fellow firearms enthusiast friends in Phoenix to do some shooting at the Rio Salado Sportsman's Club, a range on cactus land owned by the Arizona Game and Fish Department in Mesa, in the foothills northeast of the city. You don't have to be a member of the club to shoot, but membership costs $85 a year, or $95 for a family (two adults living at the same address and children eight to eighteen). It is well run and well supervised by range officers. The ambience and the atmosphere reminded me of the bowling alley my father had managed in central Massachusetts when I was growing up, except with man-shaped targets instead of tenpins down the alleys.

Whitney wanted to improve his accuracy with the Springfield Armory XD-40 subcompact pistol, made in Croatia, that he carries. "I was pulled over by a cop for speeding the other day and I mentioned that I was carrying. After the cop finished lecturing me, we talked for ten minutes about the pistol, which is half the size of the Sig Sauer the cop had to carry but just as effective. The policeman was impressed," he told me.

The range was pretty full the weekend we went, with people shooting all kinds of different guns. Whitney's friend Stuart Krone, who was a shooter on both his high school and college teams and now trains people in firearms use, had brought several guns from his collection that he thought would interest me—including a semi-automatic version of an AK-47, which I had run across often enough in my Vietnam War days to know what it sounds like to someone being shot at. This time I was pulling the trigger, at a target down-range. Mercifully, we did not check afterward to see how accurate I had been. I also got off a few rounds on Krone's M1—the first time I had one of those in my hands since my Navy Officer Candidate School days in 1966. With quite a bit more natural padding in my chest and shoulder now than I had then, the recoil was not uncomfortable at all. I could almost feel the bullet leave the barrel as I squeezed the trigger.

Then there is the allure of hunting as yet another reason to own firearms. Ted Roosevelt, like his great-grandfather, is an avid conservationist, one who believes that sensible hunting and hunting regulations play a vital role in sustaining the natural habitat that allows game to flourish. Ted and I are classmates from Harvard, but unlike me, he has a fine collection of rifles and shotguns in his New York City apartment, hunts at a rod and gun club about seventy miles upstate, and has often enjoyed hunting sharp-tailed grouse, huns (Hungarian partridge), and big game—elk—in central Montana. "The best elk I ever shot there was a couple of years ago, with my friend Jake, who grew up on that land and knows every inch of it," he told me. Jake had finally gotten a "bull tag," a license to hunt a male elk, that year. It had taken twenty years of applying for a bull permit before he was able to get one, even though he owned land in the area.

The two set off through a pine forest that they had hunted through before, often covering ten or fifteen miles in a day, but after only a few miles of walking, this time they came upon a pair of magnificent bulls. "We watched them from a distance for a time before they suddenly took off—a mule deer downwind of us had spooked them," Roosevelt recalled. They went on, and a few hours later, Jake pointed to a grove some way off, where there were two young elk. "We worked our way through the bushes to within about twenty-five yards of them. Jake motioned to me, asking if I wanted to take one, but I shook my head."

For the next four days they hunted hard but did not see another elk. On the last day, they were using field glasses to scan for animals when Jake suddenly stiffened, spotting five bulls in a clearing. "This was after the rut, when the bulls stop fighting each other and actually get together peacefully," Roosevelt said.

> We decided we'd approach by making a long circle. We went way downwind of them, into the thick woods again, and were getting pretty close when we startled another bull in the timber we were passing through. The bull jumped up and ran off towards the other five bulls. We were convinced that he would spook them into the next county. To our amazement, he joined and started to graze with them in the clearing. They were all moving slowly uphill. We had to decide which way we thought they were going to go, and, hoping we guessed correctly, went to their right.

So, flanking the group at a distance, the two men went ahead and then stopped to wait for the animals.

"At this point, we could no longer see them," Ted said. "We were there about one and a half hours, and it was cold, and I was shivering so much I was concerned that if the bulls ever did show up, I was shaking too much to shoot accurately." Then, finally, the elk came into view, one after another. "We had been very lucky. The largest bull was in the lead and we got within about 225 yards. Jake asked, 'You want to take it?' I said yes, leaning up against a tree to steady the rifle, and fired. I was using a 7-mm Remington Magnum rifle built by David Miller with a Bitterroot Bonded bullet. The combination dropped the elk instantly." Roosevelt paused in the retelling. "For a moment, it was very poignant. I felt a sad feeling come over me—here was this magnificent animal, and I had killed it, as of course I had hoped I would do, but I felt that sadness anyway." Perhaps it was admiration and respect.

After a few moments, the two men were able to turn the carcass so as to be able to start field dressing. Jake went back to the road and got his truck within reachable distance, and they took the animal back to butcher it for several hundred pounds of elk meat, which Roosevelt enjoys serving to guests in New York who appreciate the delicacy as much as his wife, Connie, does, though she came late to an appreciation of how it comes to the table, on an earlier elk hunt in Montana with her husband, a hunting partner, and two guides.

"Two hundred yards away a single bull elk stood with his nose down in a stream," she wrote of the culminating moment of this expedition, which she had accompanied mainly to find out how her husband could find such enjoyment in an activity most of her city friends thought barbaric.

> The color of early morning light, he would have been invisible if our senses had not been heightened to every stir and flicker around us. Then the peace exploded with the sound of a rifle. My eyes closed. I did not want death to be part of this experience. The men rose and ran down the hill, though they need not have hurried. The elk had fallen where it stood and did not move again. Its 700 pounds would require the pack horses to move back to camp. The men were exultant. It had been the perfect approach, the perfect shot and a venerable prize. Their celebratory rituals were primitive, their triumph contagious. Even so, I kept my distance for a while, not wanting to look at the dead elk. The carcass had little to do with the airy creature that lingered in my head like the fragment of a dream. I could not help but mourn.

But she found herself "strangely soothed by the pursuit and conquest," feeling "elementally human and more at home in the wilderness than I have ever felt in a city."[29]

However, dressing game or mourning it is not a problem if you only shoot for target practice. Henry L. Hokans of Ogunquit, Maine, a professional organist with whom I studied at All Saints Episcopal Church in Worcester, Massachusetts, in the late 1950s, had been an air force military policeman in South Korea during the Korean War and had grown up with guns on his family's farm outside of Worcester. "My father had an old .38 which he used for target practice," Hokans told me. "After the war [World War II], when my brother, David, came back from the navy, we'd go hunting together for pheasant, deer, and so on, though in Massachusetts you could only use a shotgun for that. In the early 1950s, he moved to Maine, and I'd come up for grouse and deer hunting. David used to say that deer hunting was the most wonderful sport, until you pulled the trigger."

When he was at All Saints in Worcester, he used to get a pistol from the choir (helped by one of the senior vestrymen of the church) as a present every Christmas. This was not one of those right-wing fundamentalist churches you occasionally read about, but an Episcopal church in a sophisticated urban environment in effete and certainly not gun-crazy central Massachusetts. I wonder if that would be possible there today. Eventually his collection included a .357, a .44 Magnum, and a .22 Ruger—which he used for target practice. "I never felt threatened in Worcester enough to want to carry," he told me.

New Orleans is a very different place than it was when Louis Armstrong ran afoul of the gun laws there, to be sure, but some things are still the same. Albert Ponton Jr., with whom I served in the navy in the 1960s, recently wrote to me,

> When I was a kid we never thought twice about having guns around. I shared a bedroom with 3 older brothers and it seems there were always 2 or 3 shotguns and a rifle stored in a corner of the room. We didn't own a gun cabinet or trigger guard. The attic

door was also in our room and one night someone left the attic door open. Somehow the cat had gotten in the attic and in the middle of the night the cat apparently decided it didn't want to be in the attic any more. My brother Cleo's bed was located directly under the attic opening. The commotion that erupted when the little ball of fur and claws hit my brother's face could not have been greater if a 600 pound tiger had come through the attic door. When someone turned the lights on, my other two brothers were trying to wrestle the gun away from Cleo, who was determined to shoot the cat right there in our bedroom with a 12-gauge shotgun.

Ponton said the situation was no different for many white families. "Down here in Louisiana the question is not about your rights to own guns, but whether you have a right to carry that gun into an oil refinery if you work there," he said.

Aside from self-defense and hunting, some people simply enjoy collecting guns. Dwight B. Demeritt Jr., a friend who is originally from Maine, loves antique firearms. His home in Brooklyn Heights, New York, is not far from the spot overlooking New York Harbor where George Washington decided in August 1776 to evacuate the Continental Army across the East River rather than lose it to a much superior British force that was about to attack. Washington's decision left New York City in British hands during the rest of the Revolutionary War, but ultimately saved the day for the republic.

"I grew up in Maine, where practically everybody has at least one firearm, a deer rifle, something for bird hunting, and a pistol for the fun of it," Demeritt said. "So I was taught how to handle firearms at an early age, and started collecting." His college thesis at the University of Maine in Orono was about the history of firearms manufacturing in the state, and he is the author of a definitive book on the subject.[30]

Demeritt understands why some of his fellow Brooklynites might want to have guns to defend themselves. "I was robbed at gunpoint in the early 1960s," he told me. At the time, he lived in one of those stately brownstone houses the borough is famous for, with an entrance underneath the front stairs.

> One day the doorbell rang—I was at the lower level and opened the door to find a little chrome revolver pointed at me. I was glad I had my glasses on, because I could see that the revolver was loaded. My wife and children were on the upper floors and heard me talking—there were two guys, looking for televisions. They made me lie down, one holding the gun over me, the other one going up to the parlor floor and grabbing the TV, but my wife, further upstairs, heard what was going on and called the police. I kept telling the guy holding the gun over me, "Relax, don't be nervous."

After some tense minutes, a plainclothes police officer pulled up on the street in a taxicab, and Demeritt's intruders dropped the TV and ran.

Nevertheless, Demeritt says, in all the years since, living in a New York City neighborhood where gunpoint robberies and break-ins used to be more frequent occurrences than they are nowadays, he has never felt the need for a firearm for self-defense or protection. He is not one of the 37,000 New Yorkers with a license to own a handgun in the city. "These things happen so rarely," he shrugged.

Demeritt has done more research than I ever will into the early and colonial American experience with firearms, but he thinks their importance in that period is often exaggerated. "It's not true that everybody had a gun," he told me. "In the French and Indian wars, and the Revolution, often when people were called up into the militia they'd show up without a gun, even though the law required them to own one. At Bunker Hill, a lot of the troops had no gun at all, or just a pike or a halberd. The law said they must have muskets, bayonets, but they didn't. They were farmers. In urban areas, there were practically none who had them."

Scholarship about gun rights in this country is as politically fraught and ensnared in the culture wars as the subject itself. Michael A. Bellesiles, a respected historian, lost the Bancroft Prize he had been awarded in 2001 for his book *Arming America: The Origins of a National Gun Culture* after his research, purporting to prove that colonial Americans had never had as many arms as gun-rights advocates thought they had, was challenged and found wanting.

As I spoke to gun owners and experts on guns in America, I couldn't help but wonder: Was it really true that guns were not so prevalent in those early times? I thought no one could understand the Second Amendment or its meaning today without going back and trying to understand what it meant when it was adopted, in the context of the Revolution and the colonial history that preceded it. As the next chapter will show, what I found was that history supports both sides in today's culture wars—but it does not support the hysteria that passes for discussion of the Second Amendment by gun-rights supporters and by advocates of gun control. Not by a long shot.

CHAPTER TWO

GUNS AND SURVIVAL, GUNS AND AMERICAN INDEPENDENCE

Bring every man a musket or fowling piece.
EDWARD WINSLOW, PLYMOUTH COLONY, 1621

From the very beginning, Americans in the Colonies—free white American men, at any rate—had the right to keep and use firearms, to hunt and to defend themselves. But, then and later, in the Revolution, the right was always inextricable from a duty that came with it—to bear those arms when called upon, for the common defense.

Most Americans of my generation last did any learning about early colonial history when we were in school. Growing up in Massachusetts, I should have learned more. Yes, the "Massachusetts" were the Native Americans the Pilgrims came across after they landed here, and Indian names of many towns and rivers remind us today of their past presence. But what my schoolmates and I retained about the history of relations between the natives and the colonial settlers was mostly the glow of the comforting myth of Massasoit and the Pilgrims at the first Thanksgiving. The earliest American colonists came with guns, of course, because they knew they would need to hunt game for food. And they expected to meet Native Americans, hoping to "civilize" them and share in peace the vast, apparently mostly unoccupied land. But they were also fully prepared to use weapons to defend themselves if they had to do that.

How much did they need guns for self-defense? That I had forgotten, so I began looking back into colonial history to find out. And when I did I was surprised to be reminded that there had been just as much gunfire in New England and Virginia and North Carolina in the seventeenth century as there was two centuries later in the Wild West. Battles in Massachusetts and Connecticut had often been just as deadly for the early settlers as Little Bighorn was for George Custer and the Seventh Cavalry two and a half centuries later in Montana. But the outcome, for the Native Americans, was a disaster that was foreordained—not by the God with whose blessing the early settlers thought they had come, but by their superiority in arms.

In Virginia, Captain John Smith and the men who sailed with him in May 1607 into the place they named Jamestown came with the best of intentions toward the natives. They arrived after two failures by Sir Walter Raleigh to establish a successful English colony on Roanoke Island—failures that may or may not have been due to hostilities with Native Americans. They explicitly planned to establish a new settlement without using force of arms, unlike the Portuguese and the Spanish (who had already claimed the territory, present-day Virginia and North Carolina, but not settled it), who had been such successful conquistadors in more temperate climes far to the south. Although the native peoples might not welcome them, the Virginia Company had hopes of winning them over and "civilizing" them, one of its members wrote, "not by stormes of raging cruelties (as West India was converted) with rapiers point and musket shot, murdering so many millions of naked indians, as their stories doe relate, but by faire and loving meanes, suiting to our English natures."[1]

They had cannon on the *Susan Constant,* the flagship of their three-boat fleet, to ward off pirates, and they had muskets, though the company's written instructions warned against letting the natives see them training with arms, "for if they see your learners miss what they aim at, they will think the weapon not so terrible, and thereby will be bould to assault you." Edward-Maria Wingfield, who was elected to their presidency after they set up at Jamestown, some distance up the James River from the entrance to Chesapeake Bay, ordered that initially there should be no training at all: the guns should stay stored aboard the ships. But within two weeks, the settlers were attacked by hundreds of warriors from the wary Paspahegh tribe, whose arrows killed a boy and wounded between eleven and seventeen men, one of whom also died later. The attack was repelled by a cannon shot that did not kill any Indians but terrified them by bringing down a large tree branch. John Smith, temporarily blacklisted by Wingfield as a mutineer for his opinionated criticisms during the Atlantic crossing, later complained, "Had it not chanced a crosse bar shot from the ships strooke downe a bough from a tree amongst them, that caused them to retire, our men had all beene slaine, being securely all at worke, and their armes in dry fats."[2]

The muskets came out of their "dry fats" crates and the settlers threw up fortifications, though the attacks continued for several days. Even after Jamestown became safer, the colonists proved singularly maladroit at farming and, unable to obtain much food by trading with local Indians, soon ran short of supplies. John Smith challenged Wingfield's leadership, cleared his name, and began trying to trade with tribes farther afield that had not yet become aware of English designs on their territory and were therefore less hostile. He was able to trade copper and beads and hatchets for corn and other victuals, but as autumn and then winter came on, Jamestown was in increasingly desperate shape—a disease-ridden, famine-stricken place where scores of settlers were dying.

On one of these expeditions that December, Smith was attacked and taken prisoner by Opechancanough, a chief who was a brother of the regional supreme leader, Powhatan. Taken to Powhatan, Smith would have been executed on the spot but for the famous intercession of Powhatan's daughter, Pocahontas. (The fact that there is no need to explain who Pocahontas was or what she did shows how much popular myth—and Walt Disney Studios—have romanticized and distorted early American history.)

Over the course of 1608, Smith tried alternately to charm or intimidate Powhatan into becoming a liege of his own king in England. Powhatan seems to have thought the relationship should rightly be the other way around and kept asking for swords and firearms, even cannon, as tribute in exchange for corn and food, still desperately needed by the colonists, who were singularly resistant to the idea of cultivating their own and constantly facing starvation when the Indians refused to help them out. Smith refused, though eventually others, two German glassmakers named "Adam" and "Franz," gave in to Powhatan's entreaties and smuggled some guns and ammunition to him (earning, nevertheless, his contempt and an order for their execution).

Pocahontas came to Smith's rescue again during another trade foray in early 1609 with a warning that a feast her father was sending to him was a ruse to conceal his intention of killing Smith and all the rest of the Englishmen. As David A. Price tells the story in his *Love and Hate in Jamestown:*

> Pocahontas's warning soon came to fruition. Within an hour, eight or ten large, strong men brought platters of venison. Their more sophisticated approach to disarming the English suggests that they may have been tutored that day by the German renegades. Most of Smith's men had matchlock guns, whose firing mechanisms could not operate without a length of fiber cord—the "match"—that needed to be kept aflame. (Only a few officers, such as Smith, had the more modern snaphaunce guns, fired by flint and steel.) So the food bearers complained of the smoke from the match cords, and demanded that they be extinguished. It was a dubious request in a room that was perpetually smoky from the warming fire, but it showed an acute sense of the colonists' vulnerabilities.

Smith held them off and sailed back to Opechancanough's village, hoping to buy more food to get Jamestown through another winter, but was quickly surrounded by armed warriors. Smith drew his pistol, and before the crowd, told their chief, "I see the great desire you have to kill me. . . . If I be the marke you aim at, here I stand, shoot he that dare. You promised to fraught my ship ere I departed, and so you shall, or I meane to load her with your dead carcasses. Yet if as friends you will come and trade, I once more promise not to trouble you, except you give me the first occasion."[3]

As Price points out, what John Smith and the others could not see—blinded, perhaps, by the infatuation Pocahontas had shown—was "that they might be giving offense to the natives just by being there, occupying ever-larger swaths of the riverfront."[4] Settlers chose land that looked unoccupied and unused, and therefore available, but to the Indians they still looked like squatters.

Political infighting among the Virginia colonial leaders resulted in Smith's being replaced as governor, and after he was injured in an accident in 1609, he sailed back to England. Relative peace with the Indians lasted through Powhatan's reign. After his death in 1618, Opechancanough assumed his powers as chief of chiefs, and on March 22, 1622, he launched a massive sneak attack against the colonists. Indians went to the settlements as usual that morning, joining the inhabitants unarmed in routines of trade and work. But at a prearranged signal, they then suddenly seized whatever sharp or blunt instruments the colonists had about them and used them to slaughter as many settlers as they could. Up to 400 men, women, and children, about one-third of the total number at the time, died in this attack.

This massacre marked the end of any illusions the colonists had about the possibility of peaceful coexistence. From England, Smith, who had always been skeptical, offered to lead a force of one hundred men to protect the survivors, who withdrew from exposed plantations and regrouped around Jamestown, but the Virginia Company said it could not pay. It did send forty-two barrels of gunpowder, and King James added a gift of a thousand muskets and three hundred pistols, advising the settlers to wage "perpetual warre without peace or truce," with determination "even to the measure that they intended against us, the rooting them out for being longer a people uppon the face of the Earth."

When King James dissolved the company two years later and made Virginia a Crown colony, it was a colony that was at war. And with their firearms, the settlers had a lopsided advantage over their native adversaries with their bows and arrows. Opechancanough was forced to agree to peace in 1632. But twelve years later, he struck again, killing between four hundred and five hundred settlers on April 18, 1644. Captured after two years of fighting, he was awaiting transport back to England as a prisoner of war in 1646 when an English soldier shot him in the back and killed him. By that time, the Virginia General Assembly reported, the Indians were "so routed and dispersed that they are no longer a nation."

So it was not "faire and loving meanes," or agricultural aptitude, that enabled Virginia to survive its first years—it was firearms, used in a kind of self-defense that was, to the Native Americans, no different from open aggression.[5]

I n Massachusetts, relations between the English settlers and the Massasoit and Wampanoag tribes followed much the same course as relations between the settlers and Powhatan in Virginia: assumptions that they could get along peacefully with the natives were quickly proven wrong, and they soon needed the guns the colonists had brought with them for self-defense.

After the *Mayflower* arrived at what is now Provincetown in December 1620, small parties that had put ashore to forage for food came across buried baskets of corn. Showing little curiosity about who might have actually buried the corn, and no fear of punishment if they took it, the Englishmen dug it all up to take back to the ship, as if it were manna from heaven intended for themselves all along. Small wonder that a few days later, Native Americans using bows and arrows attacked a group of the intruders at a place since known as "First Encounter Beach." Gunfire drove off the attackers.

Initial hostility subsided with a peace treaty in 1621 with the Wampanoag, who participated in the famous Thanksgiving in Plymouth that year with the Massasoit. I don't think we learned in school in Massachusetts in the 1950s that the Englishmen had brought guns with them to the feast. As one of the settlers, Edward Winslow, wrote home to England about that day, "amongst our recreations, we exercised our arms, many of the Indians coming amongst us."[6] The intention was to use guns for hunting. "Bring every man a musket or fowling piece," he told prospective settlers; "Let your piece be long in the barrel."[7]

When the Massachusetts Bay Colony a few miles up the coast was chartered in 1628, provision was made to ship "Armes ffor 100 men" from England, including eighty muskets "4 foote in the barrill." Almost immediately after they arrived in the place they named Boston, the authorities sought to forestall gun trouble with the Native Americans by keeping them unarmed. As the governor and assistants decided on September 28, 1630, "It is ordered, that no person whatsoever shall, either directly or indirectly, employ, or cause to be employed, or to their power permit, any Indian to use any piece upon any occasion or pretense whatsoever, under pain of . . . fine for the first offense, & for the 2 offense to be fined & imprisoned at the discretion of the Court."

Such efforts had little effect. French explorers and traders were active in this region and, unlike the English, had no qualms about trading firearms and ammunition for furs and other goods supplied by the natives.[8] Some of the English colonists themselves began selling or trading guns to them despite directives to the contrary, sometimes for corn or beaver pelts.

As more and more settlers arrived and it became apparent that they were going to take for themselves lands that Native Americans had always considered rightfully theirs, hostilities became inevitable, despite the authorities' best efforts to treat them decently. Settlers who stole canoes or committed other crimes against the natives could be punished by having their houses burned down and being deported back to England. Nevertheless, in 1631 it was considered too dangerous to travel alone between Boston and Plymouth, and even two or three Englishmen on the journey together were required to carry arms.[9]

By 1632, Massachusetts was legally requiring single men to furnish themselves with arms, which they believed they needed in earnest after the Pequot Indians murdered a trader in 1636. People were forbidden to go without arms farther than a mile from their houses, under penalty of fine, which shows that, as you would expect, compliance had been uneven. In 1637, the injunction against selling or giving Indians arms or gunpowder had to be repeated, and colonists were also forbidden to repair Indian guns. The fine for violations was even raised to £10, with the possibility of corporal punishment for egregious violations.

As hostilities intensified, 160 men were drafted and sent out to fight the Pequots in a war between Indians and settlers that ended on May 27 with the burning by Connecticut militiamen of the Pequot village at Mystic. They shot, beheaded, and incinerated six hundred to seven hundred native men, women, and children—nearly wiping out the entire tribe (its survivors established the country's largest gambling casino on their reservation in Ledyard in the early 1990s). They did the job so thoroughly that militiamen from Massachusetts who participated in the attack were able to return home that summer. Tensions eased so much that November that a law passed during more troubled times that required able-bodied men to bring arms to a meetinghouse—church services included—was repealed.[10]

What is obvious even from this early history is that, for these Englishmen who were also Americans, having firearms was a matter of right—a right recognized in common law. Furthermore, just as the duty to bear arms was a matter of law, the right to own them was, under common law, also subject to restrictions from earliest colonial times. About one hundred colonists in Massachusetts Bay, for example, were legally deprived of their arms in 1637 on suspicion of being heretics guided by the teachings of two religious leaders who clashed with Governor John Winthrop and were tried by the general court on charges of sedition, those leaders being Anne Hutchinson and John Wheelwright. To prevent their followers—all named, from Boston, Charlestown, Salem, Ipswich, Roxbury, and Newbury— from making "some sudden eruption upon those that differ from them in judgment," they were ordered to surrender "all such guns, pistols, swords, powder, shot, & match as they shall be owners of, or have in their custody" or face fines of £10 each.[11]

Hostilities with Indians were not general in Massachusetts at this point, and colonists were often punished by the authorities for cheating Indians or stealing from them, as well as for selling them guns or shot. But efforts to keep guns or ammunition out of their hands could not be enforced effectively. When the Narragansetts tried to organize war against the English in the colony in 1642, the legislature in Boston received intelligence that the Indians had a "great supply of powder and guns" from "some of the English in the eastern parts [Maine], which, living alone and under no government, cannot, under any ordinary way of justice, be punished or restrained," and it authorized an expedition to seize gunpowder from the miscreants, who were nevertheless left with enough powder for their own personal use.[12]

Colonial regulations in Massachusetts, as elsewhere, required all free adult (white Protestant) males in the community to own and be capable of using firearms for militia service. A law in 1645 mandated: "That all inhabitants, as well seamen as others, are to have armes in their houses fit for service, with powder, bullets, [and] match, as other souldiers, & the fishermen, shipcarpenters, (the deacons are hereby exempted from watches & wards,) & others, not exempted by lawe, shall watch or provide a sufficient man in their roome, & to traine twice a year, according to the order."[13] (The "match" or burning fuse was later replaced by more modern firing mechanisms, flints and percussion devices.) Those who could not afford weapons were sometimes lent them at town expense and required to work off the debt.[14]

Roman Catholics in New England were barred in the early days from owning firearms, as were indentured servants, slaves, and those who refused to swear allegiance to the government or non-property-owning white males.[15] Militia members did their training with degrees of enthusiasm that varied with the intensity of fear of an impending attack. When things were quiet, discipline and training were lax. But threats both to and from the Indians were mounting as the number of colonists grew and settlers began outnumbering Indians. The Puritans made attempts to convert the Indians, and established fourteen "praying towns" for those who accepted Christianity, but settlers also began building fortified villages for themselves, surrounded by log palisades with arrow-proof shelter within for all inhabitants.

As settlers with their guns and fowling pieces became more numerous, Massassoit's son Metacomet, given the Christian name Philip in Plymouth at his father's request and now sarcastically dubbed "King Philip" by the colonists, resented the fact that game for his own people had become difficult to find and hunt and that the only real way for them to acquire guns and other English products for themselves was by selling their land. The Wampanoag were being squeezed off their ancestral lands into marginal tracts and swamps, he concluded, and were also being ravaged by diseases the English had brought with them—smallpox was especially devastating. Metacomet began trying to encourage neighboring tribes to resist further colonial encroachment.

In 1671, Metacomet was summoned to Taunton, where colonial authorities demanded that he stop those efforts and surrender his firearms. Four years later, a Christian Indian who had been raised in

Natick, one of the "praying towns," warned the Plymouth governor that Metacomet was about to go on the warpath against the settlers. The informant's body was soon afterward found under the ice of a pond, and three Wampanoag men were accused by another Indian convert of the murder. Tried, convicted, and hanged for it, they provided Metacomet with a pretext for open warfare, which began in 1675. The conflict, known as King Philip's War, eventually drew in other tribes, from the Narragansett in Rhode Island to the Abenaki in Maine, and because of white superiority in firearms, it became what amounted to genocide for the Indians.

Over the next year and a half, Metacomet's allies and his forces attacked and burned scores of settlements and killed up to 2,500 colonists from Deerfield to Providence and Falmouth (in what later became Maine). The New England colonies united to muster a combined military force strong enough to defeat them, and the colonists were merciless. Thousands of Indians were killed, 40 percent of the total population at the time, and their women and children captured and sold into slavery. The "praying towns" were closed and their inhabitants moved to what amounted to concentration camps on the islands in Boston Harbor. Some smaller tribes were virtually exterminated.

In August 1676, Metacomet was shot in a Rhode Island swamp by one of the militia's Indian guides, another convert; the chief's head was put on display in Plymouth and remained there for the next twenty years. The Wampanoag, reduced to a fragment of four hundred, never again posed a threat to the colonists.[16]

But if King Philip's War taught the settlers the virtues of a well-trained militia, the lesson was all too quickly forgotten after the fighting stopped. It would be relearned when the next attacks came—as the need for preparedness against attack would be learned, forgotten, and relearned by generations of Americans over the course of the next three centuries.

These early skirmishes were crucial to forming early American attitudes about war and firearms—yet how much of this early history do most New Englanders remember today? It's much the same with New Yorkers. When they do look back on the early history of the island, most comfort themselves with the myth of peaceful relations between the natives on Manhattan—a name derived from their own tribe, the Munsees—and the Dutch explorers (who were looking for ways to keep Spain from taking over the entire continent) to whom the Indians sold the island for the equivalent of $24 in 1626. In fact, as the historian Robert Grumet reminds us, it was actually 60 guilders, the equivalent of several hundred dollars today, and the Indians and the Dutch settlers had hostilities just as deadly as the colonists who followed Massasoit and the Pilgrims in Massachusetts did.

Dutch colonial laws, like English ones, prohibited the trade of guns and the making of ammunition with the natives, but they also forbade the sale of liquor to them—a prohibition widely ignored. Although the Dutch acquired much land from the Munsees by payment recognized by deeds, disagreements over taxes and conflicts spurred by hostilities between Munsees and the Iroquois nations farther inland led to bloody conflicts between 1640 and 1645. The Dutch declared war on them and killed up to 2,000 Indian men, women, and children. Indian counterattacks killed settlers, including Anne Hutchinson and five of her fifteen children, who had taken refuge with the Dutch in Pelham after being expelled from Massachusetts. Diseases brought over the Atlantic by the Dutch may have killed more Indians than their blunderbusses. Peter Stuyvesant, who became New Amsterdam's leader in 1647, sought peace with the natives, too, but sought it with firearms, until he had to surrender to a British colonial force that came down the coast from Connecticut in 1664. By that time, the natives were decimated, and largely landless.[17]

Back in Virginia, settlers beset by attacks from the Susquehannock Indians finally rose in 1676 to their own defense with a company of militia formed by one of their own, Nathaniel Bacon. They demanded better protection from the English governor, Sir William Berkeley, who declared Bacon a traitor. Exasperated and looking for sympathy, Sir William wrote home: "How miserable that man is that Governes a People wher six parts of seaven at least are Poore Endebted Discontented and Armed."[18] Bacon later marched five hundred men into Jamestown and forced the governor to flee.

At this time there was turmoil back in the mother country as well, culminating in the "Glorious Revolution" of 1688–1689, when the struggle between the Roman Catholic monarch James II and Parliament ended with William of Orange sailing an invasion fleet in from the Netherlands and forcing James to flee to France. By legitimating the Protestants, William and his English wife, Mary, as monarchs, Parliament in effect would take the first step toward making them figureheads and would assume their political and executive power. In 1689, Parliament asserted a Declaration of Rights that spelled out the grievances against James and the constitutional guarantees William and Mary would have to make to accede to the throne. The ramifications for the colonies would be great.

The Declaration of Rights stands as one of the important foundations of modern British (and American) democracy. Although the powers of representatives of the people in Parliament, circumscribing the monarch's powers, are its main focus, the right to bear arms also figures importantly in the document. The grievances included charges that James "did endeavor to subvert and extirpate the Protestant religion and the laws and liberties of this Kingdom. . . . By causing several good subjects, being Protestants, to be disarmed at the same time when Papists were both armed and employed contrary to law" (James had increased the number of Roman Catholic officers and imported Irish Catholics to expand his army as William mounted his challenge). Article 2 of the declaration provided that "the subjects which are Protestants, may have arms for their defense suitable to their conditions, and as allowed by law."

This was far from the ringing declaration of the individual right of all Englishmen to bear arms in self-defense that the rebellious English colonists in America (and their latter-day descendants in defense of their gun rights) later saw in it. "Suitable to their conditions and as allowed by law" are important limitations, and English history ever since the declaration shows that the authorities, whether in the name of the monarchy or of Parliament, interpreted those words to apply mainly to Protestant property owners, the gentry that formed an important part of the ruling class. Guns might belong in their hands, but not in the hands of a mob.

With William's accession to the throne, the Anglo-Dutch alliance he had hoped for became a reality, and Parliament authorized him to declare war on France for taking James's side, with immediate implications for the American colonies. For the French had their own claims on the New World and were eager to push the English settlements in America into the sea for the greater glory of New France and its crown jewels, Québec and Montréal. And in the first of the resulting Anglo-French wars fought on American soil, King William's War, from 1689 to 1697, and Queen Anne's War, from 1702 to 1713, both French and British authorities used Native American allies as surrogate fighters.

They could do this because of differences among Indian tribes that had been sharpened by economic pressures brought on by the growing numbers of European settlers. Trade in furs, which besides timber were to Britain and France in North America what gold had been to Spain and Portugal in South America, created competing loyalties among the tribes, and European territorial encroachments added to conflicting interests. Tribes made shifting alliances with and against each other, with frequent battles among themselves.

The authorities of New France marshaled the Mohawk and other Iroquois tribes they had vanquished in northern New York as mercenary warriors to wreak havoc on the English settlements to the south and east. The English and Dutch, for their part, were making alliances of their own with other Iroquois tribes to the south to make mischief against the French to the north. Thus began decades of what the English colonists called the French and Indian wars.

The French were able to motivate Indians to fight with them in part because they were more inclined than the British were to let them take and keep prisoners. Indian villages had been depopulated by a low birthrate and high mortality from diseases Europeans had brought with them to the New World, and Native American women who had lost loved ones or children were permitted by their own customs to adopt prisoners taken in battle.

And yes, guns were becoming ubiquitous. Despite occasional hostilities, the Massachusetts colonial authorities often saw fit during peaceful periods to satisfy requests from the Indians for help in maintaining the firearms they had acquired—if only to keep them from turning to the French if their requests were denied. "We should be glad of a Smith here to mend our Guns," one chief requested of Lieutenant Governor William Dummer of Massachusetts during treaty negotiations in Georgetown (now Maine) in August 1717. "If you take care to pay for your work, I shall endeavor you shall have a good locksmith," Dummer replied. If he regretted decisions like this after he became governor and had to fight his own war against French and Abenaki forces in this contested area between 1721 and 1725, he showed little sign of it, negotiating similar arrangements in 1726 and 1727.[19]

Military confrontations between British and French forces and Indians allied with either side resumed again in 1754 on the western reaches of English settlement up and down the Atlantic coast, and on a larger scale, with General Edward Braddock arriving with two English regiments in Virginia as commander in chief of all English forces in the colonies—and Lieutenant Colonel George Washington commanding 450 armed colonists, Daniel Boone among them. They and the 1,400 English soldiers took on the main French military position near Fort Duquesne, at the fork of the Allegheny and Monongahela Rivers, in 1755, but nine hundred French and Indian soldiers defeated them, mortally wounding Braddock and forcing the English forces to withdraw.

Soldiers weren't the only targets, however. The French repeatedly sent out Indian marauding parties to harass settlers in western Pennsylvania. In the eastern part of the state, where Quakers were in control, the victims were advised that better treatment of the Indians, and caps on the prices of items sold to them, might make the natives friendlier. "Such admirable measures were small comfort to backwoodsmen who saw their homes in flames, their crops ruined, their wives and children scalped or captured," in Daniel Boorstin's words. Benjamin Franklin, however, supported the formation of voluntary militias in Pennsylvania for protection against French and Indian attacks in the west and against Spanish warships that occasionally made raiding forays up the Delaware River. Finally, after the governor declared war against the Delaware and the Shawnee in 1756, six Quaker members of the Pennsylvania Provincial Assembly gave up their seats in protest, effectively ending Quaker rule. The British finally took Fort Duquesne in 1758. Indian raids continued until the Pennsylvania Assembly agreed by treaty to found no new settlements west of the Alleghenies—provisions disregarded by settlers who kept streaming in anyway, despite the dangers.

The frontier was a dangerous place. All along the western regions of Virginia and the Carolina colonies, Cherokee Indians made repeated and deadly attacks against settlers and defensive forts. In the Shenandoah Valley, settlers had to keep arms at the ready for their own defense, for, again in Boorstin's words: "The backwoods was no place for the squeamish; anyone who waited for the arrival of 'troops' did not last long. The boys' pastimes early prepared them for defense. Shooting small game with a bow or a gun and throwing a tomahawk became life-saving skills when Indians attacked. By the time a boy reached the age for service in the militia he was already at home in the forest and knew the ways of the Indian." Joseph Doddridge, author of *Notes, on the Settlement and Indian Wars of the Western Parts of Virginia and of Pennsylvania from 1763 to 1783,* told how young Americans on the frontier learned facility with weapons: "A well grown boy at the age of twelve or thirteen years, was furnished with a small rifle and shot-pouch. He then became a fort soldier, and had his port-hole assigned him. Hunting squirrels, turkeys and raccoons, soon made him expert in the use of his gun."[20]

How much of that was boast and how much was reality is hard to tell. Probably it was a mixture of both. The colonists had to be familiar with arms; two centuries of their history showed that. But not all of them were as adept with them or as conscientious about their duty to common defense as the laws required.

In the eighteenth century, in towns and cities all over the colonies, the right to arms was regulated in ways that were not possible on the frontier. Boston, New York, and Philadelphia were all sizable cities by mid-eighteenth-century American standards, and local laws limited what people could do with their guns or gunpowder within city limits. Firing "a gun or a pistol" in the mainland part of Boston had been prohibited since 1713; it became a crime punishable by a fine of 40 shillings to discharge "any gun or pistol charged with shot or ball" in the town in 1746, a statute renewed in 1778; another imposed a £10 fine upon "any Person" who "shall take into any Dwelling-House, Stable, Barn, Out-house, Ware-house, Store, Shop, or other Building, within the Town of Boston, any . . . Fire-Arm, loaded with, or having Gun-Powder," but that was more because of the danger of fire than of gunfire. Philadelphia had similar restrictions, though a "governor's special license" allowed for exceptions. A Pennsylvania hunting regulation punished anyone who "shall presume to carry any gun, or hunt" on the land of others without permission, or who "shall presume to fire a gun on or near any of the king's highways," and laws in various towns there required gunpowder to be stored only in the highest room in a house—presumably to minimize the danger of fire. New York also had rules for the kinds of containers required to store gunpowder in homes.[21]

And in most parts of the colonies, slaves and indentured servants continued to be denied the right to have firearms of their own. Virginia had "An Act Preventing Negroes from Bearing Arms" as early as 1648, and in 1723 passed another law declaring that "no negro, mullatto, or Indian whatsoever" should "presume to keep, or carry any gun, powder, shot, or any club, or other weapon whatsoever, offensive or defensive." In the Carolinas, where slaves were sometimes impressed into militia service, one white trader warned in 1715 that "there must be great caution used, lest our slaves when armed might become our masters," and South Carolina required owners of slaves to keep their weapons locked and inaccessible to their servants.[22]

In many parts of the backcountry, British commanders trying to use colonist militiamen to help fight the French and Indians found them less than unquestioningly obedient. Americans were uninterested in going off to fight far from home and most responsive only to commanders they knew or had chosen personally. "The King must trust in this country to himself and those he sends," Lord Loudoun wrote in September 1756, "for this Country will not run when he calls." Loudoun was shocked, Boorstin relates, "to see men firing their guns at random after drill, sleeping on post, and taking pot shots at game while they were on the march. But the elected officers would seldom risk unpopularity by punishing offenders."[23]

Only after the French and Indian wars ended with the Treaty of Paris in 1763, with France giving up all its mainland American territories except New Orleans east of the Mississippi, did Indian attacks cease in New England. John Adams, writing to Thomas Jefferson fifty years later, said, "I remember the time when Indian murders, scalpings, depredations and conflagrations were as frequent on the eastern and northern frontier of Massachusetts as they are now in Indiana, and spread as much terror." (Hostilities with Native Americans had continued on that "western" frontier, though, and at the time of Adams's letter, Indians were once again fighting on the side of the enemy around the Great Lakes—only this time the enemy was the British.)

But the shortcomings the British officers had noticed in the colonial militias during the French and Indian wars had fateful consequences for relations between colonists and imperial authority. The militias by themselves could not defend the colonies from the French and Indian threat, and the Crown had been forced to send in large numbers of regular forces. But that had been enormously expensive, forcing the Exchequer to raise taxes and go heavily into debt. Members of Parliament began asking themselves: for whom had they gone to such great trouble and expense? The colonists who benefited from British military protection ought to help pay for it, and there was also no reason they shouldn't be buying more British goods instead of making supplies themselves and selling them for profit.

We all know what happened next: a series of steadily more onerous measures that imposed taxation or customs duties even on ne-
cessities of life, "taxation without representation" to support the cost
of keeping a standing army in the colonies, an army the colonists
were obliged by the Quartering Act to provide with room and board
on their own properties.

But the colonists still had the right and the duty to bear those
firearms they had. And now their thoughts began turning to using
those arms against the increasing oppression they were suffering at
the hands of the mother country across the sea. The colonists had
always felt they were entitled to manage their own affairs, but Parliament in London didn't see it that way. After lifting one of the most
onerous revenue fees, the Stamp Act, in 1766, Parliament had gone
so far as to claim "the absolute right . . . to bind the colonies in all
cases whatsoever." It was a fatal miscalculation.

British officials kept enforcing that right, and when customs officers in 1768 ordered the seizure of the *Liberty*, a ship owned by the
well-known Boston merchant (and much-admired Boston smug-
gler) John Hancock, for not paying the required duty on its cargo of
Madeira wine, an angry mob forced them to take refuge in Castle
William in Boston Harbor and call for English troops to come to
their rescue.

Encouraged by Samuel Adams's success in getting the Massachusetts general court to approve a circular letter to the other colonies
to resist these new English acts of oppression, patriots convened an
unofficial provincial conference in Faneuil Hall as British warships
were sailing into the harbor at the end of September. Delegates from
ninety-six towns called on inhabitants who were "unprovided" to
obey colonial laws requiring soldiers and householders to have "a
well fix'd Firelock, Musket, Accouterments and Ammunition"—in
case rumors of impending hostilities (with France, they were careful
to say) should prove true. And "A.B.C.," perhaps Samuel Adams,

wrote in the *Boston Gazette* of September 26 that "the Governor has said, that he has Three Things in Command from the Ministry, more grievous to the People, than any Thing hitherto made known. It is conjectured 1st, that the Inhabitants of this Province are to be disarmed. 2d. The Province is to be governed by Martial Law."[24]

Two English infantry regiments from Halifax, Nova Scotia, arrived on October 1 and were quartered by orders of the British governor, Sir Francis Bernard, in the settled parts of the city, whose newspapers were soon filled with daily accounts of outrages visited on proper Bostonians by arrogant, brutish louts in uniform who knocked them around, used foul language in the presence of ladies, threatened them with arrest or worse, and had the indecency to parade noisily through the streets with fife and drum while Sunday church services were going on. Governor Bernard sternly threatened punishment for anyone calling citizens to arms, leading Samuel Adams to complain (pseudonymously) in the *Boston Evening Post* that "it is certainly beyond human art and sophistry, to prove the British subjects, to whom the *priviledge* of possessing arms is expressly recognized by the Bill of Rights, and, who live in a province where the law requires them to be equip'd with *arms, &c.* are guilty of an *illegal act,* in calling upon one another to be provided with them, as the *law directs.*"[25]

Commentaries like this, by various pseudonymous authors and all labeled "A Journal of the Times," were widely recirculated in other colonial newspapers during Boston's military occupation. Another essay by Samuel Adams, published on February 27, 1769, observed, "How little do those persons attend to the rights of the constitution, if they know anything about them, who find fault with a late vote of this town, calling upon the inhabitants to provide themselves with arms for their defense at any time; but more especially, when they had reason to fear, there would be a necessity of the means of self preservation against the *violence of oppression.*" Adams cited the leading British constitutional authority of the time, William Blackstone, on the right of "having and using arms for self-preservation and defense" in the Bill of Rights of 1689: "*Having arms for their defense* he tells us is 'a public allowance, under due restrictions, of the *natural right of resistance and self preservation,* when the sanctions of society and laws are found *insufficient* to restrain the *violence of oppression.*'" Blackstone, in his "Commentaries on the Laws of England," had described the right to arms as the fifth auxiliary right of British subjects, auxiliary to the three natural rights of personal security, personal liberty, and private property.[26] But Blackstone, too, noted that the right was circumscribed. British subjects had the right, "suitable to their condition and degree, and such as are allowed by law."[27]

But, as has been shown, the British Bill of Rights was the result of the struggle over sovereignty between the monarchy and Parliament. It is Parliament that had the right to arm British subjects in militias, and Parliament that finally emerged supreme and made the monarch essentially a figurehead. It was Parliament, through acts expressed in the name of the monarchy, that had driven the Americans to revolution, not the royal whim of King George III.

And in America a century after 1689, Samuel Adams clearly wasn't talking about a danger to the individual right of self-preservation. What he had in mind was the collective right to arms to resist oppression—the right to resist armed attempts by the faraway Parliament and king to encroach on the colonists' power to govern themselves, a power they thought had been promised them by the original colonial charters.[28]

In the *Boston Gazette* on December 12, 1768, complaining about the high-handedness of the occupation, Adams wrote:

> It is a very improbable supposition, that any people can long remain free, with a strong military power in the very heart of their country: Unless that military power is under the direction of the

people, and even then it is dangerous.—History, both ancient and modern, affords many instances of the overthrow of states and kingdoms by the power of soldiers, who were rais'd and maintain'd at first, under the plausible pretence of defending those very liberties which they afterwards destroyed. Even where there is a necessity of the military power, within the land, which by the way but rarely happens, a wise and prudent people will always have a watchful & a jealous eye over it; for the maxims and rules of the army, are essentially different from the genius of a free people, and the laws of a free government. Soldiers are used to obey the absolute commands of their superiors. . . .[29]

Samuel's cousin John Adams was called upon to defend that principle as counsel for the British soldiers tried for shooting Crispus Attucks and four others to death in the Boston Massacre of March 5, 1770, when a mob used snowballs, clubs, and a sword (but no guns) to protest the brutality of the occupation. The incident whipped up a frenzy in all the colonies, not just in Massachusetts. As Adams also told the court, "Here every private person is authorized to arm himself, and on the strength of this authority, I do not deny that the inhabitants had a right to arm themselves at that time, for their defense, not for offense."[30] The jury found most of the accused soldiers not guilty of murder; two privates were pronounced guilty of manslaughter and had their hands burned in open court— before being discharged as free men.

But the Crown backed down later on duties imposed on goods the colonies had to import, except for tea. Gradually, tempers cooled—too much so for Samuel Adams, who called a town meeting in Boston in 1772 that endorsed his "State of the Rights of the Colonists." The Boston Tea Party in December 1773 got their juices flowing again, and the British responded with another military occupation.

General Thomas Gage, the commander of all British troops in North America, replaced the governor of Massachusetts Bay in 1774, and four British regiments followed him to Boston. He ordered the seizure of the Massachusetts Colony's arsenal in Charlestown in September but complained that the rebellious colonists were hoarding powder anyway, "and arms are carried out openly by every man that goes out of Boston without molestation." In November, he wrote that he found "the whole country in a Ferment, many parts of it, I may say, actually in Arms, and ready to unite." He warned, presciently, "If Force is to be used at length, it must be a considerable one, and Foreign Troops must be hired, for to begin with Small Numbers will encourage Resistance and not terrify; and will in the End cost more Blood and Treasure."[31]

John Adams wrote a series of essays in the *Boston Gazette* in 1774 addressing objections to possible independence. In his words,

> The colonies south of Pennsylvania have no men to spare, we are told. But we know better; we know that all those colonies have a back country, which is inhabited by a hardy, robust people, many of whom are emigrants from New England, and habituated, like multitudes of New England men, to carry their fuzees or rifles upon one shoulder, to defend themselves against the Indians, while they carry their axes, scythes, and hoes upon the other, to till the ground. . . . But, "have you arms and ammunition?" I answer, we have; but if we had not, we could make a sufficient quantity of both. What should hinder? We have many manufacturers of firearms now, whose arms are as good as any in the world. Powder has been made here, and may be again, and so may saltpetre. What should hinder? We have all the materials in great abundance, and the process is very simple.[32]

Meanwhile, Americans were making changes to the traditional system of general militia service in response to the threat of sustained occupation by a large British regular force. Companies of ordinary militia, free males aged sixteen to sixty who were scattered over the countryside, took time to round up and assemble, rifles at the ready, where they were needed. So in September 1774, a town meeting in Concord, Massachusetts, decided "that there be one or more Companys Raised in this Town by Enlistment and that they Chuse their officers out of the Body So Inlisted and that Said Company or Companies Stand at a minutes warning in Case of an alarm. . . ."[33] Still, it took until the end of January, and several unsuccessful musters, to raise the hundred enlistments of "Minutemen" that Concord set as its quota, as Robert A. Gross found in his groundbreaking 1976 study, *The Minutemen and Their World*.[34] Their own townsmen kept them in arms: guns, saltpeter, holsters, and cartridge cases were all made by fellow citizens. "Minutemen trained twice a week on the common and carried their muskets everywhere, in the fields, in shops, even in church," Gross wrote.[35] Organized in two companies, they were expected to provide the first line of defense when fighting started. And by March 1775, they were ready.

Parliament in London then declared Massachusetts to be in a state of rebellion, but the colonies were by that time united in determination to resist imperial coercion. That July 6, the Second Continental Congress issued a "Declaration Setting Forth the Causes and Necessity of Their Taking Up Arms," written by Thomas Jefferson and John Dickinson, that declared that the right was God-given:

> We gratefully acknowledge, as signal instances of the Divine favor towards us, that his Providence would not permit us to be called into this severe controversy, until we were grown up to our present strength, had been previously exercised in warlike operation, and possessed of the means of defending ourselves. With hearts fortified with these animating reflections, we most solemnly, before

God and the world, declare, that, exerting the utmost energy of those powers, which our beneficent Creator hath graciously bestowed upon us, the arms we have been compelled by our enemies to assume, we will, in defiance of every hazard, with unabating firmness and perseverance, employ for the preservation of our liberties; being with one mind resolved to die freemen rather than to live slaves.

An Anglican minister wrote home from Maryland that year:

In this country, my lord, the boys, as soon as they can discharge a gun, frequently exercise themselves therewith, some a fowling and others a hunting. The great quantities of game, the many kinds, and the great privileges of killing making the Americans the best marksmen in the world, and thousands support their families by the same, particularly riflemen on the frontiers, whose objects are deer and turkeys. In marching through woods one thousand of these riflemen would cut to pieces ten thousands of your best troops.[36]

Indeed, as Adams had noted, Americans had been making improvements to the arms they knew so well how to use. Flintlock muskets were still the most common weapons—single-shot, about five feet long, firing lead balls weighing about an ounce and muzzle-loaded—but more accurate rifles, the rifling inside the barrel ensuring that the projectiles flew with greater accuracy, had been developed. Gunsmiths in Pennsylvania in the second half of the eighteenth century, working from rifles made in Germany, developed the "Pennsylvania" rifle, which later evolved as the better-known "Kentucky" rifle. With stocks of maple, curly maple, or sometimes walnut, these rifles usually had a fixed sight, an octagonal barrel for a bore with slow-pitch rifling, and were about .50 caliber, with a ball of half-inch diameter weighing only half an ounce, fired at high velocity. "Hence at anything under 100 yards the aim was correct within an inch or so with the same sight; and consequently it made no difference whether the savage peeking over a fallen log, or the squirrel squatting on a branch, was 20, 50, or 90 yards away; if he was truly covered, down he went," as one twentieth-century arms expert described its effectiveness.[37] British regulars would soon discover just how deadly the colonists could be as armsmen.

On April 19, 1775, General Gage truly found out what he was up against. He had ordered eight hundred grenadiers and infantrymen to Concord to seize the "considerable quantity of arms and military stores" that had been deposited there at the order of the Massachusetts Provincial Congress for its militia forces. On the way to Concord, in Lexington, he was also expecting to arrest the leaders of the insurgency, Samuel Adams and John Hancock. Paul Revere made his famous ride to summon militiamen from towns between Boston and Lexington to keep all this from happening—but he forgot his pistol, and so he was unable to prevent British troops from stopping him.

Redcoat officers implored the seventy or so militiamen they found waiting in Lexington, "Lay down your arms, Damn you, why don't you lay down your arms!" British muskets fired the first shots and killed eight patriots. Militiamen were, in fact, streaming toward the fight, to Concord; some of them, passing through Braintree, found eight-year-old John Quincy Adams, son of Abigail and John, at their farm, executing the manual of arms with a musket taller than he was.[38] At Concord, the British forces began seizing arms and supplies from the taverns, barns, and farmhouses where the citizens had hidden them and set fire to the "liberty pole" near the courthouse, which soon caught fire as well. Minutemen and militia troops waiting on the outskirts of the village on the west end of the North

Bridge over the Concord River saw the smoke and resolved "to march into the middle of the town to defend their homes, or die in the attempt."[39]

Minutemen, militia volunteers, and three British companies now all converged at the bridge, the Americans on the west end, and on the east the Redcoats, who fired the first volley. "Fire, fellow soldiers, for God's sake, fire," Major John Buttrick commanded in return, and their shots—heard 'round the world—felled nearly a dozen British regulars.

As Timothy Dwight IV, president of Yale College, recounted a generation after the Revolution, the British then withdrew back toward Lexington. "On their way to Lexington they were continually harassed by an irregular, and not ill-directed fire from the buildings and walls on their route," Dwight reported. Nine hundred more British troops arrived to reinforce them, and with their fieldpieces kept the Americans at a distance.

> The neighboring country was now in arms, and moving both to attack the enemy and to intercept their retreat. The troops, therefore, speedily re-commenced their march. From both sides of the road issued a continual fire, directed often by excellent marksmen, and particularly dangerous to the officers . . . Everywhere the retreating army was pursued and flanked. Their enemies descended from every new hill, and poured through every new valley. Perplexed by a mode of fighting, to which they were strangers, and from which neither their valor nor their discipline furnished any security; exhausted by fatigue, and without a hope of succor, the troops wisely withdrew from impending destruction with the utmost celerity.

After the battle, sixty-five British soldiers lay dead, 180 were wounded, and twenty-eight were taken prisoner. The American losses were fifty killed, thirty-four wounded, four missing.[40]

Dwight's telling of the tale shows how powerfully the mythology of the day had already taken hold. The marksmanship of the militiamen, for example: even George Washington at first encouraged the troops of the Continental Army to wear "Hunting Shirts, with long Breeches made of the same Cloth . . . it is a dress justly supposed to carry no small terror to the enemy, who think every such person a complete Marksman."[41] What did not pass into myth were the weaknesses the militia had shown as a body. With little discipline and training in tactics, provincial and regular units at Concord coordinated poorly, leaving the British with time to regroup and withdraw, and after the shooting stopped, many of the soldiers simply went home on their own authority. Later, Washington would often express extreme frustration about the shortcomings of the militia.

In Boston, General Gage saw no choice but to impose a state of siege, promising its citizens permission to leave if they surrendered their arms. Many of them did—1,778 "firearms," primarily muskets; 634 pistols, 973 bayonets, and 38 blunderbusses (short-barreled shotguns) were given up, but Gage did not keep the promise. To those who complained, he replied: "You ask why is the town of Boston now shut up? I can only refer you, for an answer, to those bodies of armed men, who now surround the town, and prevent all access to it . . . I am surrounded by an armed country."

Indeed, the Massachusetts Provincial Congress had appointed Artemus Ward commander in chief of a force of 13,600 quickly mobilized militia soldiers, and Samuel Adams drafted a letter to the Mohawk and other Indian tribes on May 15, saying the British wanted to "take away our liberty and your liberty . . ." and "to make you and us their servants and let us have nothing to eat, drink, or wear, but what they say we shall; and prevent us from having guns and powder to use, and kill our deer, and wolves, and other game, or to send to you, for you to kill your game with, and to get skins and fur to trade with us for what you want: but we hope soon to be able to supply you with both guns and powder, of our own making." The Kahnawake in Québec supposedly wrote back that if they were obliged to take up arms on either side, "they shall take part on the side of their brethren, the English in New England, all the chiefs of the Caughnawaga [Kahnawake] tribe being of English extraction, captivated in their infancy."[42] Gage proclaimed martial law in Boston and offered a pardon to all who would lay down their arms and take a loyalty oath to the Crown—all except John Hancock and Samuel Adams. Doggerel published in several newspapers made fun of his order:

> That whoso'er keeps gun or pistol,
> I'll spoil the motion of his systole—
> Meanwhile let all, and every one
> Who loves his life, forsake his gun. . . .[43]

After the Battle of Bunker Hill in June, won by the British at terrible cost, with nearly triple the losses of their opponents, General Gage wrote: "The Tryals we had shew that the Rebels are not the despicable Rabble too many have supposed them to be, and I find it owing to a Military Spirit encouraged amongst them for a few years past, joined with an uncommon Degree of Zeal and Enthousiasm that they are otherwise."[44] A year later, with the Declaration of Independence, the die was cast.

Some Americans, of course—an estimated 500,000 of them, about 19 percent of the white population during the Revolutionary War—did not renounce loyalty to the Crown. Most remained quiet about it, since the rebelling colonies eventually passed laws disarming and seizing and disposing of the property of those who spoke or acted against independence. About 80,000 loyalists emigrated, to

Britain, Canada, and other places, but many who remained defied laws that made their opposition a form of treason and served in militias that fought with the British army. Some paid for their loyalty with their lives.[45]

Native Americans were caught in the middle of the conflict in parts of New York, and as in the French and Indian wars, both of the principal combatants did all they could to enlist Indian warriors as allies. And, in the Revolutionary War, the Indians lost even more than the British—their native land, in many instances. In New York, Iroquois tribes were drawn into the fighting by both sides. In one of the most violent battles of the entire war, in 1777 at Oriskany Creek in the Mohawk River Valley between the present-day cities of Rome and Utica, a force of eight hundred to one thousand Mohawks and Senecas fought alongside the British, and a smaller number of Oneida warriors sided against their compatriots with the colonial militia. The fighting was intense and bitter, and was hailed as an American victory despite the fact that the revolutionaries suffered five hundred dead, more than in any other battle of the war. But losses were even more telling for the Native Americans. Seventeen Seneca chiefs were killed, most of them in a direct assault against militiamen who felled them with a sheet of flame in volleys from .75-caliber muskets, destroying much of the tribe's leadership. In Richard Berleth's account of the battle, "Twenty feet up from the fire-swept road, one Seneca recalled, the trees were riddled with shot, the leaves torn, and branches down. No one had ever seen so much lead discharged in so small a space."[46] With Oneidas fighting on the other side, the Iroquois Confederacy was in effect destroyed.

By the end of the war, the Mohawk Valley was a wasteland, and the Iroquois tribes numbered only 6,000. In control of half the present territory of New York state in 1784, they were sold out by their British allies and then bought, bamboozled, and bowled out of their lands over the next two decades, driven west like so many other Native American tribes by the inexorable pressure and energy of white settlement. An Oneida chief, dubbed by the victorious Americans Good Peter, lamented, "The voice of the birds from every quarter cried out 'You have lost your country—You have lost your country—You've lost your country! You have acted unwisely and done wrong.' And what increased the alarm was that the birds who made this cry were white birds."[47] It was no different for other tribes: the Catawba Nation in the Piedmont, the Cherokee elsewhere in the South, the Delawares in Pennsylvania.

Americans won their land at a terrible cost to the people who had originally inhabited it and thought it was theirs. And the settlers had won it, for better or for worse, with firearms. This legacy would shape the country the United States became. And American firepower would eventually change the world.

CHAPTER THREE

GUNS AGAINST TYRANNY

Standing armies in time of peace are dangerous to liberty.
FROM VIRGINIA'S PROPOSED BILL OF RIGHTS FOR THE
CONSTITUTION OF THE UNITED STATES, 1788, NO. 17

The values that have shaped our nation do not rest on firepower alone; they have been moral and philosophical since the beginning, though in contemporary discourse they have often been distorted or poorly understood. Although some on the left today would like to think the Second Amendment an aberration, the freedom it protects was included in the Bill of Rights for the same reason that freedom of speech, the right to jury trials, and the right to be secure against unreasonable searches and seizures were included: to protect Americans from tyranny that could be imposed by a strong federal government.

The language itself does no favors to those looking for its true meaning: "A well regulated Militia, being necessary to the security of a free State, the right of the people to keep and bear Arms, shall not be infringed."

Start with this: does "the right of the people to keep and bear arms" mean your right and mine, or only the right of the state we live in to arm its militia? Lawyers, judges, lobbyists, and politicians argued about this for fifty years before the two Supreme Court decisions in the *Heller* and *McDonald* cases in 2008 and 2010, both narrowly decided by 5–4 conservative majorities that concluded that the right, for us today, is an individual and not a collective one, connected more to self-defense than to defense of the state.

I am not a legal historian, much less a Supreme Court originalist who thinks that what the men who wrote and debated and finally adopted the Bill of Rights thought the Second Amendment meant then is the only thing it can mean today. Nevertheless: as a journalist with an interest in history and no animus for or against gun rights, I wanted to find out what "the right of the people to keep and bear arms" meant to the men who wrote the Second Amendment—by going back to see what the founders were actually *saying* and *writing* about it.

I would be the first to admit that interpreting things that were said and written more than two centuries ago with only partial context to go on is a process fraught with uncertainty. The Supreme Court majority, and I and many others have all read the identical documents, and yet we have come to profoundly unidentical conclusions about what they mean.

But one thing is clear: the founders shared an idea of what they thought was the greatest danger to freedom, something very hard for us to imagine as a danger today—the threat of tyranny imposed on an unwilling population by a standing army. Little wonder that they had such a fear back then; the king's Redcoats and Hessian mercenaries had tried to impose just such tyranny on the colonies. The

Constitution to replace the failed Articles of Confederation that was agreed upon at the Constitutional Convention in Philadelphia in 1787 had created a strong new federal government and given its legislature, Congress, the authority to "raise and support Armies" in case of need. But the framers knew that tyranny could arise, as one of them said, "from our own bowels," especially if the federal government had to create a powerful standing army. However, they thought tyranny could not prevail if citizens remained armed and answerable to the call to civic duty in the militias of the separate states, the political entities closest to the people.

There was so much concern that the new federal government should not be overpowering that the founders realized that to get this new Constitution ratified by a majority of the thirteen states, they would have to amend it with guarantees that Congress and the president could not overstep their bounds. Thus the Second and the other amendments that ended up in what later became known as the Bill of Rights were intended to accomplish a political purpose—to ensure ratification of the new Constitution by attenuating the fears it inspired. Fear that a federal government could deprive Americans of their right to bear arms was not the central concern, but it was one of many that supporters of the Constitution wanted to address. Distrust of big government is not something invented by the twenty-first-century Tea Party—it has been a powerful element of American political thought since the original eighteenth-century Boston Tea Party.

Supporters of the new Constitution sought to ensure ratification by making formal guarantees that the new national government would not deprive Americans of the individual rights they had fought for under the Articles of Confederation. It was not an easy sell.

But . . . see for yourself.

In January 1776, John Adams wrote a letter, "Thoughts on Government," to George Wythe of Virginia. Earlier in the Revolution,
Wythe had asked Adams what plan of government he would envi-
sion in preparation for the formation of a republic. In his response,
among Adams's thoughts was this:

> A militia law, requiring all men, or with very few exceptions besides
> cases of conscience, to be provided with arms and ammunition, to
> be trained at certain seasons; and requiring counties, towns, or
> other small districts, to be provided with public stocks of ammu-
> nition and entrenching utensils, and with some settled plans for
> transporting provisions after the militia, when marched to defend
> their country against sudden invasions; and requiring certain dis-
> tricts to be provided with field-pieces, companies of matrosses
> [gunnery troops], and perhaps some regiments of light-horse, is
> always a wise institution, and, in the present circumstances of our
> country, indispensable.[1]

Adams also recognized, as the common law did, that citizens
could use arms "at individual discretion" in "private self-defense"—
but mainly he saw in the right to have firearms a connection to the
civic duty of militia service: "To suppose arms in the hands of citizens, to be used at individual discretion, except in private self-
defense, or by partial orders of towns, counties, or districts of a state,
is to demolish every constitution, and lay the laws prostrate, so that
liberty can be enjoyed by no man; it is a dissolution of the government. The fundamental law of the militia is, that it be created, di-
rected, and commanded by the laws, and ever for the support of the
laws."[2] So much for the persistent claims by the Branch Davidians
and other misguided fringe groups two hundred years later that the
founders gave them the right to form citizens' militias to resist any
kind of government authority.

Most of the earliest state constitutions or declarations of rights also tied the right to carry arms to service in the state militia. Virginia's was the first, adopted in 1776. Thomas Jefferson, who wrote three drafts of the state constitution, tried at first to make the right a more clearly personal entitlement. An admirer of the Italian eighteenth-century thinker Cesare Beccaria's idea that "the laws that forbid the carrying of arms . . . disarm only those who are neither inclined nor determined to commit crimes,"[3] Jefferson wrote, in his first draft, "No freeman shall ever be debarred the use of arms"—slaves, of course, were not entitled to them. In the second and third drafts, he narrowed this down slightly: "No freeman shall be debarred the use of arms (within his own lands or tenements)."[4]

But when it was adopted, the Virginia constitution included none of these words, nor any other explicit description of the individual right to have firearms or use them for private purposes. It did have in its Declaration of Rights, drafted by George Mason, what can be read as an implicit recognition of the right of self-defense, an acknowledgment that citizens "have certain inherent rights, of which, when they enter into a state of society, they cannot, by any compact, deprive or divest their posterity," first among them "the enjoyment of life and liberty. . . ." But all the declaration says about arms is: "That a well regulated militia, composed of the body of the people, trained to arms, is the proper, natural and safe defense of a free state; that standing armies, in time of peace, should be avoided, as dangerous to liberty; and that, in all cases, the military should be under strict subordination to, and governed by, the civil power." A year earlier, Mason had explained that he thought a well-regulated militia should be "composed of gentleman freeholders, and other freemen"—led, in other words, by property-holding gentry, the same class to which the right to bear arms in the British Bill of Rights was later applied in practice.[5] What Virginia's constitution left unsaid, but clearly assumed, was that the "body of the people" could not be "trained to arms" unless the individuals in it had the right to own arms and knew how to use them.

Much like Virginia, North Carolina proclaimed in its 1776 constitution "that the people have a right to bear arms for the defense of the state," with a warning against standing armies and a statement of the need to subordinate the military to civilian authority. Maryland and Delaware both adopted declarations of rights that did not explicitly include the right to bear arms but proclaimed a "well-regulated militia" the natural defense of free government and a standing army a danger to liberty.

Were all these states trying to say that only men subject to militia service had the right to keep and bear arms? If so, it wouldn't have amounted to much of a limitation, because at the time virtually all adult males were obliged, in theory, to serve in the militia. Pennsylvania (later followed by Vermont, when it became a state) clearly did not do this in its Declaration of Rights in 1776, which proclaimed for its citizens "the right to bear arms for the defense of themselves and the state." But joined to that clause was another: "and as standing armies in the time of peace are dangerous to liberty, they ought not to be kept up." The "defense of themselves" right that Pennsylvanians were concerned about was, some historians say, most probably not the common-law right of individual self-defense but the result of the long prior refusal by the Quaker-dominated colonial legislature to pass a militia law urged by Benjamin Franklin and others to help settlers along the western border defend themselves against Indian attacks. Franklin had argued that volunteers could provide their own weapons, "most People having a Firelock of some kind or other already in their hands."[6]

Later, during his mission to Paris to get French support for the Revolution, Franklin wrote in response to a pseudonymous "secret and confidential" note in English attacking the Americans that somebody had tossed over the gate of his lodgings, "Our militia you find by experience are sufficient to defend our lands from invasion....We therefore have not the occasion you imagine of fleets or standing armies, but may leave those expensive machines to be maintained for the pomp of princes, and the wealth of ancient states."[7]

In 1779, drafting a declaration of rights for the constitution of the Commonwealth of Massachusetts that was adopted the following year, John Adams began with "All men are born free and equal, and have certain natural, essential, and unalienable rights, among which may be reckoned the right of enjoying and defending their lives and liberties...." Article 17 of the Massachusetts Declaration of Rights, as finally adopted, begins: "The people have a right to keep and bear arms for the common defense...."[8] The meaning is clear: the state constitutional right that "the people" had was connected to their duty to the common defense.

At first glance, "keep and bear," in this context, seems clearly a military term of art. But the phrase can equally be read to mean that the people have a right to keep arms, and to bear arms for the common defense. And how could "the people" bear arms for the common defense if individuals had no personal right to have arms for their own purposes? Adams's wording did not specify that only "people subject to militia service" could have arms. A few years later, in his defense of the constitutions of government of the United States of America, he made clear what he meant, by writing that "the people, or public, comprehends more than a majority, it comprehends all and every individual."[9]

This "common defense" wording sailed through almost every one of the well over one hundred Massachusetts town meetings that were called to adopt the state constitution. Almost every one of them ended with a unanimous vote of approval. In only a couple of towns, both of them on what a hundred years earlier had been the

dangerous Massachusetts "frontier" where Indian raids were a constant danger, was there any hint that people found that the declaration too narrowly defined their right to arms. In one of these,
Northampton, the townsfolk thought that Article 17 was "not expressed with that ample and manly openness and latitude which the
importance of the right merits" and wanted it changed to "the people
have a right to keep and bear arms as well for their own as the common defense." Their wording was almost identical to what people in
nearby Williamsburg had voted to adopt in their own meeting two
weeks earlier, as explained by Josiah Dwight, the town clerk: "1st
that we esteem it an essential priviledge to keep Arms in Our houses
for Our Own Defense and while we Continue honest and Lawfull
Subjects of Government we Ought Never to be deprived of them.
Reas. 2 That the legislature in some future period may Confine all
the fire Arms to some publick Magazine and thereby deprive the
people of the benefit of the use of them."[10]

In the twentieth century, proponents of the idea that the Second
Amendment created a constitutional individual right to keep and
bear arms for self-defense would cite the reservations expressed in
Williamsburg and Northampton as proof of general nationwide concern at the time that the individual right was under threat from government. But outside of those two neighboring towns in what had
long been the state's western frontier, exposed to Indian attacks, the
people of Massachusetts generally voiced no such concern and even
overwhelmingly backed a state constitution that made clear that it
was not individual self-defense but the collective "common defense"
that it meant to guarantee with the right to arms. No other towns
joined Williamsburg and Northampton, and Massachusetts adopted
the constitution with the wording as it was, "common defense." That
did not mean that people in Massachusetts could not have arms for
self-defense or hunting; that went without saying, as it had from the

beginning. It was a right in common law, but not a right elevated to protection by the state constitution.

But state constitutions and declarations of rights alone did not ensure that the militia would be well trained and well organized— "well regulated"—and capable of providing that common defense. As a reality, the militia sometimes fell short of that level. For all the lore and legend about the Minutemen, who were in fact more specialized and better trained than the broader militia, none other than George Washington said, after victory had been won, that "if I was called upon to declare upon Oath, whether the Militia have been most serviceable or hurtful upon the whole; I should subscribe to the latter."[11] Much earlier, after the French and Indian wars, he had written: "Militia, you will find, Sir, will never answer your expectation, no dependence is to be placed upon them; They are obstinate and perverse, they are often egged on by the Officers, who lead them to acts of disobedience, and, when they are ordered to certain posts for the security of stores, or the protection of the Inhabitants, will, on a sudden, resolve to leave them, and the united vigilance of their officers can not prevent them."[12]

Washington knew what he was talking about. He had taken command of what the Continental Congress proclaimed as the Continental Army just outside Boston on July 2, 1775, and it was a force of New England citizen-soldier volunteers from militias that were far from "well regulated." They included sharpshooters who inflicted heavy casualties on the British, but also troops who were dirty, undisciplined, untrained, and greatly inclined to drink. "Many had volunteered on the condition that they could elect their own officers, and the officers, in turn, were inclined out of laziness, or for the sake of their own popularity, to let those in the ranks do much as they pleased," as David McCullough described them in his book *1776*. "For every full-fledged deserter there were a half-dozen others inclined to stroll off on almost any pretext, to do a little clam digging perhaps, or who might vanish for several weeks to see wives and children, help with the harvest at home, or ply their trades for some much-needed 'hard money.' . . . It was not that they had no heart for soldiering, or were wanting in spirit. They simply had had little experience with other people telling them what to do every hour of the day."[13]

Washington and his officers, Alexander Hamilton, Nathanael Greene, Henry Knox, and others, had whipped discipline into this Continental Army, but it had not been easy, in large part because the political forces of the thirteen colonies that had established it had great mistrust—"fatal jealousy," Washington called it in 1780—of a standing army. Congress was always behind in payments to finance its operations, and through Valley Forge and later, troops, short of clothing, even short of food, were paid in currency that was, if not worthless, shaky (because the sovereign states were slow to respond to requests from Congress for money to pay for the war). Washington had to beg Congress and, when that was unavailing, had to plead with the individual states to pay up and provide the troops he requisitioned, all the way through the war, as Ron Chernow's biography *Washington: A Life* makes clear: "One half the year is spent in getting troops into the field," he wrote to his brother Samuel in 1780, "the other half is lost in discharging them from their limited service." Later that year, he wrote to Congress, "*No militia* will ever acquire the habits necessary to resist a regular force . . . The firmness requisite for the real business of fighting is only to be attained by a constant course of discipline and service."[14]

Even after the final victory at Yorktown, Congress neglected its bills, leaving most soldiers unpaid while the peace negotiations dragged on. As a result, in early 1783, there was a near-mutiny of officers at the Continental Army's encampment near Newburgh, New

York, after an anonymous pamphlet urged the army to refuse to defend the country and march on Philadelphia to force Congress to pay up. It took a speech by Washington himself to bring the restive officers to their senses:

> This dreadful alternative, of either deserting our Country in the extremest hour of her distress, or turning our Arms against it, (which is the apparent object, unless Congress can be compelled into instant compliance) has something so shocking in it, that humanity revolts at the idea. My God! What can this writer have in view, by recommending such measures? Can he be a friend to the Army? Can he be a friend to this Country? Rather, is he not an insidious Foe? Some Emissary, perhaps from [still British-held] New York, plotting the ruin of both, by sowing the seeds of discord and separation between the Civil and Military powers of the Continent?[15]

When he took out his glasses and said that he had gone not only gray but nearly blind in the service of his country, insurrectionary feelings were washed away in a flood of tears. Congress did finally pay, but the end of the Continental Army was more like gradual collapse than organized demobilization. Most soldiers just decided themselves when to go home. Military preparedness in peacetime would not come easily to Americans for many years to come.

Under the Articles of Confederation, in 1784, Congress refused Washington's request to establish a small standing army and a trained national militia, though it later authorized a First American Regiment force of about seven hundred soldiers provided by the states to defend against foreign attack, Indian raids, or domestic insurrection. The states provided indifferent support, and the regiment was incapable of dealing with Shays' Rebellion in western

Massachusetts in 1786–1787, an armed uprising against the state government by debt-ridden farmers forced into bankruptcy because of the high taxes that had been levied on them to help pay off the state's Revolutionary War debt. After farmers organized an armed Minuteman force and shut down courthouses in Northampton and Worcester to prevent foreclosures on distressed properties, the governor called out the state militia, but eight hundred of them joined forces with the rebels. The Continental Congress then stepped in to help Massachusetts draft more obedient troops, and when 1,200 rebels moved on the national arsenal at Springfield, the government militia routed them, sending Daniel Shays and Eli Parsons fleeing to New Hampshire. A year later, Major Samuel Nasson of the Massachusetts province of Maine tried to make the best of the militia's performance: "If during the last winter, there was not much alacrity shown by the militia in turning out, we must consider that they were going to fight their countrymen."[16]

Inadequate provision for dealing with insurrections and for the national defense was but one of the many defects of the Articles of Confederation. Seeking resolution, the founding fathers, Washington among them, met again in Philadelphia in 1787 to try, first, to fix it—and then to replace it altogether with a new Constitution that created, for the first time, a strong national government, but one whose powers were to be balanced with those of the states, not to replace them. Unlike the unwritten British constitution, in which government is entirely the creature of Parliament, the American design split legislative and executive power so that one could balance the other, with an independent federal judiciary to check both of them.

As far as military matters were concerned, the new Constitution left to the states the power to appoint officers and train troops but gave Congress the power to set standards and call up men from the militias for national service to enforce laws, suppress insurrections, and repel invasions. The "militia" whose effectiveness these provisions wanted to ensure was not the body of all armed adult male citizens age seventeen to forty-five but a "select"—better trained, equipped, and disciplined—force that would make it unnecessary to resort in all cases to a standing national army. Indeed, it was not a "federalist" but George Mason of Virginia who proposed it on August 18, the notes of the debates show: "Mr Mason introduced the subject of regulating the militia. He thought such a power necessary to be given to the general government. . . . Thirteen states will never concur in any one system, if the disciplining of the militia be left in their hands. If they will not give up the power over the whole, they probably will over a part, as a select militia." Mason it was, as well, who first moved a proposal to leave to the states the authority of appointing militia officers, so as to preserve a federal-state balance.[17] James Madison, more concerned about the nation as a whole, argued, "The states neglect their militia now, and the more they are consolidated into one nation, the less each will rely on its own interior provisions for its safety, and the less prepare its militia for that purpose. . . . The discipline of the militia is evidently a *national* concern, and ought to be provided for in the *national* constitution."[18]

When the convention finally finished its work in September, it was agreed that the states and the national government would share the responsibility of equipping and training the force: Article 1, Section 8, of the Constitution gave Congress the responsibility to organize, arm, and discipline the militia, and reserved to the states the right of appointing militia officers and training troops to the standards set by Congress. Crucially, the new Constitution also gave Congress the power "to raise and support" a national army and to create a navy, but it limited budget appropriations for the army to

two years at a time, to ensure that, leashed by such short congressional purse strings, it would remain under civilian control. Mason
was one of the participants who decided he could not agree to the
Constitution as it was, and he suggested it should have a bill of rights.
Mason was convinced, he told the convention on September 15, that
the system established by the Constitution "would end either in
monarchy or a tyrannical aristocracy—which, he was in doubt—
but one or other, he was sure."[19]

Mason was far from alone in fearing the effects of strengthened
federal power over the states, and demands arose for amendments to
ratify the perceived defects, with Thomas Jefferson and Elbridge
Gerry of Massachusetts, notably, viewing the lack of a bill of rights as
the most glaring omission. "Federalists," as people like Hamilton,
Madison, and John Jay cleverly dubbed themselves to throw sand in
the eyes of critics of the new Constitution—who, wanting to preserve
powers for the states, considered themselves the true federalists—
countered their arguments in essays published in the newspapers in
New York that were widely circulated in other states as well—the *Federalist Papers*.

Madison, writing as "Publius" in *Federalist 46* in January 1788, argued that the militia was the best single guarantee against the danger
a standing national army could pose to states' rights. Although the
scenario he outlined to prove the point may seem far-fetched today,
his reasoning assumes that the American common-law individual
right to arms would enable the state militias to counterbalance any
tendency toward tyranny by the national government. The United
States, by his calculations, could not raise a national army of more
than 25,000 or 30,000 men. Even if its commanding general ran
amok and tried to impose tyrannical rule with military force,

> To these would be opposed a militia amounting to near half a mil-
> lion of citizens with arms in their hands, officered by men chosen

from among themselves, fighting for their common liberties, and united and conducted by governments possessing their affections and confidence. . . . Besides the advantage of being armed, which the Americans possess over the people of almost every other nation, the existence of subordinate governments, to which the people are attached, and by which the militia officers are appointed, forms a barrier against the enterprises of ambition, more insurmountable than any which a simple government of any form can admit of.[20]

Hamilton, one of Washington's most talented generals, had a realistic view of how much intensive training would be required to create a true "well-regulated militia" out of the entire armed citizenry, but in *Federalist 29*, the same month, he also showed no doubts that they were entitled to arms, provided by the government if need be: "Little more can reasonably be aimed at, with respect to the people at large, than to have them properly armed and equipped; and in order to see that this be not neglected, it will be necessary to assemble them once or twice in the course of a year," he wrote; a "select corps" would provide "an excellent body of well-trained militia, ready to take the field whenever the defense of the State shall require it" and would banish the tyrannical danger of a standing army. Hamilton believed that "the State governments will, in all possible contingencies, afford complete security against invasions of the public liberty by the national authority." "When," he asked in *Federalist 28* at the end of 1787, "will the time arrive that the federal government can raise and maintain an army capable of erecting a despotism over the great body of the people of an immense empire, who are in a situation, through the medium of their State governments, to take measures for their own defense, with all the celerity, regularity, and system of independent nations?"[21]

Still, the anti-federalists were not convinced.

One of them in New York, "Brutus" (thought to be Robert Yates), warned that mistrust of a standing army was not a far-fetched concern, reminding his readers what George Washington had spared the country from in that near-mutiny in the last days of the Continental Army in 1783. "I firmly believe," he wrote in January 1788,

> no country in the world had ever a more patriotic army, than the one which so ably served this country, in the late war. But had the General who commanded them, been possessed of the spirit of a Julius Caesar or a Cromwell, the liberties of this country, had in all probability, terminated with the war. . . . When an anonymous writer addressed the officers of the army at the close of the war, advising them not to part with their arms, until justice was done them—the effect it had is well known. It affected them like an electric shock. He wrote like Caesar; and had the commander in chief, and a few more officers of rank, countenanced the measure, the desperate resolution had been taken, to refuse to disband. What the consequences of such a determination would have been, heaven only knows. The army were in the full vigor of health and spirits, in the habit of discipline, and possessed of all our military stores and apparatus. . . . We should in all probability have seen a constitution and laws, dictated to us, at the head of an army, and at the point of a bayonet, and the liberties for which we had so severely struggled, snatched from us in a moment. It remains a secret, yet to be revealed, whether this measure was not suggested, or at least countenanced, by some, who have had great influence in producing the present system. Fortunately indeed for this country, it had at the head of the army, a patriot as well as a general. . . .

The remedy, "Brutus" suggested, was a constitutional amendment to make it impossible for the central government to raise troops for a standing army in peacetime without a two-thirds majority in both House and Senate, and to limit its function to guarding the frontiers and meeting the threat of any foreign invasions. Again, not a word about any threat to the individual right to bear arms or the need of a constitutional amendment to protect it.[22]

A minority of twenty-one members of the Pennsylvania convention that ratified the Constitution at the end of 1787 dissented after the majority refused to include their reservations in the official report of the vote. There were fourteen such reservations in all, questioning the lack of a guarantee of freedom of conscience, of freedom of speech, and so on. In point 7, the dissenters, much like the townsfolk of Northampton and Williamsburg in Massachusetts before them, wanted a guarantee "that the people have a right to bear arms for the purpose of defense of themselves and their own state, or the United States, for the purpose of killing game; and no law shall be passed for disarming the people or any of them, unless for crimes committed, or real danger of public injury from individuals. . . ." But the words that follow add this crucial justification: "as standing armies in the time of peace are dangerous to liberty, they ought not to be kept up: and that the military shall be kept under strict subordination to and be governed by the civil powers." They added that the right to fowl and hunt and fish in all the several states should go to all inhabitants "without being restrained therein by any laws to be passed by the legislature of the United States."[23]

The proposed Constitution would inevitably "produce a despotism," the Pennsylvania minority report explained, not least if Congress had complete control of the militia, which could then become "the unwilling instruments of tyranny." Congress could create a "select" militia and use it as a standing army to destroy liberty: "The militia of Pennsylvania may be marched to New England or Virginia to quell an insurrection occasioned by the most galling oppression, and aided by the standing army, they will no doubt be successful in subduing their liberty and independency. . . ." And "the rights of conscience may be violated, as there is no exemption of those persons who are conscientiously scrupulous of bearing arms," as the Quakers were in Pennsylvania.[24]

But when they listed "those unalienable and personal rights of men, without the full, free and secure enjoyment of which there can be no liberty," that they wanted in a bill of rights, what were those? They were "the rights of conscience, personal liberty by the clear and unequivocal establishment of the writ of habeas corpus, jury trial in criminal and civil cases, by an impartial jury of the vicinage or county, with the common-law proceedings, for the safety of the accused in criminal prosecutions; and the liberty of the press, that scourge of tyrants, and the grand bulwark of every other liberty and privilege; the stipulations heretofore made in favor of them in the state constitutions, are entirely superseded by this constitution." Did they think that the right to carry arms for self-defense did not rise to the level of "unalienable and personal rights" without which there could be no liberty? A greater fear, clearly, was what control of the militia by the new national Congress could do to liberty; most of the discussion of arms in the Pennsylvania dissent is about that.[25]

The Pennsylvania minority's views were much on the minds of supporters of the Constitution when the Massachusetts ratifying convention met in January 1788, but few of the concerns expressed by the doubters in Boston had much to do with the right to arms, and there again, those that did related to the militia. More serious were doubts about the wisdom of letting Southern states count slaves for the apportionment of congressional seats, about the federal power of taxation, and other matters of fundamental importance. Those doubts even made it seem possible that Massachusetts would not ratify. Finally, in hopes of averting that danger, Samuel Adams proposed a compromise that he hoped would also be adopted later by other states and ensure ratification of the Constitution. The essence of his compromise was the promise of certain amendments as a condition of approval. As another delegate had put it, Massachusetts would "instruct our first members in Congress to exert their endeavors to have such checks and guards provided as appear to be necessary in some of the paragraphs of the Constitution."

After considerable debate, John Hancock, the president of the Massachusetts ratifying convention, formally presented a list of suggested amendments, and it was finally adopted. But, significantly, it did not include a guarantee of the right to bear arms. Adams did try, almost at the end of the convention, to add one, thinking it might win over opponents of ratification, and gun-rights advocates ever since have quoted what he said as support for the view that what the authors of the Second Amendment must have meant it to do was to ensure that Congress could never prevent law-abiding individual American citizens from having firearms for self-defense.

Here is the language Samuel Adams actually proposed:

And that the said Constitution be never construed to authorize Congress, to infringe the just liberty of the press, or the rights of conscience; or to prevent the people of the United States, who are peaceable citizens, from keeping their own arms; or to raise standing armies, unless when necessary for the defense of the United States, or of some one or more of them; or to prevent the people from petitioning, in a peaceable and orderly manner, the federal legislature, for a redress of grievances; or to subject the people to unreasonable searches and seizures of their persons, papers or possessions.

Samuel Adams, the firebrand who had fomented the Boston Tea Party, certainly did want gun rights made explicitly clear—for "peaceable citizens"—but his proposal links that concern with the worry about standing armies. He did not even put the right to keep arms ahead of the right to freedom of the press. He may have believed that the Constitution needed an amendment to protect the right of individual Americans to have firearms for self-defense, but he didn't put those words into his proposal—you have to infer them to believe that this is what he meant. (Supreme Court Justice Stephen Breyer inferred something else, though, in his dissent from the *Heller* decision in 2008: "Samuel Adams doubtless knew that the Massachusetts Constitution contained somewhat similar protection. And he doubtless knew that Massachusetts law prohibited Bostonians from keeping loaded guns in the house. So how could Samuel Adams have advocated such protection *unless* he thought that the protection was *consistent* with local regulation that seriously impeded urban residents from using their arms against intruders?")

Adams soon saw that his proposals were having the opposite of the intended effect on the delegates and stirring up more opposition to the Constitution. As the journal of the convention reported laconically, on the same day as he submitted them, "after they were debated a considerable time," he withdrew his proposals as "not meeting the approbation of those gentlemen whose minds they were intended to ease." Massachusetts ratified the Constitution, with the suggested amendments listed by Hancock, by 187 votes to 168, with nary a word about the right to keep arms.[26]

In June 1788, New Hampshire adopted a similar list but added a proposal that did what Adams had wanted to do for Massachusetts: "Congress shall never disarm any Citizen unless such as are or have been in Actual Rebellion." Live free or die, perhaps, but the last thing the founders intended militias to do, despite the many misreadings of their intent by twentieth-century radical libertarians, was to give discontented citizens the right to take up arms against the state. As Hamilton had written in *Federalist 28* at the end of the previous year:

"An insurrection, whatever may be its immediate cause, eventually endangers all government"; and "if insurrection should pervade a whole State, or a principal part of it, the employment of a different kind of force might become unavoidable," a more powerful and "more regular" force "constituted differently from the militia, to preserve the peace of the community and to maintain the just authority of the laws against those violent invasions of them which amount to insurrections and rebellions."

Hamilton would later be seen as a crypto-monarchist by such anti-federalist "republican" leaders as Jefferson and Patrick Henry, who warned at the ratifying convention in Virginia that same June about the dangers to state sovereignty that a too-powerful national government would pose. "Have we the means of resisting disciplined armies, when our only defense, the militia is put into the hands of Congress?" he asked in a speech on June 5.[27] Congress could starve a state militia of arms by not providing any. Or a powerful president at the head of a centralized government could easily misuse the army to seize all power in his own hands like a king, he warned two days later: "The army will salute him Monarch; your militia will leave you and assist in making him King, and fight against you: And what have you to oppose this force? What will then become of you and your rights? Will not absolute despotism ensue?" The record of the proceedings inserts at this point, "Here Mr. Henry strongly and pathetically expatiated on the probability of the President's enslaving America and the horrible consequences that must result."[28]

Influenced, perhaps, more by the Massachusetts compromise than by the best efforts of Hamilton, Madison, and Jay, Virginia ratified the Constitution despite such objections and attached a recommendation for a bill of rights with twenty points. Number 17 was this, in language very much like that of the state's own declaration of rights: "That the people have a right to keep and bear arms; that a well regulated Militia composed of the body of the people trained to arms is the proper, natural and safe defense of a free State. That standing armies in time of peace are dangerous to liberty, and therefore ought to be avoided, as far as the circumstances and protection of the community will admit; and that, in all cases, the military should be under strict subordination to, and governed by, the civil power."[29] Defining the militia as "the body of the people trained to arms" rather than a "select" smaller corps implied that for Virginians it was the right of all the people—meaning individuals—to have arms and be trained to use them. Indeed, that was their right under common law. But the focus of the proposed amendment was on ensuring that the state militia would be a counterweight to federal power.

New York, where the anti-federalists were also strong, ratified the new Constitution a month later, on July 27, also with a long list of proposed amendments, including guarantees of freedom of the press and the right to trial by jury, and the right to bear arms: "That the people have a right to keep and bear arms; that a well-regulated militia, including the body of the people capable of bearing arms, is the proper, natural, and safe defense of a free state." New York's ratification expressed confidence that these proposals for amendments would receive "an early and mature consideration."[30] And so they did.

With the Constitution ratified by the necessary majority of states, Madison did what he and other supporters had agreed to do. After the new House of Representatives convened on June 8, 1789, Madison introduced a proposed list of rights to be inserted into the Constitution (though he wanted them sewn into the original articles at appropriate points, not appended separately as they finally were).

What became the Second Amendment started out as this, in Madison's draft, which he intended to be inserted in Article 1, Section 9, with the guarantee of habeas corpus and the ban on bills of attainder and ex post facto laws, rather than among the militia clauses in Section 8: "The right of the people to keep and bear arms shall not be infringed; a well armed, and well regulated militia being the best security of a free country: but no person religiously scrupulous of bearing arms, shall be compelled to render military service in person."[31] Notable is that lack of mention of self-defense, hunting, or target practice. Was this because he and others had argued from the beginning that the Constitution gave only limited powers to the central government and that regulating individual self-defense, hunting, or target practice was not among them? That seems to me to be the most logical explanation, because the individual right was, as I have repeatedly pointed out, clearly established in the common law of the land.

Weeks of debate followed in the House, with a select committee report on proposed amendments and then consideration by the committee of the whole. Representative Frederick A. Muhlenberg of Pennsylvania, the Speaker, noted in a letter to Benjamin Rush that the report of the Committee of the Whole House "takes in the principal amendments which our minority had so much at heart." But the House did not adopt any of the Pennsylvania minority's wording—did not expand the scope of the right to include hunting and self-defense—in the version that it passed on August 24. Was that because members of the House did not believe that Americans had this individual right? The lack of a record of debate on that point, and all the other evidence already examined of how much Americans in the 1780s took for granted their right to have guns, makes that seem extremely unlikely. The House version that was finally adopted was: "A well regulated militia, composed of the body of the People,

being the best security of a free State, the right of the People to keep
and bear arms, shall not be infringed, but no one religiously scrupulous of bearing arms, shall be compelled to render military service
in person."[32]

In the Senate, the conscientious-objector provision was deleted,
and a proposal that would have made the meaning of "keep and bear
arms" even clearer (and more restrictive) by adding to it "for the
common defense" was rejected. Why? Because senators thought it
was clear enough that this is what it meant, or because they thought
"for the common defense" would imply that individuals did not have
the right to keep arms for their own self-defense? It is not possible
to tell.[33] But it is clearly wrong, and illogical, to assert, as some gun-
rights enthusiasts and others have done, that the intention was to
guarantee the individual right of self-defense *rather than* the common defense.[34] That conclusion ignores the whole context of the debate, which was squarely focused on the militia and how the states
and the federal government should share responsibility for providing
for it.

What the states were finally asked to approve in the Bill of Rights
was the wording that has come down to us in our day: "A well regulated militia, being necessary to the security of a free State, the right
of the people to keep and bear arms, shall not be infringed." After
Virginia ratified it in 1791, the Bill of Rights, with this as the Second
Amendment, went into effect (though it was not formally ratified by
Massachusetts, Connecticut, and Georgia until 1939!).

It is beyond dispute, it seems to me, that what the authors of the
amendment intended—the original purpose at the time—was to
ensure that the *states* could not be deprived of their militias by the
federal government. They saw the states as the political entities closest to the people, and the state legislatures as the surest obstacle to
federal overreach. In late eighteenth-century America, there was little

reason for law-abiding individuals of sound mind to fear being deprived of their individual common-law right to arms for self-defense or hunting. And the framers knew the militias would be useless to either the federal or the state governments unless the citizens who served in them had the right to have arms in their homes and knew how to use them, so that they could do their duty when duty called. All able-bodied free men, white men between eighteen and forty-five, at any rate, had that right, an individual right. They all had that duty as well.

The framers did not set out to create a new individual constitutional right. The language makes that clear: the amendment does not say, "the people shall have the right to keep and bear arms"; it says, "the right of the people to keep and bear arms shall not be infringed," thus recognizing, acknowledging, and protecting an individual right that Americans had already, a preexisting right. And it conjoined the right to keep arms with the *duty* to bear arms in what, at that time, amounted to civil defense. When the founders said "rights," they meant rights that came with civic responsibilities. But they did not say, or write, that people had the right to keep and bear arms only if they were serving in a militia. The militia needed people equipped with and trained to use guns. But those people did not need to belong to a militia to have the right to own them.

Major Samuel Nasson wrote to a friend in mid-1789, after Madison had submitted his first proposal to Congress:

Amendments are once again on the carpet. . . . Then there will be no Dispute Between the people and rulers in that may be secured the right to keep arms for Common and Extraordinary Occasions such as to secure ourselves against the wild Beast and also to amuse us by fowling and for our Defense against a Common Enemy. You know to learn the Use of arms is all that can Save us from a foreign

foe that may attempt to subdue us, for if we keep up the Use of arms
and become well acquainted with them, we Shall always be able to
look them in the face that arise up against us.[35]

He believed the Second Amendment recognized that right implicitly.

T he Second Amendment was not effective in achieving its original purpose of ensuring a well-regulated militia. States could
not form militias if the able-bodied men living in those states in the
late eighteenth century did not have the right to own firearms and
know how to use them—but neither could they form effective militias unless they regarded it as a duty and took their duty seriously.
In peacetime most of them did not, until the late twentieth century.
Thomas Jefferson, in *Notes on the State of Virginia,* said that there
were 49,971 men serving in the militia in that state in 1787, but that
some served poorly indeed. "The law requires every militia-man to
provide himself with arms usual in the regular service. But this injunction was always indifferently complied with, and the arms they
had have been so frequently called for to arm the regulars, that in the
lower parts of the country they are entirely disarmed," Jefferson
wrote. "In the middle country a fourth or fifth part of them may have
such firelocks as they had provided to destroy the noxious animals
which infest their farms; and on the western side of the Blue Ridge
they are generally armed with rifles."[36]

The Uniform Militia Act passed by Congress in 1792, a year after
the Bill of Rights was adopted, made clear, in principle, what a mili-
tiaman's duty was:

Each and every free able-bodied white male citizen of the respective states, resident therein, who is or shall be of the age of eighteen
years, and under the age of forty-five years (except as is herein after

excepted) shall severally and respectively be enrolled in the militia by the captain or commanding officer of the company, within whose bounds such citizen shall reside.... Every citizen so enrolled and notified, shall, within six months thereafter, provide himself with a good musket or firelock, a sufficient bayonet and belt, two spare flints, and a knapsack, a pouch with a box therein to contain not less than twenty-four cartridges, suited to the bore of his musket or firelock, each cartridge to contain a proper quantity of powder and ball: or with a good rifle, knapsack, shot-pouch and powder-horn, twenty balls suited to the bore of his rifle, and a quarter of a pound of powder; and shall appear, so armed, accoutred and provided, when called out to exercise, or into service.[37]

The force envisioned by the Uniform Act was not the "select militia" that Secretary of War Henry Knox had originally proposed in 1790, a plan for a national militia divided into an "advanced corps," a "main corps," and a "reserved corps." That was the kind of thing that many of the founders had considered almost as potentially dangerous to liberty as a standing army itself. The House debated how Congress should live up to its constitutional responsibility to provide arms for the militia, but Roger Sherman of Connecticut, according to a newspaper account of the debate in 1790, thought that

there were so few free men in the United States incapable of procuring themselves a musquet, bayonet and cartouchbox, as to render any regulation by the general government respecting them improper. If the people were left to themselves, he was pretty certain the necessary warlike implements would be provided without inconvenience or complaint, whereas if they were furnished by Congress, the public arsenals would be speedily drained, & from the careless manner in which many persons are disposed to treat such public property, he apprehended they would be speedily lost or destroyed.[38]

Sherman had been instrumental in formulating the earliest changes to the Constitution as a separate set of amendments rather than interpolating them into the original articles. A few years later, St. George Tucker, a jurist and federal judge who had been a colonel in the Virginia militia during the revolution, noted that lack of uniform standards, training, and discipline among the various militias had been responsible for "a very large portion of those disgraces, which attended the militia of almost every state, during the revolutionary war," shortcomings that George Washington had complained about.[39] Tucker also warned that neglect in properly providing for the militia would "pave the way for standing armies, the most formidable of all enemies to genuine liberty in a state."

Having failed to bring about its first goal, neither did the Second Amendment achieve the secondary goal of its original purpose—that of avoiding the establishment of a large standing army. President Washington used the militia to suppress the Whiskey Rebellion in 1794 and 1795 when distillers rose up against federal duties imposed on them to help pay off the Revolutionary War debt taxes. The rebels countered by calling on armed citizens to help them defend "republican liberty." Secretary of State Edmund Randolph feared some of the militia might sympathize as they had in Massachusetts during Shays' Rebellion and find common cause with the rebels, raising the specter of a civil war. "There is another enemy in the heart of the Southern States who would not sleep with such an opportunity of advantage," he warned Washington on August 7, 1794. The militia rallied to the federal cause and did its duty. The Whiskey Rebels were defeated, and Washington then gave their leaders a pardon. But, a month later, Secretary Knox reported that fewer than one-third of the Americans required to be ready for militia service owned any arms, despite the requirements of the Uniform Act.[40]

In the War of 1812, on the whole, the performance of the militia left much to be desired. The governors of three New England states refused at first to answer President Madison's call to summon their militias to federal service, and there was individual resistance to being called up for duty.[41] British forces were able to penetrate the defenses of the national capital and torch the White House—after the Fifth Maryland Militia cut and ran in a battle at Bladensburg. Their compatriots from Tennessee, Louisiana, and Kentucky acquitted themselves better in the Battle of New Orleans on January 8, 1815, under the command of Andrew Jackson—after peace had been negotiated across the sea, unbeknownst to the combatants. Jackson's forces, which besides 2,100 militiamen using five-foot-long, high-velocity Kentucky rifles also included five hundred regulars, took negligible casualties but killed or wounded over 2,000 British troops wielding less accurate smooth-bore weapons. "Many of the dead were shot accurately in the center of the forehead; scores had two or more bullet holes in the skull; hundreds were literally riddled with bullet holes," an arms expert boasted a century later of the militiamen's feats in this, "the first large battle between the smooth bore and the rifle."[42]

But after the war, most of the militiamen laid down their arms and went back to peaceable pursuits. William H. Sumner, the adjutant general of Massachusetts, found public apathy toward the militia so great there in 1823 that he published a pamphlet in the form of a letter to ex-president John Adams in Quincy, warning about the dangers of letting its readiness deteriorate. The framers of the Constitution had made provisions "for arming the whole body of active citizens and for organizing, officering, and disciplining them, as soldiers, as the surest safeguard of their liberties," he wrote. Adams, whose brief answer was published with the pamphlet, agreed that there was danger in letting the militia devolve into a "select" corps of the few who would volunteer: "You have proved it to be the most essential foundation of national defense. . . . These American states have owed their existence to the militia for more than two hundred years. Improve its constitution by every prudent means, but never destroy its universality. A select militia will soon become a standing army, or a corps of Manchester yeomanry. . . . Whenever the militia comes to an end, or is despised or neglected, I shall consider this union dissolved, and the liberties of North America lost forever."[43]

A decade later, the distinguished jurist Joseph Story noted in his commentaries on the Constitution:

> It cannot be disguised that, among the American people, there is a growing indifference to any system of militia discipline, and a strong disposition, from a sense of its burdens, to be rid of all regulations. How it is practicable to keep the people duly armed without some organization, it is difficult to see. There is certainly no small danger, that indifference may lead to disgust, and disgust to contempt; and thus gradually undermine all the protection intended by this clause of our national bill of rights.[44]

Besides another war with Great Britain, there were a lot of things that few people besides Hamilton in the 1790s had been able to foresee—most important, the Civil War, the first shots of which were fired at federal troops in Fort Sumter by the Palmetto Guard, a unit in the South Carolina militia. Standing armies replaced the militias in both the Confederacy and the Union during the war. After the shooting stopped, things took different courses on either side.

In the Northern states, the Union army rapidly shriveled after winning the war—from 1 million men in 1865 to fewer than 30,000 in 1870, remaining below that level in the decades following. The general unorganized militia still existed in theory, but the only militia troops that could be called up were those serving in volunteer units (gradually becoming known as "National Guard" units) that were in fact "select" militias, and those were few and far between. When militia troops were called out, it was often to put down a strike against a railroad or a coal mine, and often they did a poor job.

When war broke out with Spain in 1898, the army had no organized system of drafting recruits and President William McKinley had to issue a special call for volunteers. Theodore Roosevelt was among those who came to its rescue with his Rough Riders, but after the war, as president, he told Congress at the end of 1901:

> Action should be taken in reference to the militia and to the raising of volunteer forces. Our militia law is obsolete and worthless. The organization and armament of the National Guard of the several States, which are treated as militia in the appropriations by the Congress, should be made identical with those provided for the regular forces. The obligations and duties of the Guard in time of war should be carefully defined, and a system established by law under which the method of procedure of raising volunteer forces should be prescribed in advance. It is utterly impossible in the excitement and haste of impending war to do this satisfactorily if the arrangements have not been made long beforehand. Provision should be made for utilizing in the first volunteer organizations called out the training of those citizens who have already had experience under arms, and especially for the selection in advance of the officers of any force which may be raised; for careful selection of the kind necessary is impossible after the outbreak of war.

In 1903, Congress separated the "organized militia, to be known as the National Guard," from the "reserve militia," which was thenceforth little more than the pool of all American men subject to the draft.

It took two world wars and the cold war to change American thinking to accept the necessity of a strong national defense force, intricately bound with the National Guard, to ensure the security of the country. Today, the US Army and the US Air Force could not accomplish their assigned missions without the National Guard units that serve regularly with them. National Guard units are fully integrated into the regular military command when they are called up to serve, as they have been constantly, for the wars in Iraq and Afghanistan.

But is the Second Amendment now completely unmoored from any connection with civic duty, in or outside of the militia? And when did self-defense come to be understood as its main purpose? The history of gun rights in America over the two centuries after the Revolution provides the answers.

CHAPTER FOUR

GUNS AND SELF-DEFENSE IN NINETEENTH-CENTURY AMERICA

*Full and equal benefit of all laws and proceedings concerning
personal liberty [and] personal security, including the constitutional right to bear arms.*

FREEDMEN'S BUREAU ACT, 1866

I magine: the eighteenth-century gentlemen who wrote the founding documents believed, or hoped, that the Constitution they created had codified a social compact. As Americans civilized the
wilderness, they would eventually be able to rely not just on their
own skill at individual self-defense for protection against thieves and
criminals, but on the laws and civil authorities and the other institutions of government they were building. Nothing shows more
clearly the spirit of these early years than the preface to the *Travels*

in New-England and New-York that Timothy Dwight IV, president of Yale College, began in 1796, published in London in 1823 after his death as letters "to an English Gentleman":

> In both New-England and New-York, every man is permitted, and in some, if not all the states, is required to possess fire arms. To trust arms in the hands of the people at large has, in Europe, been believed, and so far as I am informed universally, to be an experiment fraught only with danger. Here by a long trial it has been proved to be perfectly harmless; neither public nor private evils having ever flowed from this source, except in instances of too little moment to deserve any serious regard. If the government be equitable; if it be reasonable in its exactions; if proper attention be paid to the education of children in knowledge and religion, few men will be disposed to use arms, unless for their amusement, and for the defense of themselves and their country. The difficulty here has been to persuade the citizens to keep arms, not to prevent them from being employed for violent purposes.[1]

Would Dwight have been surprised by the rampant gun violence of our time? And is the Second Amendment to blame for it, or are other factors? Looking at the way Americans have thought about gun rights over time provides one set of answers. Yet, curiously, looking at the way American courts have thought about them provides a different set, as we shall see.

In the beginning, in the decades immediately after the Revolutionary War, the problem for state and national governments was not that too many people had guns but that, as Dwight had observed, too few took seriously enough the duty to have and know how to use them in case they were called up for militia service. Until the nineteenth century, muskets and long arms had been cumbersome, unwieldy, and expensive—slow to load and fire and too expensive for many people to acquire. And despite the 1792 militia law, many adult white males who did not need guns for self-defense ignored the duty to acquire them for militia service. Long arms had to be imported or handmade by artisans, limiting their availability, until Eli Whitney and others introduced what he called the Uniformity System (mass production) for firearms after Napoleon threatened the United States with war in 1798.

After the turn of the century, as they became more easily available, guns came to be seen less as adjuncts to civic duty than as means of individual empowerment and self-defense. With that change came abuses of the right to own and use firearms, and, consequently, increased regulation. These changes did not come all at once; they came in different ways, and they also produced backlashes—indeed, one that began in the 1960s that has led to the present-day ascendancy of the view that the right to own and carry personal weapons for self-defense is paramount.

But then, we've always been schizophrenic about firearms. Going back two hundred years, take the problem posed by duels, for example. Dueling had been relatively uncommon until the Revolution, and after the turn of the century it was even illegal in New Jersey and New York, but in New Jersey the law against it was not enforced severely and in New York it was. So when Alexander Hamilton and Aaron Burr, both New Yorkers, though Burr was then vice president of the United States, agreed to settle an affair of honor with a duel in 1804, they decided to do it across the Hudson River in Weehawken, New Jersey. They had no problem finding guns; Hamilton picked the weapons, as was his right. They were the same pistols, owned by his brother-in-law, that had been used in the duel in which his son Philip had died in 1801—.544-caliber smooth-bore flintlocks made by the London gunsmith Wogden in the 1790s, "with lacquered walnut handles, ornamental designs, and gold mountings along their brass barrels" and bullets that weighed a full ounce.[2]

Burr and Hamilton embarked at dawn on July 11 in separate boats to cross the river, and two hours later were at the dueling ground twenty feet above the water on the Hudson Palisades. Hamilton had intended to miss his first shot, and it went into the trees nowhere near his opponent, but, firing almost simultaneously, Burr dealt Hamilton a fatal wound in the abdomen above his right hip. Both men went back to New York separately with their seconds, but Hamilton was able to tell his friends before he died there that he had thrown away his shot, and Burr was indicted for murder. The charge was later reduced, but Burr fled through Philadelphia and Washington, DC, to an island off the coast of Georgia. In late October, a New Jersey grand jury did charge him with murder, but he had no problem returning to Washington, presiding over the Senate when it reconvened on November 4, or dining with President Thomas Jefferson, no political friend of Hamilton's, in the White House more than once. The state indictment was eventually dismissed because Hamilton had not died in New Jersey.[3]

This custom of settling matters of honor with firearms continued to spread in the decades immediately following, especially among the political-military elite, and in the South. Henry Clay dueled against Humphrey Marshall in 1809; James Barron killed Stephen Decatur in a duel in 1820; Governor James Hamilton of South Carolina wounded opponents in fourteen duels. Andrew Jackson, who may have participated in as many as a hundred of these contests, stretched the code by pulling the trigger twice on Charles Dickinson of Nashville, Tennessee, in 1806. Dickinson had been allowed to shoot first and had fired one shot that struck Jackson, who was not wounded so severely that he could not take his turn. But when he pulled the trigger, his pistol failed to fire. He fired again and wounded his opponent, fatally. The question of honor in this case was Dickinson's, having called Jackson "a worthless scoundrel, poltroon and a coward," an insult Jackson considered a more serious offense than attempted murder. Jackson went on to become president and survive an assassination attempt in 1835, when a housepainter tried to shoot him with two flintlock pistols, both of which misfired.[4]

States in the South, starting with Virginia in 1810, passed anti-dueling laws, but Southern gentlemen who defied the law and yet managed to survive were often able to rely on the reluctance of juries of their peers to convict them. But there were other sanctions. Duelists were often blacklisted from society, barred from prestigious clubs and positions. So those offended took to less socially risky (if physically just as risky) alternatives. Carrying concealed weapons that could be pulled out to avenge honor on the spot was one of them, allowing satisfaction (for one of the parties, perhaps, anyway) and avoiding the potential complications of a formal duel, with its need for a formal challenge and for finding people to serve as seconds, and its complicated rules.[5]

On his travels to America, Alexis de Tocqueville talked to a young Alabama lawyer from Montgomery in 1832 ("I have forgotten his name which anyhow is very obscure," he wrote in his notes) who told him: "There is no one here but carries arms under his clothes. At the slightest quarrel, knife or pistol comes to hand. These things happen continually; it is a semi-barbarous state of society." But, de Tocqueville asked, when a man is killed like that, is his assassin not punished?

> He is always brought to trial, and always acquitted by the jury, unless there are greatly aggravating circumstances. I cannot remember seeing a single man who was a little known, pay with his life for

such a crime. This violence has become accepted. Each juror feels that he might, on leaving the court, find himself in the same position as the accused, and he acquits. Note that the jury is chosen from all the free-holders, however small their property may be. So it is the people that judges itself, and its prejudices in this matter stand in the way of its good sense.[6]

Far from being restricted to use in militia service, firearms for personal use became more readily available as manufacturing techniques improved after the mid-1830s. A riot in Philadelphia in 1844 that started in a clash between Irish immigrants and "native" Protestants over the exclusive use of the Protestant Bible in public schools was marked by so much gunfire, and so many deaths and injuries, that one member of the militia that was called in wrote, "We have never had anything like it before, but now that firearms have been once used & become familiar to the minds of the mob, we may expect to see them employed on all occasions, and our riots in future will assume a more dangerous character."[7]

American enthusiasm for small arms in private hands grew even after the assassinations of three presidents, Abraham Lincoln, James A. Garfield, and, in 1901, William McKinley (during an organ recital at a World's Fair in Buffalo). Before the establishment of regular police forces in midcentury, outright murders had been taking place on the streets so often, particularly after the Colt revolver (a mass-produced product, like Whitney's rifles, made in Connecticut) came into use in 1838, that by the time of the Civil War, Kentucky, Louisiana, Georgia, Virginia, Alabama, and Ohio had all passed laws to make it illegal to carry concealed weapons—not just guns, but knives, picks, and anything else that could be used to do bodily harm.

What did the courts of the time have to say about such laws? Generally, they found them consistent with the right to keep and bear arms. There was no disputing that the right to bear arms openly was one all white male Americans had—but state courts, for the most part, ruled that concealing deadly weapons was craven and cowardly (rulings that gun owners didn't like, even back then, a century before concealed-carry laws permitted the practice almost everywhere). A decision in 1840 by the supreme court of Tennessee, whose state constitution provided "the free white men of this state" with "a right to keep and bear arms for their common defense," for example, upheld a law that said, "if any person shall wear any bowie knife, or Arkansas tooth-pick, or other knife or weapon, that shall in form, shape or size resemble a bowie knife or Arkansas tooth-pick, under his clothes, or keep the same concealed about his person, such person shall be guilty of a misdemeanor, and upon conviction thereof, shall be fined in a sum not less than two hundred dollars, and shall be imprisoned in the county jail, not less than three months and not more than six months."

One William Aymette had been caught the previous June carrying not just one but two such knives concealed, and in *Aymette v. The State,* the Tennessee court channeled the thinking that had gone into the national debates about the Second Amendment more than half a century earlier. It came to the conclusion that the right guaranteed by its equivalent in Tennessee's constitution was the right to use weapons that could be used for the common defense, not concealed weapons like bowie knives that were only good for private purposes:

> King James II, by his own arbitrary power, and contrary to law, disarmed the Protestant population, and quartered his Catholic soldiers among the people. This, together with other abuses, produced the revolution by which he was compelled to abdicate the throne of England. William and Mary succeeded him, and, in the first year of their reign, Parliament passed an act recapitulating the abuses

which existed during the former reign, and declared the existence of certain rights which they insisted upon as their undoubted privileges. Among these abuses they say, in sec. 5, that he had kept a "standing army within the kingdom in time of peace, without the consent of Parliament, and quartered soldiers contrary to law." Sec. 6. "By causing several good subjects, being Protestants, to be disarmed, at the same time when Papists were both armed and employed contrary to law."

In the declaration of rights that follows, sec. 7 declares that "the subjects which are Protestant may have arms for their defense, suitable to their condition and as allowed by law." . . . No private defense, was contemplated, or would have availed anything. If the subjects had been armed, they could have resisted the payment of excessive fines, or the infliction of illegal and cruel punishments. When, therefore, Parliament says that "subjects which are Protestants may have arms for their defense, suitable to their condition, as allowed by law," it does not mean for private defense, but, being armed, they may as a body rise up to defend their just rights, and compel their rulers to respect the laws.

Judge Nathan Green, who wrote the decision, saw the British situation correctly. As anybody who knows the history of England or has lived in Britain long enough to see how very different British parliamentary democracy is from its American, republican (with a small r) form will recognize, the British Declaration of Rights was, first and foremost, an expression of Parliamentary control over the monarchy, not an expression of individual rights like our own Bill of Rights. *Aymette* went on:

With us, every free white man is of suitable condition, and, therefore, every free white man may keep and bear arms. But to keep and bear arms for what? If the history of the subject had left in doubt the object for which the right is secured, the words that are employed must completely remove that doubt. It is declared that they may keep and bear arms for their common defense. . . . The object, then, for which the right of keeping, and bearing arms is secured is that of the public. The free white men may keep arms to protect the public liberty, to keep in awe those who are in power, and to maintain the supremacy of the laws and the constitution. . . . They need not, for such a purpose, the use of those weapons which are usually employed in private broils, and which are efficient only in the hands of the robber and the assassin. These weapons would be useless in war. They could not be employed advantageously in the common defense of the citizens. The right to keep and bear them is not, therefore, secured by the constitution.[8]

That conclusion, of course, was drawn from the explicit "common defense" language in Tennessee's constitution, not from the Second Amendment to the federal Constitution, with its language acknowledging the right to have private weapons and use them. The *Aymette* decision did not go so far, but still, it left the right to military-type rifles and pistols and bayonets "such as are usually employed in civilized warfare" secure, even in Tennessee. (Tennessee later revised its constitution to add a provision giving the legislature "power by law to regulate the wearing of arms with a view to prevent crime," and in *Andrews v. The State* in 1871 its supreme court found that a law making it illegal to carry a pocket pistol or revolver or knife was consistent with this provision, again because these were not military weapons protected by the state constitution's "common defense" clause.)

Most states had passed laws or adopted constitutional provisions protecting the right to keep and bear arms, some tying it to the common defense, many not. Kentucky protected the individual right to own and use guns, not limiting the right to militia service, in 1792. When thirty years later its supreme court ruled that a law against carrying concealed weapons violated the state constitution, it was then amended to allow such a ban.[9] In Missouri, which became a state in 1820 (under the Missouri Compromise, which allowed slavery there and barred it in Maine, which was admitted at the same time), the state constitution said that the people's right to bear arms "in defense of themselves and of the state, cannot be questioned." (Maine's right was "for the common defense" but was also unquestionable.) Texas, in 1845, proclaimed, "Every citizen shall have the right to keep and bear arms in the lawful defense of himself and the State." Similar constitutional provisions in many of the sixteen other states that were admitted to the union between 1790 and 1860 protected the right for individual self-defense, or family defense, as well as for collective purposes.[10]

But concealed carrying was still against the law in many places, including in states that protected the right to have guns. Local regulations didn't violate the federal Constitution because it was thought to apply only to federal actions. In 1850, the Louisiana supreme court upheld a statute making concealed carrying of a pistol (or knife) a misdemeanor with these words:

> This law became absolutely necessary to counteract a vicious state of society, growing out of the habit of carrying concealed weapons, and to prevent bloodshed and assassinations committed upon unsuspecting persons. It interfered with no man's right to carry arms (to use its words) "in full open view," which places men upon an equality. This is the right guaranteed by the Constitution of the United States, and which is calculated to incite men to a manly and noble defense of themselves, if necessary, and of their country, without any tendency to secret advantages and unmanly assassinations.[11]

The state of Georgia, "to guard and protect the citizens of the State against the unwarrantable and too prevalent use of *deadly weapons,"* passed a law in 1837 forbidding most pistols altogether and barring concealed carrying of other weapons such as the usual dirks and bowie knives, and so on. But in 1846, the state supreme court found that one Hawkins H. Nunn had been unconstitutionally indicted, not for concealing but for openly brandishing a pistol. Georgia could make concealed *carrying* of pistols or other weapons illegal, the court said, but it could not keep people from *having* pistols. The reasoning was out of the ordinary range in 1846, but it would be echoed 162 years later in the *Heller* decision:

> Does it follow that because the people refused to delegate to the general government the power to take from them the right to keep and bear arms, that they designed to rest it in the State governments? Is this a right reserved to the *States* or to *themselves*? Is it not an inalienable right, which lies at the bottom of every free government? We do not believe that, because the people withheld this arbitrary power of disfranchisement from Congress, they ever intended to confer it on the local legislatures. This right is too dear to be confided to a republican legislature. . . .
>
> The right of the people, old and young, men, women and boys, and not militia only, to keep and bear arms of every description, and not such merely as are used by the militia, shall not be infringed, curtailed, or broken in upon, in the smallest degree; and all this for the important end to be attained: the rearing up and qualifying a well-regulated militia, so vitally necessary to the security of a free State. Our opinion is, that any law, State or Federal, is repugnant to the Constitution, and void, which contravenes this right, originally belonging to our forefathers, trampled under foot by Charles I. and his two wicked sons and successors, re-established by the revolution of 1688, conveyed to this land of liberty by the colonists, and finally incorporated conspicuously in our own Magna Charta! And Lexington, Concord, Camden, River Raisin,

Sandusky, and the laurel-crowned field of New Orleans plead elo-
quently for this interpretation! And the acquisition of Texas may
be considered the full fruits of this great constitutional right.[12]

But this was not the commonly held judicial view at the time. In
Texas, for example, in 1871, the legislature passed a law making it a
misdemeanor for anyone to carry—even in a saddle—a pistol, a dirk,
or a dagger "unless he has reasonable grounds for fearing an unlawful
attack on his person, and that such grounds of attack shall be immediate and pressing" (with exceptions for militiamen, police, and others). The next year, in *English v. The State*, the Texas supreme court
found that William English had been lawfully convicted of violating
the law because he had been wearing a pistol while drunk in the city
of Jefferson. The law, the court said, was not in conflict with the Texas
constitution, which provided that "every person shall have the right
to keep and bear arms in the lawful defense of himself or the state,
under such regulations as the legislature may prescribe." And it found
that the Second Amendment protected the bearing of arms only in
connection with militia service:

> To refer the deadly devices and instruments called in the statute
> "deadly weapons," to the proper or necessary arms of a "well-regu-
> lated militia," is simply ridiculous. No kind of travesty, however sub-
> tle or ingenious, could so misconstrue this provision of the
> constitution of the United States, as to make it cover and protect
> that pernicious vice, from which so many murders, assassinations,
> and deadly assaults have sprung, and which it was doubtless the in-
> tention of the legislature to punish and prohibit. The word "arms,"
> in the connection we find it in the Constitution of the United
> States, refers to the arms of a militiaman or soldier, and the word is
> used in its military sense. . . . It will doubtless work a great improve-

ment in the moral and social condition of men, when every man shall come fully to understand that, in the great social compact under and by which states and communities are bound and held together, each individual has compromised the right to avenge his own wrongs, and must look to the state for redress. We must not go back to that state of barbarism in which each claims the right to administer the law in his own case; that law being simply the domination of the strong and the violent over the weak and submissive. It is useless to talk about personal liberty being infringed by laws such as that under consideration. The world has seen too much licentiousness cloaked under the name of natural or personal liberty; natural and personal liberty are exchanged, under the social compact of states, for civil liberty.[13]

Arms in military service, as the Texas court said, were another matter. After the outbreak of the Mexican-American War in 1846, "I can shoot straight" was all the qualification that the Southwest frontier guide "Kit" Carson, at the age of sixteen, had needed to offer Colonel Stephen W. Kearny, who then ordered him to lead a wagon train of 1,600 volunteers, all good shots, from Missouri to the Mexican stronghold at Santa Fe. It fell without a shot in September 1846, after Mexican forces fled the field rather than fight.

Carson and Kearny later found more fight in the enemy in California, but once the Mexicans were defeated, all that stood in the way of fulfilling the American "manifest destiny to overspread the continent allotted by Providence for the free development of our yearly multiplying millions," in the memorable words of the journalist John L. O'Sullivan, were the Native American tribes that thought Providence had allotted the same continent to them. These— Navajo, Apache, Comanche, and Ute—would later prove to be formidable adversaries to the "New Men," as the Navajo chief Narbona called the Americans, and Kit Carson would himself serve with the army to do battle with them. Except that a large number of white settlers speaking Spanish instead of English had preceded the Americans this time, the dynamic was much the same as it had been for the Abenaki, Narragansett, Massasoit, Pequot, and Powhatan in frontier Massachusetts, Maine, or Virginia two centuries before. On top of Andrew Jackson's Removal Act and the relocation or forced removal west of the Mississippi of the Cherokee, Choctaw, Seminole, Creek, and other Southern Indian nations, the outcome, for the Indians, was disastrous, right up to the Battle of the Little Bighorn in 1876, the defeat of Custer in that last stand notwithstanding.

Noted landscape architect Frederick Law Olmsted spent the years 1863–1865 in California as manager of a gold mine in Bear Valley. There, practically every man carried a gun. He wrote of his experience that "a night seldom passed in which there was not a quarrel in which pistols were used by a number of persons" and someone was killed. "A large proportion of those who lost their lives appear to have been Mexicans or Negroes (Indians never count)," he wrote. Of conflict between white settlers and Indians along the western frontier in general, he observed:

Indians driven from their traditional hunting and camping grounds occasionally attack white settlers. Occasionally these attacks, especially the bolder ones, create great excitement in a cluster of white settlements, perhaps a panic occurs, and a period of furious, half-mad, savage fear and hatred of Indians, in which, throughout the communities affected, no red man, no Mexican or Negro who can be imagined to have affinity with red rather than white men, are safe. Finally the army cooperates with the settlers, or some sort of systematic movement is made against the real enemy. He is driven farther back, the frontier advances, the settlements move up correspondingly, and henceforth those who last suffered from Indian barbarities are a little more safe.

And something like this, the incidents varying infinitely, has, I repeat, been going on for the last two hundred years, all along the crooked frontier lines—a distance of from one to three thousand miles.[14]

Yes, settlers used arms to win the West, shortening long rifles so that weapons could be more easily used on horseback against Indian attack, but the lawlessness that Olmsted observed was succeeded, even in the "wilderness," by surprisingly restrictive state and municipal regulations on the ownership and use of firearms, as the Texas law cited above shows. Concealed carry was banned in Montana, Oklahoma, and in fact in most states by the end of the nineteenth century, but many states and municipalities in the "Wild West" considered themselves free even to ban wearing guns openly. The famous shootout at the OK Corral in Tombstone, Arizona, in 1881 started after Ike Clanton was fined $27.50 for violating a local ordinance—one that forbade openly carrying firearms within the city limits. In Dodge City, Kansas, cowboys on cattle drives were obligated to "check" their weapons at the edge of town, to minimize mayhem in the saloons and whorehouses they had come to visit. "Frontier communities like gun control because small towns on the border of civilization wanted to become bigger towns filled with civilized people," Adam Winkler writes. "The growth and economic development they wanted required attracting investors, who were going to come only if the towns were stable and crime was low."[15]

The fear that the people could be disarmed had been an abstraction for the founding fathers, though they held on to vivid memories of how the British had tried to make it a physical reality.

After independence, the founders imagined disarmament as one of the ways homegrown tyrants might try to subvert the new Constitution. But on a smaller, less abstract scale, in the South during the years leading up to the Civil War, and during Reconstruction afterward, concern about disarmament had a different meaning, intimately connected with racism, and more directly with the right to self-defense than with the right to resist tyranny.

Many white Southerners began carrying weapons in the early nineteenth century for reasons that had nothing to do with dueling. Some carried them "as a protection against slaves," as Richard Hildreth, a contemporary journalist, wrote, particularly after the discovery of a rebellion planned by Denmark Vesey, a former slave in Charleston, in 1822 to encourage a mass uprising, kill all the slave masters, and flee to safety in Haiti. Vesey's plan was nipped in the bud, and he and thirty-four of his followers were hanged. But another slave uprising, the one led by Nat Turner in Virginia in 1831, killed at least fifty-seven whites. Although Turner's followers had used mostly knives, axes, and blunt instruments, not guns, many Southern legislatures moved after the violence to deny the right to own firearms not only to slaves but also to free blacks.

In 1840, for example, North Carolina passed a law providing "that if any free negro, mulatto, or free person of color, shall wear or carry about his or her person, or keep in his or her house, any shot gun, musket, rifle, pistol, sword, dagger or bowie-knife, unless he or she shall have obtained a license therefor from the Court of Pleas and Quarter Sessions of his or her county, within one year preceding the wearing, keeping or carrying thereof, he or she shall be guilty of a misdemeanor, and may be indicted therefor." When a free black man, Elijah Newsom, was convicted of violating the law by having a shotgun in his possession, the state supreme court ruled in 1844 that the law and the conviction were in accordance with North Carolina's constitution, which at the time denied "free people of color" the right to vote and meant that they "cannot be considered as citizens, in the largest sense of the term,"[16] a view later reinforced by the United States Supreme Court.

Blacks had not been recognized by the Constitution as citizens, Chief Justice Roger B. Taney wrote in the *Dred Scott v. Sandford* case in 1857; the large slaveholding states would never have agreed to that. "It would give to persons of the negro race, who were recognized as citizens in any one State of the Union, the right to enter every other State whenever they pleased . . . to go where they pleased at every hour of the day or night without molestation . . . and it would give them the full liberty of speech in public and in private upon all subjects upon which its own citizens might speak, to hold public meetings upon political affairs, and to keep and carry arms wherever they went." In the antebellum South, guns were for whites only, a situation that was increasingly infuriating to Northern supporters of abolition.

Parts of the West became a new theater of confrontation between supporters and opponents of slavery after the Kansas-Nebraska Act of 1854 opened the possibility of slavery in those territories if enough settlers there wanted it. Supporters and opponents in Kansas elected rival governments and rushed, bringing plenty of firearms with them, to populate settlements. Abolitionists in the anti-slavery states began supplying their Kansas allies with breech-loading rifles made by the Sharps Rifle Manufacturing Company of Connecticut. Henry Ward Beecher, the firebrand abolitionist preacher of Brooklyn, told the *New York Tribune* in 1856 that Sharps rifles had "more moral power," at least against pro-slaveholding gangs in Kansas, than a hundred Bibles. Sharps rifles were shipped by the crateload to anti-slavery forces in Kansas, labeled as books—"Beecher's Bibles."

Olmsted, now back in New York City, signed up as the official representative of the militia of the Kansas abolitionist stronghold of Lawrence, and raised $400 to supply the corps with arms. As his biographer Witold Rybczynski writes, Olmsted "went on a shopping spree at the New York State Arsenal and purchased a mountain howitzer together with fifty rounds of canister and shell and, for good measure, added five hand grenades, fifty rockets, and six swords. He told the private sellers that the shipment was intended for 'landing in boats on some foreign coast.'"[17]

Disarm the abolitionist settlers, their pro-slavery opponents and their supporters cried. In Washington, in the Senate chamber, as armed pro-slavery thugs were marching on Lawrence to sack the place, Charles Sumner of Massachusetts thundered against Andrew Pickens Butler of South Carolina:

> The rifle has ever been the companion of the pioneer and, under God, his tutelary protector against the red man and the beast of the forest. Never was this efficient weapon more needed in just self-defense, than now in Kansas, and at least one article in our National Constitution must be blotted out, before the complete right to it can in any way be impeached. And yet such is the madness of the hour, that, in defiance of the solemn guarantee, embodied in the Amendments to the Constitution, that "the right of the people to keep and bear arms shall not be infringed," the people of Kansas have been arraigned for keeping and bearing them, and the Senator from South Carolina has had the face to say openly, on this floor, that they should be disarmed—of course, that the fanatics of Slavery, his allies and constituents, may meet no impediment.[18]

Senator Butler was incensed, and his cousin, Congressman Preston Brooks, later thrashed Sumner nearly to death on the Senate floor with his cane.

During the Civil War, 180,000 former slaves served with the Union armies, usually in segregated units, not always happily. Some of the 11,000 free blacks in New Orleans offered to serve with General Benjamin F. Butler's forces after he seized New Orleans in April 1862, but the next February, eighteen of their officers resigned, saying white soldiers had treated them with "scorn and contempt."[19] Emancipation, when it came, finally brought to African Americans the common-law right to have arms for hunting and self-defense. They did not have the right to vote, but after the end of the war, white Southerners moved to disarm them.

Mississippi adopted a "black code" in late 1865 forbidding any "freedmen, free negro, or mulatto" not serving in the occupying army to have or carry firearms or knives without a license from the local police, and Alabama's black codes did the same. The Mississippi militia wore Confederate uniforms and even confiscated weapons from black veterans of the Union army who had been allowed to take their rifles home with them. In Florida, blacks found to be keeping firearms could be punished by whiplashing. South Carolina passed a law at the same time excluding blacks from the state militia and forbidding them to keep weapons that could be used in military service—a sort of negative Second Amendment law—though "owners of a farm" could keep a shotgun or a hunting rifle.[20] Black South Carolinians sent a petition asking Congress to invalidate this law "as a plain violation of the Constitution,"[21] and General Daniel E. Sickles issued a military order suspending it, proclaiming, "the constitutional rights of all loyal and well-disposed inhabitants to bear arms will not be infringed."[22]

Many in Congress in Washington, dominated by Republicans who thought the whole point of Union victory was being subverted, were outraged. A joint congressional committee report in 1866 noted that in South Carolina, "armed parties are, without proper authority, engaged in seizing all firearms found in the hands of the freemen. Such conduct is in clear and direct violation of their personal rights

as guaranteed by the Constitution of the United States, which declares that 'the right of the people to keep and bear arms shall not be
infringed.'"[23] Here, again, the view of what the Second Amendment
meant was not the founders' original vision of protecting the right
so as to guarantee the preservation of the state militias—indeed, in
1867, Congress voted to disband those in Virginia, North Carolina,
South Carolina, Georgia, Florida, Alabama, Louisiana, Mississippi,
and Texas because of what they were doing to blacks. Now the right
had come to mean something directly connected to individual self-
defense. Blacks in the South were faced with tyranny, all right, but it
was not the tyranny of the federal government in Washington.

The congressional response to the black codes also included new
authority for the Bureau of Refugees, Freedmen and Abandoned
Lands, the "Freedmen's Bureau," a War Department agency created
to help former slaves during Reconstruction. The Freedmen's Bureau
Act of 1866, passed over President Andrew Johnson's veto, specified
that neither race nor color nor "previous condition of slavery" could
be used to deny to anyone the right "to have full and equal benefit
of all laws and proceedings concerning personal liberty, personal security, and the acquisition, enjoyment and disposition of estate, real
and personal, including the constitutional right to bear arms." The
Civil Rights Act of 1866, passed about the same time, also over President Andrew Johnson's veto, guaranteed equal rights for all former
slaves but did not enumerate the right to have arms. Neither piece
of legislation mentioned their right to vote, at that point still denied
to free black men in many places (and all women, white or black) in
the North.

Fearing that the Supreme Court could declare such laws unconstitutional, Republican members of Congress wrote the Fourteenth
Amendment, but as adopted and later ratified, in 1868, it also made
no explicit mention of the right to bear arms: "No State shall make

or enforce any law which shall abridge the privileges or immunities of citizens of the United States; nor shall any State deprive any person of life, liberty, or property, without due process of law; nor deny to any person within its jurisdiction the equal protection of the laws." Neither did supporters use that as a "selling point" for the amendment. As the Second Amendment scholar Saul Cornell speculates, "While inspirational appeals invoking the struggles of heroic freedmen defending their homesteads with rifle in hand might resonate in the halls of Congress, the image of armed African-Americans was more likely to have frightened many voters."[24]

In 1868, Congress began restoring the right of Southern states to reestablish militias, which were to be formed of both black and white soldiers. Whites quickly dismissed them as the "Negro militia" and refused to serve. Organizing all-black militias of freedmen to resist white violence only infuriated the whites further and exposed blacks to more deadly attacks by militia-like, all-white armed gangs bent on disarming them—raiders who began calling themselves members of the Ku Klux Klan. As the struggle over Reconstruction intensified, so did violence. By 1870, when the Fifteenth Amendment finally extended the right to vote to black (male) citizens in both North and South, the Ku Klux Klan and organizations like it that were dedicated to the restoration of the prewar social order had become entrenched in every Southern state. The Klan could and did easily outgun the few rural blacks who owned firearms—usually shotguns, not the rifles and revolvers Klansmen had access to. "The ku kluks klan is shooting our familys and beating them notoriously," a man named W. A. Patterson wrote to the Reconstruction governor of North Carolina in 1868, adding, "We do not know what to do."

But, as the historian Eric Foner wrote, some of the Reconstruction governments did not know what to do, either. "Deep South governors had little confidence in the freedmen's prospects when

confronting well-trained Confederate veterans, and feared the arming of a black militia would inaugurate all-out racial warfare," in
Foner's words. The governor of South Carolina, Robert K. Scott,
was an exception, enrolling thousands of blacks in the militia there
in 1870. "The only law for these people [the white irredentists] was
the Winchester Rifle," he allegedly boasted, but after he won reelec-
tion he did not deploy the militia units when violence swept the up-
lands.[25] Things were better in Arkansas and Texas, where there were
large populations of whites who supported Reconstruction, and the
Klan was neutralized there.

But altogether, violence set the stage for the failure of the whole
Reconstruction effort. Blacks and whites in the South both wanted
guns for personal self-defense, but for different reasons, and the
Klan's interpretation of "self-defense" was certainly not the same as
that of the African Americans they were persecuting. And, importantly, violence in the South would lead the Supreme Court to significantly restrict its view of the protection given by the Second
Amendment to the individual right to bear arms. For almost the next
hundred years, the Court's rulings permitted an unprecedented expansion of gun-control laws—yet, at the same time, there was an
equally unprecedented expansion of the number of guns in private
American hands. How and why this happened is the subject of the
rest of this book.

CHAPTER FIVE

THE SECOND AMENDMENT AND THE SUPREME COURT

There seems to us no doubt, on the basis of both text and history, that the Second Amendment conferred an individual right to keep and bear arms.

JUSTICE ANTONIN SCALIA, MAJORITY OPINION, *DISTRICT OF COLUMBIA V. HELLER*, 2008

T he courts, as Chief Justice John Marshall put it in *Marbury v. Madison* in 1803, are empowered "to say what the law is," and the Supreme Court has the last word on what the Constitution means. But about the Second Amendment, about the firearms, despite the proliferation of guns in private hands and the numerous conflicting local statutes, the high court maintained silence for most of a century. When it finally spoke in 1876, it supported the view that the Second Amendment did not protect an individual right against state or local regulation. It seemed to take a similar view again in 1939. But seven decades later, in 2008, it contradicted itself, ruling 5–4 that the right to keep and bear arms is an individual right—just as an overwhelming majority of Americans, by that time convinced by a wave of conservative argument in favor of that position, agreed that it was. Perhaps the Chicago humorist Finley Peter Dunne had been right in 1901 when he had his Mr. Dooley character observe that "th' Supreme Coort follows th' election returns." But did the five conservative justices in the majority in the 2008 decision finally get the Second Amendment right? I think they did, though I disagree with how they got there.

The Court's long silence on the subject until 1876, and conflicting lower court opinions, contributed to considerable confusion. Two years earlier, an article in an influential journal of the time described the state of the law on firearms as "unsatisfactory." John Forrest Dillon, a federal appeals court judge and Columbia Law School professor, wrote in the *Central Law Journal:* "There would seem to remain no doubt that if the question should ever arise" in the high court that "it would be held that the Second Amendment of the federal Constitution is restrictive upon the general government merely, and not upon the states, and that every state has power to regulate the bearing of arms in such manner as it may see fit, or to restrain it altogether."

There was a contradiction, he noted, between the right to be armed for self-defense and the right to be safe from violence.

On the one hand, as long as the machinery which society has afforded for the prevention of private injuries remains in its present ineffective state, society cannot justly require the individual to surrender and lay aside the means of self-protection in seasons of personal danger; and it will be in vain that the laws of society denounce penalties against the citizen for arming himself when his life is menaced by the attacks of wild beasts, of highwaymen, or of dangerous and persevering enemies. On the other hand, the peace of society and the safety of peaceable citizens plead loudly for protection against the evils which result from permitting other citizens to go armed with dangerous weapons, and the utmost that the law can hope to do is to strike some sort of balance between these apparently conflicting rights.[1]

Those words bear repeating today.

All that the Supreme Court had said about the Second Amendment up to that point was merely by implication, in an opinion by Chief Justice Marshall in an 1833 case that had nothing to do with guns (*Barron* ex rel. *Tiernan v. Mayor of Baltimore*). He ruled that the entire Bill of Rights applied only to actions by the federal government, not to the states, and the federal government was not regulating gun rights (except by expecting all able-bodied men subject to militia service to have guns and know how to use them!).

It took a terrible massacre in Colfax, Louisiana, on Easter Sunday of 1873, one of the tragedies of the failure of Reconstruction, for the Supreme Court to finally offer up its first pronouncement on the right to bear arms. The elections of 1872 had led to a standoff between Republicans and anti-Reconstruction Democrats in the governorship, and to similar impasses in many other places in the state, including Grant Parish. "Freedmen who feared Democrats would seize the government cordoned off the county seat of Colfax and began drilling and digging trenches under the command of black veterans and militia officers," Eric Foner wrote. "They held the tiny town for three weeks; on Easter Sunday, whites armed with rifles and a small cannon overpowered the defenders and an indiscriminate slaughter followed, including the massacre of some fifty blacks who lay down their arms under a white flag of surrender. Two whites also died." The total number of blacks killed was at least 150, making this "the bloodiest single instance of racial carnage in the Reconstruction era."[2]

State authorities took no action, but the federal government brought charges against ninety-eight white men for murder and conspiracy to oppress or threaten citizens to prevent them from exercising rights "*granted or secured*" to them by the Constitution. One of those rights, according to the indictment, was the freedmen's right "to keep and bear arms for a lawful purpose," self-defense. Only six of those charged were tried, and three were acquitted; the three others were convicted of conspiracy. They, including William Cruikshank, a cotton planter, appealed their convictions in *United States v. Cruikshank*, and in 1876 the Supreme Court dealt a heavy blow to black civil rights in its ruling.

Neither the Fourteenth Amendment and its guarantee of equal protection nor the Civil Rights Act of 1866 applied to the case, Chief Justice Edward Douglass White wrote, because the indictment had not specified clearly what the defendants had conspired to do; it was "nowhere alleged in these counts that the wrong contemplated against the rights of these citizens was on account of their race or color."

But, he also proclaimed, the Second Amendment right of bearing arms for a lawful purpose, like the other amendments in the Bill of Rights,

> is not a right granted by the Constitution. Neither is it in any manner dependent upon that instrument for its existence. The Second Amendment declares that it shall not be infringed; but this . . . means no more than that it shall not be infringed by Congress, leaving the people to look for their protection against any violation by their fellow-citizens of the rights it recognizes, to what is called . . .

the "powers which relate to merely municipal legislation, or what was, perhaps, more properly called internal police," "not surrendered or restrained" by the Constitution of the United States.[3]

So if states or localities restricted or limited the right to bear arms, it was not a right that individuals, black or white, could look to federal courts to protect on constitutional grounds. And blacks could not look to the Fourteenth Amendment to protect them from discriminatory state or local laws.

Ten years later, in the case of *Presser v. Illinois* in 1886, the Supreme Court reinforced the view of the right to bear arms that it had expressed in *Cruikshank*. The Second Amendment, Justice William B. Woods wrote for the unanimous Court, "is a limitation only upon the power of congress and the national government, and not upon that of the state." Herman Presser, the leader of a private German-style shooting club with civic aspirations, the Lehr und Wehr Verein, that was not part of the 8,000-man organized militia, the Illinois National Guard, had paraded his troops bearing rifles through the streets of Chicago and had been convicted of violating a state law requiring paramilitary organizations to be licensed by the governor. Presser had argued that the law's provisions violated the constitutional articles on the militia and the Second Amendment.

The state, Justice Woods ruled, had the right to decide which armed militias were legal, as it had the right "to disperse assemblages organized for sedition and treason, and the right to suppress armed mobs bent on riot and rapine." He added: "The States cannot, even laying the constitutional provision in question out of view, prohibit the people from keeping and bearing arms, so as to deprive the United States of their rightful resource for maintaining the public security, and disable the people from performing their duty to the General Government," but the Illinois statute did not do that. As to the Second Amendment, "the amendment is a limitation only upon the power of Congress and the National government, and not upon that of the States."[4]

So state and local governments remained free to devise and impose gun regulations. And with handguns proliferating rapidly— even by the end of the 1870s, some fifty companies like Colt, Sharps, Smith and Wesson, and Winchester were making them and selling them under names like "Protector" and "Banker's Pal"—city authorities were more inclined to impose some degree of control.

Even in the early twentieth century, though, few of them did so with a heavy hand. In New York City, for example, the legendarily stingy millionaire businesswoman Hetty Green had no trouble when she applied at the Leonard Street police station for a permit to carry a revolver in May 1902. An article in the *New York Times* painted the scene:

> "Now, young man," Ms. Green told Sergeant Isaac Frank, "I want permission to carry a pistol. Because I am a rich woman, some people want to kill me."
>
> "Do you think the carrying of a pistol will protect you?" Sgt. Frank asked.
>
> "Certainly," she responded. "And I want everyone to know I have one. Those who have any knowledge of me will not doubt my ability or courage to use it."

She was going to Boston, she said, and wanted a permit right away. "But a New York permit will be no good in Boston," Sgt. Frank told her, but she brushed off the objection: "Well, I can get another there. . . . You see I often carry many valuables and vicious people know it." She received Permit No. 13,854 on May 8.[5]

New York tightened its gun laws, however, after Mayor William J. Gaynor was shot on a cruise ship in the harbor by a disgruntled city employee in August 1910. In 1911, the Sullivan Law, still in force a decade into the twenty-first century, made it a felony to carry a weapon small enough to be concealed, and a misdemeanor to own one, unless the bearer had a permit. Permits were (and still are) hard to get. Illegal guns brought in from other states were not. So gun violence continued to rise.

I t was not until 1939, five years after the National Firearms Act had been passed to deal with the growing problem of organized crime on a national scale, that the Supreme Court again addressed the scope of the Second Amendment, in a case called *United States v. Miller.*

The Firearms Act applied to sawed-off shotguns, concealable rifles, silencers, and machine guns and the like—weapons that Murder, Inc., the enforcement-thug branch of the crime syndicate, and people like John Dillinger had been using since Prohibition, until mounting public outrage forced Congress to take action. The Roosevelt administration had also wanted to put handguns on the list but could not get enough legislative support to do that. The act was the first major federal government gun-control measure, requiring anyone who wanted to own or transport weapons like tommy guns to be fingerprinted and register a written order with federal authorities, and pay a federal tax of $200 on each one of them, a lot of money in those days. Jack Miller and Frank Layton had been indicted for taking a double-barreled 12-gauge shotgun with barrels of less than eighteen inches across state lines from Oklahoma to Arkansas in violation of the law, and a lower federal court had ruled that the indictment should be dismissed because it violated their Second Amendment rights.

For the Supreme Court in *Miller* in 1939, federal gun control on that type of weapon did not violate the Second Amendment. "In the absence of any evidence tending to show that possession or use of a 'shotgun having a barrel of less than 18 inches in length' at this time has some reasonable relationship to the preservation or efficiency of a well regulated militia, we cannot say that the Second Amendment guarantees the right to keep and bear such an instrument," Justice James McReynolds wrote. "Certainly it is not within judicial notice that this weapon is any part of the ordinary military equipment or that its use could contribute to the common defense," he went on, citing the *Aymette* decision by the Tennessee court a century earlier.[6] Because the Second Amendment's purpose was to ensure the effectiveness of the militia, he said, "It must be interpreted and applied with that end in view." Machine guns and sawed-off shotguns weren't in common use at the time of the Second Amendment, so the National Firearms Act could be used to keep them out of the hands of gangsters in organized crime syndicates, the national problem that had led to passage of the act in 1934.

McReynolds's opinion did not say explicitly that the Second Amendment gave constitutional protection for the right to be armed only to people in some sort of connection with militia service, but that was what federal courts across the country understood *Miller* to mean for most of the rest of the twentieth century. Indeed, many of their rulings went even further beyond what the opinion actually said and found that the Second Amendment did not guarantee an individual right at all, but a collective one, the right of the states to have their militias.

Would the men who framed and adopted the Second Amendment have agreed that they were trying to protect this collective right? Yes, because their original intent was to preserve the state militias, and they would have had no trouble with the idea of denying weapons to criminals, as common law had permitted since colonial times. They recognized a common-law individual right that was, to be sure, connected to a civic duty. But a civic duty to have and know how to use firearms when answering a call to military service cannot be fulfilled unless individuals have the right to keep those arms. It is therefore almost inconceivable that the founders would have agreed that the right did not belong to individuals at all, but only to the states.

They might well have agreed, though, with Justice John Paul Stevens's interpretation of the effect of the *Miller* decision in his dissent from *Heller* in 2008: "The view of the Amendment we took in *Miller*—that it protects the right to keep and bear arms for certain military purposes, but that it does not curtail the Legislature's power to regulate the nonmilitary use and ownership of weapons—is both the most natural reading of the Amendment's text and the interpretation most faithful to the history of its adoption," he observed. "Since our decision in *Miller*, hundreds of judges have relied on the view of the Amendment we endorsed there; we ourselves affirmed it in 1980," he wrote.[7]

That 1980 decision, in a case that did not discuss the Second Amendment at all, *Lewis v. United States,* found that the 1968 Gun Control Act's provision denying convicted criminals the right to own firearms clearly met the "rational basis" test that was the least restrictive hurdle for laws affecting constitutional rights. "The legislative history of the gun control laws discloses Congress' worry about the easy availability of firearms, especially to those persons who pose a threat to community peace. And Congress focused on the nexus between violent crime and the possession of a firearm by any person with a criminal record," the Supreme Court found in that 1980 decision. (The petitioner had argued that his conviction had been unconstitutional because he had not been represented by counsel at trial, but the Supreme Court said, more or less, that he should have gotten it overturned or gotten a pardon before buying a gun.)[8]

A federal appeals court in Chicago two years later addressed a handgun ban in a nearby suburb, in the case of *Quilici v. Village of Morton Grove.* The lower court decision that the plaintiff, Victor D.

Quilici, had appealed held that Morton Grove's ban of working handguns in its village limits for all but a few (police, security guards, members of the armed forces, licensed collectors, and so on) did not violate any Second Amendment constitutional right to own a gun. The three-judge appeals court split, 2–1, but the majority held that the constitutional right to keep and bear arms extended only to arms necessary to maintain a well-regulated militia, as the Supreme Court decision in *Miller* had implied in 1939—and that, anyway, the Second Amendment did not apply to the states or to Morton Grove in Illinois. "As the Village correctly notes, appellants are essentially arguing that *Miller* was wrongly decided and should be overruled. Such arguments have no place before this court. Under the controlling authority of *Miller* we conclude that the right to keep and bear handguns is not guaranteed by the second amendment," the appeals court ruled. Quilici appealed to the Supreme Court, but a quarter century too early; in 1983, the Court did not deign even to hear the case. The law on the Second Amendment seemed settled—at least to judges and Supreme Court justices.[9]

But outside the courts, it was not settled at all. As racial and social turmoil increased in the 1960s, public attitudes about firearms shifted, as we have seen. And if judges and Supreme Court justices were not changing their view of firearms laws, students and authors in influential law journals were, and so were conservative politicians who were exploiting popular resentment against taxes and intrusive government regulations—including gun-control laws.

Skepticism about the soundness of the *Miller* decision had been building since 1960, when a law school student, Stuart R. Hays, in an article in the *William and Mary Law Review*, argued that the courts had, by and large, misunderstood the Second Amendment if they thought it applied only to the militia. The right of self-defense was a fundamental individual right, and the right to bear arms flowed directly from it, he asserted; the militia was an army of individuals, the people who the Second Amendment said had the right to keep and bear arms, and the amendment made that right an individual constitutional right. "It would seem that as long as there is danger to the life of man that the society has not eliminated the right of self-defense. As long as this right lives, then also should coexist the right to bear arms," Hays wrote.[10]

Many more law journal articles arrived at a similar conclusion over the next four decades. Don B. Kates Jr., for example, started off an article in the *Michigan Law Review* in 1983: "Believing that a militia (composed of the entire people possessed of their individually owned arms) was necessary for the protection of a free state, they [the founding fathers] guaranteed the people's right to possess those arms." Kates continued: "The amendment's use of 'right' without further definition suggests that its purpose was to constitutionalize the right to arms which the Founders knew from the common law." It might "suggest" that, but all it literally did was to recognize—and, admittedly, to protect—the common-law right. Kates then returned to the reason he thought the founders added the amendment: "Since the Constitution contained no guarantee of the citizenry's right to arm, the new federal government could outlaw and confiscate them, thereby destroying the supposed barrier to federal despotism."[11]

Still, Kates added, "Neither [gun] registration nor permissive licensing are per se violative of the amendment since they operate only to exclude gun ownership by those upon whom the amendment confers no right." Militia laws at the time the amendment was adopted, he wrote, required males reaching the age of required service to show they had guns, and they had to be submitted for inspection periodically to make sure that they were fit for service. "In sum, the historical background of the Second Amendment seems inconsistent with any notion of anonymity or privacy insofar as the mere fact of one's possessing a firearm is concerned."[12] Kates, as a student at Yale Law School, had gone to North Carolina to help fight the legal battles for civil rights in the summer of 1963, but the guns he had taken with him had been more important than any legal arguments one night when he and others stood guard for an activist who had received death threats but thought the police would be more likely to side with the Ku Klux Klan than with her.[13]

Law journal articles questioning previous interpretations of the meaning of the amendment continued to appear, supporting the individual-right view—notably, one in the *Yale Law Journal* in 1989 with the provocative title, "The Embarrassing Second Amendment," by Sanford Levinson of the University of Texas at Austin. "Although the record is suitably complicated, it seems tendentious to reject out of hand the argument that the one purpose of the Amendment was to recognize an individual's right to engage in armed self-defense against criminal conduct," Professor Levinson wrote, but he also saw civic implications in the way the amendment was designed to work, implications that "might push us in unexpected, even embarrassing, directions; just as ordinary citizens should participate actively in governmental decision-making, through offering their own deliberative insights, rather than be confined to casting ballots once every two or four years for those very few individuals who will actually make the decisions, so should ordinary citizens participate in the process of law enforcement and defense of liberty rather than rely on professionalized peacekeepers, whether we call them standing armies or police." The Second Amendment should be taken as seriously as the First, or the Fifth: "If protecting freedom of speech, the rights of criminal defendants, or any other parts of the Bill of Rights were always (or even most of the time) clearly costless to the society as a whole, it would truly be impossible to understand why they would be as controversial as they are," Levinson wrote.[14]

There were fifty-eight articles along similar lines in the 1990s, according to Robert J. Spitzer, a political science professor and constitutional law specialist whose Second Amendment writings come to opposite conclusions. This "blizzard" of writing, he concluded, soon "transformed agreed-upon meaning into a debate where both sides seemed equally legitimate—as if supporters of 'scientific creationism' had succeeded in flooding science journals with articles about evolution to produce an apparent academic stalemate between seemingly equivalent dueling scientific interpretations."[15] But why not? The courts had also found much in the amendment—including much "agreed-upon meaning" ever since *Miller*—that was arguably never really there.

By the mid-1990s, there had been so many articles building the case for an individual-right interpretation of the amendment that supporters were calling that view the "standard model." By its lights, the "people" who had the right were the same "people" who had the right of freedom of speech and assembly; the right to keep and bear arms was not subordinate to the militia, but the other way around. As Glenn Harlan Reynolds put it in an article summarizing the "standard model" in the *Tennessee Law Review* in 1995,[16] the Second Amendment recognized the right that individuals had always had in the colonial days to defend themselves and hunt for food, and the amendment's purpose was "to ensure an armed citizenry, from which can be drawn the kind of militia that is necessary to the survival of a free state."

Even Laurence H. Tribe, a Harvard Law School professor who was a staunch defender of comprehensive gun control, came close to the individual-rights view in 2000, when he wrote in a revision of his book *American Constitutional Law* that the amendment recognized "a right (admittedly of uncertain scope) on the part of individuals to possess and use firearms in the defense of themselves and their homes," one that Congress and the executive branch, and perhaps also states and cities, could not deny without unusually strong justification.[17]

There was opposition to the emerging "standard model" view, of course, but the main new competing view, dubbed the states' right model, was far less persuasive: What the Second Amendment protected was not an individual right but a collective one, the right of the states to have their militias. As opponents of the view pointed out, in practical application, it allowed states to pass restrictive gun-control laws for whatever reasons they wanted. Soon cracks began to appear in the judicial consensus against the individual-right interpretation.

The first notable departure from the idea that the Second Amendment did not protect an individual right came in a Fifth Circuit Court of Appeals decision in 2001 in New Orleans. It was *United States of America v. Timothy Joe Emerson*, the case of a doctor indicted for purchasing a pistol while subject to a restraining order obtained by his wife in a nasty divorce. A lower court in Texas had found that he had been denied his Second Amendment rights and dismissed his indictment on those grounds, among others. The appeals court panel concluded, but only after forty-nine pages of "standard-model," exhaustively researched examination of the history and antecedents of the Second Amendment, that the prevailing federal court doctrines about it were all wrong: "We agree with the district court that the Second Amendment protects the right of individuals to privately keep and bear their own firearms that are suitable as individual, personal weapons and are not of the general kind or type excluded by *Miller*, regardless of whether the particular individual is then actually a member of a militia."

But it was nonsense, the New Orleans appeals court judges said, to rely on *Miller* to support rulings that the Second Amendment does not apply to individuals at all, but "merely recognizes the right of a state to arm its militia," or that it applies only to individuals serving in a militia. Yet a number of "our sister circuits," the judges said, other federal appeals courts, had embraced precisely such legal theories, which it dismissively cited, as academics were increasingly doing, as the "collective rights theory" or the "sophisticated collective rights theory." In the twenty-first century, in any case, there was no such thing as the "militia," which the founders had understood as the general population of all men capable of bearing arms when civic duty called. The closest thing to that nowadays was the National Guard, which is provided with arms by the federal government. That would have seemed to the founders more like the "select militia" they dreaded as a tyrannical menace just as much as they feared a standing army would be.

But, the appeals court added, "Although, as we have held, the Second Amendment does protect individual rights, that does not mean that those rights may never be made subject to any limited, narrowly tailored specific exceptions or restrictions for particular cases that are reasonable and not inconsistent with the right of Americans generally to individually keep and bear their private arms as historically understood in this country." And it reinstated Emerson's indictment.[18]

With George W. Bush, a gun-rights supporter, in the presidency in 2004, the Justice Department's Office of Legal Counsel (OLC) prepared a memorandum opinion for Attorney General John Ashcroft along similar lines, this one endorsing the "standard model" lock, stock, and barrel. The "people" whose rights to keep and bear arms were not to be infringed upon were not collective entities or the states, but the same individuals as the "people" whose right of free speech was protected—all Americans. Only individuals could "keep" arms; so it must be individuals who had the right to "keep and bear" arms. "It is true that 'bear arms' often did refer to carrying arms in military service," the memorandum conceded, but arms "also could be 'borne' for private, non-military purposes, principally tied to self-defense."

Some of the analysis in the memorandum was based not on what the founders wrote and said about it but on later exegesis. It relied heavily on post–Revolutionary War interpretations of it by St. George Tucker, William Rawle, and Justice Joseph Story, who in 1833 wrote, "One of the ordinary modes, by which tyrants accomplish their purposes without resistance, is, by disarming the people, and making it an offence to keep arms, and by substituting a regular army in the stead of a resort to the militia." The memorandum also cited post–Civil War legislation like the Civil Rights Act of 1866, many congressional supporters of which, the memorandum said, had sought to ensure for freed slaves the right to bear arms, though the 1866 act does not specify that. The memorandum found that what the Supreme Court had said in *Miller,* with all its emphasis on the militia context for the Second Amendment, did not mean that the right was restricted to that context; the restriction simply put weapons like sawed-off shotguns and machine guns beyond the pale of protection. "We conclude," the memorandum said, "that the Second Amendment secures a personal right of individuals, not a collective right that may only be invoked by a State or a quasi-collective right restricted to those persons who serve in organized militia units."[19]

Congress in Washington was, by then, on the same wavelength. In 2005, both houses passed the Protection of Lawful Commerce in Arms Act, barring lawsuits seeking to hold gun manufacturers or licensed dealers responsible for criminal acts committed with firearms made or sold by them. Signed into law by President Bush on October

26, it includes among its "findings" by Congress this one: "The Second Amendment to the United States Constitution protects the rights of individuals, including those who are not members of a militia or engaged in military service or training, to keep and bear arms."[20]

The Supreme Court of the United States didn't find that for three years, until Justice Scalia's majority opinion in *District of Columbia v. Heller* in 2008. Much of his opinion tracks very closely with the OLC memorandum. It goes over the same historical grounds, finds the same historical quotations, makes the same—sometimes indisputable, sometimes highly dubious—interpretations of those quotations, and of course arrives at the same overall conclusion. One thing in particular is very different about the *Heller* decision: its insistence that individual self-defense was the *main reason* for the amendment, protecting the individual right to keep and bear arms.

So a ban on handguns, the firearm most commonly used for self-defense, was unconstitutional. *Heller* left open the question of what kind of gun-control regulation, short of outright bans on handguns, would pass muster (the question of whether it was binding on the states as well as the District of Columbia was settled two years later in the case of *Otis McDonald et al. v. City of Chicago et al.*). "Nothing in our opinion should be taken to cast doubt on longstanding prohibitions on the possession of firearms by felons and the mentally ill, or laws forbidding the carrying of firearms in sensitive places such as schools and government buildings, or laws imposing conditions and qualifications on the commercial sale of arms," Scalia noted in *Heller*. "We also recognize another important limitation on the right to keep and carry arms. *Miller* said, as we have explained, that the sorts of weapons protected were those 'in common use at the time.' We think that limitation is fairly supported by the historical tradition of prohibiting the carrying of 'dangerous and unusual weapons.'"

The case was a set piece from the beginning. It was the creation, the *New York Times* Supreme Court writer Linda Greenhouse reported in 2007, "of a wealthy libertarian, Robert A. Levy, senior fellow in constitutional studies at the Cato Institute, a prominent libertarian research organization. With the blessing of Cato, Levy financed the lawsuit and recruited six plaintiffs, all of whom wanted to keep handguns in their homes for self-defense."[21] One of them, Dick Anthony Heller, a government security guard, had applied for a handgun permit so that he could bring and keep at home the handgun he carried on duty, and the district authorities had turned him down. The federal appeals court for the District of Columbia ruled in 2007, in a 2–1 decision written by Senior Circuit Judge Laurence H. Silberman,[22] that Heller had been deprived of an individual right protected by the Second Amendment, and the district appealed to the Supreme Court. Judge Silberman had also allowed that the right was subject to "reasonable restrictions."

However, it's not the setup of the case so much as how the conservative majority arrived at its opinion in *Heller* that struck me as tortuous. The five justices appeared to be torturing texts until they gave up the answers they were looking for. They construed some historical quotations to make it seem that fear of personal disarmament, rather than of political tyranny, was the dominant American obsession of the last decade of the eighteenth century. It is hard from fragmentary evidence hundreds of years old to reach definitive conclusions about what speakers and writers really had on their minds then, but the Court's conclusions sometimes make you wonder instead what the justices in the *Heller* majority could have been thinking. For example: "During the 1788 ratification debates, the fear that the federal government would disarm the people in order to impose rule through a standing army or select militia was pervasive in Antifederalist rhetoric. See, *e.g.,* Letters from The Federal Farmer III

(Oct. 10, 1787) . . . John Smilie, for example, worried not only that Congress's 'command of the militia' could be used to create a 'select militia,' or to have 'no militia at all,' but also, as a separate concern, that 'when a select militia is formed, the people in general may be disarmed.'"

Yes, John Smilie did say "disarmed," but the meaning is clearly "powerless to resist tyranny." What Smilie, one of the members of the Pennsylvania minority that had refused to ratify the Constitution, actually feared was not that despotic federal authorities would take arms away from individuals, but that they would deprive the state militias of arms, the militias that he believed to be the best guarantee that citizens could resist despotism:

> The militia, regulated and commanded by the officers of the general government, will be warped from the patriotic nature of their institution, and a standing army, that most prevailing instrument of despotism, will be ever ready to enforce obedience to a government by which it is raised, supported and enriched. If, under such circumstances, the several States should presume to assert their undelegated rights, I ask again what balance remains with them to counteract the encroachments of so potent a superior? To assemble a military force would be impracticable; for the general government, foreseeing the attempt would anticipate the means, by the exercise of its indefinite control over the purses of the people. . . .[23]

Nor was "The Federal Farmer" giving a warning in Letter 3 that the government could leave individual citizens unable to protect themselves against felons or wild beasts by forbidding them to have firearms. The author, a pseudonymous opponent of the new Constitution, writing letters to "The Republican" at the end of 1787 in the *Poughkeepsie Country Journal,* was concerned about the balance of power between the federal government and the states, and in Letter 3 he wrote about the dangers of a standing army and federal control over the militia:

> I see so many men in America fond of a standing army, and especially among those who probably will have a large share in administering the federal system; it is very evident to me, that we shall have a large standing army as soon as the monies to support them can be possibly found. . . . It is true, the yeomanry of the country possess the lands, the weight of property, possess arms, and are too strong a body of men to be openly offended—and, therefore, it is urged, they will take care of themselves, that men who shall govern will not dare pay any disrespect to their opinions. It is easily perceived, that if they have not their proper negative upon passing laws in congress, or on the passage of laws relative to taxes and armies, they may in twenty or thirty years be by means imperceptible to them, totally deprived of that boasted weight and strength: This may be done in a great measure by congress, if disposed to do it, by modelling the militia. Should one fifth, or one eighth part of the men capable of bearing arms, be made a select militia, as has been proposed, and those the young and ardent part of the community, possessed of but little or no property, and all the others put upon a plan that will render them of no importance, the former will answer all the purposes of an army, while the latter will be defenseless.[24]

Again, is it not clear that "defenseless" is used in the sense of politically powerless? This is a political argument about how control of the militia figures in the balance of power, not a warning about the danger that the federal authorities would leave individual citizens unable to defend themselves because their private arms had been confiscated. Nor does the Federal Farmer give any such warning in this stirring defense of the importance of an armed citizenry to the preservation of liberty, in Letter XVIII:

> But, say gentlemen, the general militia are for the most part employed at home in their private concerns, cannot well be called out, or be depended upon; that we must have a select militia; that is, as I understand it, particular corps or bodies of young men, and of men who have but little to do at home, particularly armed and disciplined in some measure, at the public expense, and always ready to take the field. These corps, not much unlike regular troops, will ever produce an inattention to the general militia; and the consequence has ever been, and always must be, that the substantial men, having families and property, will generally be without arms, without knowing the use of them, and defenseless; whereas, to preserve liberty, *it is essential that the whole body of the people always possess arms, and be taught alike, especially when young, how to use them*; nor does it follow from this, that all promiscuously must go into actual service on every occasion.[25]

Even setting these dubious interpretations aside, it is the underlying logic of the core conclusion of the *Heller* decision that has always stumped me. "It has always been widely understood that the Second Amendment, like the First and Fourth Amendments, codified a *pre-existing* right," the opinion says. "The very text of the Second Amendment implicitly recognizes the pre-existence of the right and declares only that it 'shall not be infringed.' As we said in *United States* v. *Cruikshank*, 92 U.S. 542, 553 (1876), 'this is not a right granted by the Constitution. Neither is it in any manner dependent upon that instrument for its existence. The Second Amendment declares that it shall not be infringed.'"[26] So far, so good. Yet now *Heller* contradicts itself, asserting that the Second Amendment did indeed make it a right granted by the Constitution: "There seems to us no doubt, on the basis of both text and history, that the Second Amendment conferred an individual right to keep and bear arms. Of course the right was not unlimited, just as the First Amendment's right of free speech was not. . . ."[27] The opinion conceded that the preamble, with its "a well regulated Militia, being necessary" wording, set forth the purpose of the Second Amendment—"to prevent elimination of the militia"—but then concluded nonetheless that self-defense was the "central component" of the right to arms that it said should not be infringed upon.[28] "A prefatory clause does not limit or expand the scope of the operative clause," it said—the right to arms could mean whatever the court decided it meant, "a well regulated Militia" notwithstanding. And what the majority opinion found was that the Second Amendment "surely elevates above all other interests the right of law-abiding, responsible citizens to use arms in defense of hearth and home."[29] Well, where did it do that? There is not a single word about self-defense in the Second Amendment.

For one distinguished conservative federal judge, J. Harvie Wilkinson III of the United States Court of Appeals for the Fourth Circuit, this was originalism run amok, "originalist activism," flying in the face of "inconclusive" historical evidence of how the founders understood the amendment.[30] Other flaws in the decision were found by Justice John Paul Stevens and liberal Justice Stephen Breyer in two powerful dissents, and they were joined by Justice Ruth Bader Ginsburg and Justice David Souter. But the majority opinion by Justice Scalia was now law, in the district at least, and the law was that the right to own firearms, for self-defense or anything else that was legal, is an individual right.

And on that crucial point, I think the conservative majority was right. If I were writing the opinion I would have said that the Second Amendment "recognized" or "acknowledged," rather than "conferred," a preexisting individual right, but I disagree with Judge Wilkinson and believe the founders had no doubt that it was an individual right, one that predated the Constitution. The right may no longer serve the constitutional purpose for which they wrote the Second Amendment—ensuring the continued existence of state militias—but it was never limited to that purpose, and it lives on without it today.

If you could ask John Adams (let alone Samuel, a real firebrand), if you could ask Thomas Jefferson, Alexander Hamilton, or John Hancock after the adoption of the Bill of Rights whether they had an individual right to carry arms and use them for self-defense, or to hunt, or to exercise or pursue any other lawful purpose, they would have laughed at you. Of course they had that right, they would have said. The Second Amendment didn't give it to them; it simply recognized a right Americans had always had in common law and protected it.

The District of Columbia revised its gun regulations after the decision, no longer banning handguns but requiring that firearms be registered with the police (a requirement not challenged by Heller and his earlier fellow plaintiffs) and banning "assault" weapons (semiautomatic weapons based on or resembling full-automatic military assault weapons, some with enough firepower to bring down a stag or a bear) in its crowded urban territory. Dick Heller, the DC special police officer who had brought the original challenge, and the NRA and others promptly launched a new case against these new laws, finding the registration requirement "prohibitive" and objecting to the bans on assault weapons and large-capacity magazines.

In March 2010, Federal District Judge Ricardo M. Urbina rejected their challenge. Judge Urbina explicitly based his decision on the *Heller* opinion and applied the standard of "intermediate scrutiny" to decide if the District of Columbia's new regulations squared with the constitutional right to keep and bear arms. He found that the regulations were "substantially related to an important governmental interest"—public safety in the nation's capital—and thus permitted by the Constitution. The District of Columbia Council had carefully deliberated over the new regulations, which did "not interfere with the 'core right' the Second Amendment protects by depriving the people of reasonable means to defend themselves in their homes," he ruled. Applicants for gun permits could be required to register their guns, and to do more: to submit photographs of themselves and be fingerprinted, to pass a firearms training or safety course, to submit to a background check every six years, and to let the DC police keep records of their weapons' ballistics profiles, among other requirements, because none of them, in the judge's opinion, infringed the core right to use arms for self-defense and all of them were demonstrably related to public safety in the district. Requiring a wait of thirty days after the purchase of a handgun for an individual to buy another one was reasonable, and so was the ban on military-style assault weapons or large-capacity magazines (of more than ten rounds of ammunition), because neither infringed on the core right of self-defense.

Dick Heller vehemently disagreed, in a written statement he submitted to a DC Council committee at a public hearing later in 2008:

> Criminals are walking the streets, carrying concealed, and YET for some reason the city council thinks there is a NEED to monitor ME, a CERTIFIED ARMED DC Special Police officer, and to monitor the rest of our good citizens with gun registration. SOMETHING is wrong with this picture.
>
> What the council needs to do is, to NOT monitor the good guys, but to design laws that strongly dis-incentivise the few bad guys from using firearms in crimes. A MANDATORY 5 or 10

years in the Slammer for gun crimes cuts the crime rates in many other jurisdictions.[31]

Gun-rights supporters backing Heller agreed and then appealed on the grounds that deciding on the constitutionality of laws affecting a right protected by the Constitution required "strict scrutiny." The District of Columbia should have to show that it had a "compelling" interest in passing and enforcing the legislation, and that the laws were narrowly tailored to achieve that interest, in the least restrictive way possible.

Two of three judges on a District of Columbia federal court of appeals panel in 2011 upheld Judge Urbina's finding that an intermediate level of scrutiny was sufficient to pass on the constitutionality of the new DC gun laws. The panel also upheld his ruling upholding the ban on assault rifles and large-capacity magazines for them, finding sufficient evidence in the record that such weapons figured far more often in mass shootings and attacks on police officers than they ever did in self-defense in the home. Somewhat bafflingly, the appeals court said Heller and his lawyers had not made clear whether they were also appealing a ban on assault *pistols* and large-capacity magazines for them, making no pronouncement on those.[32]

The appeals judges found nothing objectionable about requiring gun owners to register their guns, as seven states and many other cities do. But it sent the more unusual registration requirements— the thirty-day wait after buying a handgun before buying a second one is allowed, the ballistics records, and so on—back to the lower court for reconsideration, finding that the District of Columbia had presented insufficient justification.

So, as of 2011, the last word had not been heard on the new DC gun laws. But because having handguns in the home was now a constitutional right in the district, it was inevitable that the Supreme Court would find that it was a right in other places as well. That happened two years after the *Heller* decision, in the case of *McDonald v. Chicago*. Otis McDonald, the lead plaintiff, was an African American man in his late seventies whose home in Chicago's high-crime South Side had been broken into three times. According to the *AARP Bulletin* in June 2010, "He once called 911 after spotting a bad guy leveling a pistol at a fleeing car in the alley next to his front porch. For that, three thugs threatened to 'put him down,'" and he wanted a pistol at home to protect his family. But Chicago had an effective ban on handguns much like the one the Supreme Court had struck down in DC. The criminals in the South Side had plenty of illegal guns; why should the law deny law-abiding people the freedom to have guns in their homes for self-defense? McDonald asked.

Justice Samuel Alito, writing the opinion for the conservative majority in the Supreme Court—himself, Chief Justice John Roberts, Justice Scalia, and Justice Clarence Thomas—and joined by Justice Anthony Kennedy, gave McDonald his answer on June 28, 2010:

> The city of Chicago (City) and the village of Oak Park, a Chicago suburb, have laws that are similar to the District of Columbia's, but Chicago and Oak Park argue that their laws are constitutional because the Second Amendment has no application to the States. We have previously held that most of the provisions of the Bill of Rights apply with full force to both the Federal Government and the States. Applying the standard that is well established in our case law, we hold that the Second Amendment right is fully applicable to the States.[33]

The obligations the Fourteenth Amendment imposed on the states in 1868 incorporated the right to have and use arms for self-defense that the Court had found in the Second Amendment in the *Heller* case, the majority opinion held; the precedents that the federal appeals court in Chicago had relied on in denying the right to McDonald no longer applied, so that court was now obliged to think again. "The right to keep and bear arms," Alito wrote, "is not the only constitutional right that has controversial public safety implications. All of the constitutional provisions that impose restrictions on law enforcement and on the prosecution of crimes fall into the same category."[34]

The dissenters were, again, Justice Breyer and Justice Stevens, who asserted in vain that the right to have and use firearms had to be balanced with the right to be safe from armed violence. "The idea that deadly weapons pose a distinctive threat to the social order—and that reasonable restrictions on their usage therefore impose an acceptable burden on one's personal liberty—is as old as the Republic," Justice Stevens wrote, noting as well that *Heller* had unleashed "a tsunami of legal uncertainty, and thus litigation" about what kind of gun laws would now pass constitutional muster.[35] As Judge Wilkinson later lamented, "The Court henceforth would say what the people of Texas and Rhode Island or Chicago and Tallahassee could and could not enact."[36]

Justice Breyer, whose dissent was joined by Justice Ginsburg and the Court's newest member, Justice Sonia Sotomayor, observed:

> Thus, the specific question before us is not whether there are references to the right to bear arms for self defense throughout this Nation's history—of course there are—or even whether the Court should incorporate a simple constitutional requirement that firearms regulations not unreasonably burden the right to keep and bear arms, but rather whether there is a consensus that so substantial a private self-defense right as the one described in *Heller* applies to the States. . . . On this question, the reader will have to make up his or her own mind about the historical record. . . . In my view,

that record is insufficient to say that the right to bear arms for private self-defense, as explicated by *Heller*, is fundamental in the sense
relevant to the incorporation inquiry.... States and localities have
consistently enacted firearms regulations, including regulations
similar to those at issue here, throughout our Nation's history.
Courts have repeatedly upheld such regulations.[37]

Three days after the decision, Mayor Richard M. Daley pushed a
substitute law through the Chicago City Council requiring applicants for permits to have training including four hours in a classroom
and an hour on a firing range, which might be reasonable if firing
ranges were allowed within Chicago's city limits, but they aren't. Applicants who managed to find training somewhere else could register
only one handgun a month and could keep only one assembled, and
then only inside the home—not in the garage, not on the front
porch, and not in the yard, places where arguably one might be more
needed in a self-defense emergency. Understandably, the NRA and
others went right back to court to challenge the new ordinance. Such
measures only make it easier for the NRA to convince its supporters,
and the lawmakers who answer to them and everybody else, that *any*
gun-control regulation is really just a stealth attempt to impose a ban
on guns.

But the question remained: Would the tsunami of challenges to
gun-control laws that Justice Stevens said he feared after the *Heller*
and *McDonald* decisions sweep them all away? Interestingly, the wa-
ters have remained relatively calm since 2008. The NRA ridicules
New York City's strict gun laws, as will be seen, but as of mid-2012,
it had not mounted any kind of serious legal challenge to them on
constitutional grounds. Even the Supreme Court seemed, at that
point, more inclined to let things drift than to look for opportunities
to hear more cases on the right to bear arms outside the home—

indeed, in late 2011 it declined to hear one such case, *Williams v. Maryland*. But though no tsunami, the tide keeps rising slowly. In another Maryland case soon afterward, a federal judge in Baltimore found in March 2012 that the state law requiring "good and substantial reason" for a handgun permit inside or outside the home was unconstitutional. The case was filed by a gun-rights organization, the Second Amendment Foundation, on behalf of Raymond Woollard, who had obtained a permit in 2002 after a struggle with an intruder in his home but had been unable to get it renewed in 2009 because he could not demonstrate that he was still threatened enough to need a gun. "A citizen may not be required to offer a 'good and substantial reason' why he should be permitted to exercise his rights," Judge Benson E. Legg wrote. "The right's existence is all the reason he needs." The state and the Brady Center to Prevent Gun Violence said they would immediately appeal the ruling.[38] No doubt the question will arise in other cases.

CHAPTER SIX

GUN CONTROL AND GUN VIOLENCE

Well then, I'm often asked, what kind of gun laws are you for?
I reply that I am for laws of common sense.
BARRY GOLDWATER, 1975

The United States, with something close to 300 million guns in private hands, has more guns than any other advanced industrial country, and more gun violence. "Across US regions and states, where there are more guns, children are at significantly greater risk for dying," David Hemenway, professor of health policy at the Harvard School of Public Health, has written, also noting that in at least four other studies drawing on data from the 1980s to 2003, in states with more guns, there were higher rates of homicide; and 70 percent of homicides are committed with guns, mostly handguns, at that.

Indisputably, the firearm homicide rate in the United States is higher, by far, than it is in Canada, Australia, and twenty-three other wealthy nations—it was seventeen times as high as their average rate in the 1990s.[1] Surely, if it were possible to make handguns and rifles disappear from the United States, there would be fewer homicides and fewer suicides (because other means are less efficient). But a closer look at the statistics shows that strict gun-control laws by themselves do not lead to less gun violence. Census Bureau figures show that the homicide rate in Massachusetts, where the gun laws are pretty strict, was much lower in 2008 than it was in Georgia or Mississippi, where they are pretty lax. But the Massachusetts rate was barely below Vermont's, a state that has no statewide gun laws at all, and it was almost twice as high as the rate in Utah,[2] where gun laws are also very relaxed (Utah adopted the Browning M1911 .45 pistol, invented by a native son, as the state firearm, in 2011).

Even in cities where handgun ownership has been so severely restricted that it amounted to a ban, it is hard to see what effect that has on gun violence. Chicago banned handguns in 1982. Yet in the years that followed, the crime rate and the murder rate rose steadily. The rate of murders involving handguns in Chicago was 9.65 per 100,000 residents in 1983, the Supreme Court was told in the *McDonald* case, but by 2008, with the ban in effect, it was even higher, at 13.88 per 100,000. Similarly, in the District of Columbia, the homicide rate also rose in the 1980s, after the district banned handguns—in fact it rose even more than it did in forty-nine other comparable major cities, as Justice Breyer conceded in his dissent in the *Heller* case.[3] In 2008, the murder rate per 100,000 of population in the District of Columbia was 31.4, far higher than the rates of 6.3 per 100,000 in New York City (where handguns are not banned, but only 37,000 people are licensed to own them and only 4,000 have concealed-carry permits[4]) and 3.1 in Austin, Texas, where as everybody knows, it's a lot easier for anybody legally to get a gun.

These data can't be taken as the final word on gun-control laws. Obviously, strict gun laws in the District of Columbia don't mean a whole lot when the laws in adjoining states are lax, and criminals don't obey any of them anyway. Nevertheless, what becomes clear is that there are many factors besides the availability or prevalence of guns that go into explaining violent crime rates. The most important single reason that gun violence rose sharply in Chicago and the District of Columbia and many cities across the country between the mid-1980s and the early 1990s was drugs—specifically, crack cocaine, bursting upon the scene at the time. Juvenile and young adult males were recruited to sell the drugs in troubled neighborhoods and were armed, or armed themselves, with handguns. One result was the rise of a culture of what a study by two criminologists called "irresponsible and excessively casual use of guns by young people" in inner cities. In 1993, the peak year of this drug-induced surge in violent crime, more than 3,000 adolescents and young people (age fifteen to nineteen) were murdered with guns nationwide.[5]

Likewise, the most important single reason that violent crime and gun violence have been falling sharply since the mid-1990s is this: that's when the crack epidemic began to wane. Crime rates have been falling sharply since then all over the United States, even though the number of guns has not. (At least, as far as anybody knows—much information comes from surveys that ask people if they own guns, how many, and whether they have used them in self-defense, and the answers should be taken with more grains of salt than their purveyors usually sprinkle over them. The percentage of households that acknowledged having guns of any kind in the home in one such survey dropped, from 54 percent in 1977 to 34.5 percent in 2006,[6] most respondents saying they owned rifles and shotguns, not handguns.) In the first half of 2009, newspaper reports said the violent crime rate (crimes per 100,000 population) was at its lowest level nationwide since the 1960s. In New York City, there were one-fourth as many murders in 2010 as there were in 1990—536, compared to 2,262 then, according to police statistics.

Many other things besides the decline in drug availability have contributed to the decline in crime rates in American cities. Possible explanations range from the high number of perpetrators away in prison for earlier crimes, to the gradual aging of urban populations, to the gentrification of many previously crime-ridden neighborhoods in big cities. It's not possible to tie the crime rate directly to a rise or a decline in the number of guns. Only about 10 percent of the average annual 8.9 million incidents involving victims of violent crimes of all kinds between 1993 and 2001 involved guns, according to Justice Department surveys—though, importantly, homicides are a huge exception, as most of them are committed with handguns.

Not all deaths caused by firearms are the result of violent assault. Even though about 30,000 people in America are shot to death every year, the truth is that most of them do it themselves. In 2007, according to the national Centers for Disease Control and Prevention's definitive National Vital Statistics Reports, 17,352 people committed suicide with firearms, compared to 12,632 murdered by assailants using guns of all kinds. The suicide rate was 4.2 per 100,000 Americans of all age groups and races—but highest, at 11.0, among those fifteen to twenty-four, and a slightly lower 9.2 among those twenty-five to thirty-four. Accidental firearms deaths were at a low of 613, but again, the rate was highest among fifteen- to twenty-four-year-olds. Less complete FBI estimates for years after that show violent crimes continuing to decline nationally, to 8,775 homicides by gunfire (6,009 of them involving handguns) in 2010.

Overall, the death rate from firearms has run between 10.1 per 100,000 to 10.4 per 100,000 in recent years, double or triple the rate in European countries, where gun ownership is tightly restricted. But America is a younger society than any in Europe, and youths, young males in particular, commit most of the violence. Americans more highly prize aggressiveness (which can easily morph into physical aggression) in business, and in sports like football and hockey in particular, than most Western Europeans. Americans have historically committed (or suffered) homicides without guns at a rate higher than the total homicide rate in most other comparable countries (with and without firearms).

To sum up: more people are killed by guns in America (31,224 in 2007) than die from falls (22,631), but fewer than die in motor vehicle accidents (43,945).[7]

Now, think about this: cars have become much safer in recent years, and enforcement of drunk-driving laws has become stricter. Whatever the reason, the number of people killed in traffic accidents in 2010 was estimated by the National Highway Traffic Safety Administration as 32,788, the lowest number since 1949, before the days of seat belts, air bags, antilock brakes, and rumble strips. The purpose of automobiles is not to inflict death or injury, unlike handguns, for which it is a primary purpose. Government regulations did not try to limit the number of automobiles people were allowed to buy; they aimed instead at requiring or encouraging carmakers to make their products safer, and at changing driver behavior patterns. It made sense to require people riding in cars to use safety belts and put small children in safety car seats, and to deter drunk driving with strict enforcement of laws that provide for heavy punishments; more recently it makes sense to do the same for people who try to text and drive at the same time. The careful collection of statistics correlated with the causes of deaths and injuries enabled government authorities and legislators to craft regulations aimed at improving the odds against fatality.

The same approach could be used in devising better ways of keeping the guns out of the hands of those who everybody—or at least everybody with any common sense—agrees should not have them. Our society could take up more effective ways of changing or deterring self-destructive or antisocial behavior patterns, as well as ways of making guns safer to use. Figuring out what would work requires accurate data collection and careful analysis. But Congress, driven by fears fanned by the NRA that Big Brother will use data collection to attack gun rights, has severely limited the ability of government agencies to collect and release data connected with firearms.

Americans willingly submit to requirements to get driver's licenses and buy liability insurance on automobiles. We have federal agencies to monitor prescription drugs, food, aviation, transportation, and other things that can cause death—even children's toys. But legislators—under the whip of the NRA and other gun lobbies—balk at the idea of gun registration, or creating a safety agency to monitor whether guns are made to be safe. The national background check database that federally licensed firearms dealers are required to use to make sure maniacs or criminals cannot legally buy guns is riddled with holes. The Bureau of Alcohol, Tobacco, Firearms and Explosives, the agency that checks on dealers, is barred by law from collecting data about them and has been hamstrung by years of starvation budgets imposed on it by Congress.

On March 1, 2010, the NRA sent out a tocsin to members against a bill that would allow the federal government to keep records of firearms purchases, a proposal by Senator Frank Lautenberg of New Jersey for a "Preserving Records of Terrorist and Criminal Transactions Act." The broadside by Chris W. Cox, the executive director of the NRA's congressional lobbying branch, warned in boldface type and fully underlined text: "The truth is that this legislation would effectively create a NATIONAL GUN REGISTRATION system. And if this bill becomes law, it could set the stage for gun-banners to achieve their ultimate goal—confiscation of our firearms and the end of the Second Amendment!!!"

Why do they blow it out of proportion like this?

His letter went on: "Under this national gun registration scheme, your *name, personal information,* and *gun purchase records* will be stored in a centralized government database where it can be accessed by countless government officials in Washington, D.C. and across the country."

Cox concluded: "Throughout history, freedom-hating tyrants have used gun registration as the key first step in their march to disarm law-abiding citizens. In fact, there is NO OTHER REASON for the government to know which citizens own which guns, and which guns they own."

Senator Lautenberg, a Democrat, has repeatedly introduced legislation to require private sellers at gun shows to carry out the same instant background check on buyers that licensed firearms dealers must do. He supports reinstating and strengthening the "assault" weapons ban that expired in 2004. He has sponsored legislation that would allow federal authorities to deny people whose names are on the terrorist watch list—suspected terrorists—the right to buy guns if there is reason to believe they might use them to carry out terrorism. Lautenberg has long tried to get a law passed that would permit the FBI to keep for 180 days records of NICS background checks that cleared gun purchasers within twenty-four hours, so that the FBI can do a better job of tracking down straw buyers who supply criminals with weapons, cracking down on dealers who knowingly sell to them or falsify sales records, or catching up with gun buyers whose disqualifying backgrounds were missed in the twenty-four-hour check.

The reason the FBI cannot do that is legislation originally proposed by a member of Congress on the other side of the cultural divide in the gun wars, Representative Todd Tiahrt, Republican of Kansas. Since 2004, "Tiahrt amendments" to appropriations bills for the ATF have required destruction of the data gathered in those background checks within twenty-four hours of the sale. Tiahrt, strongly supported by the NRA, ran unsuccessfully for the Senate in 2010 and is no longer a member of Congress, but it is more than likely that his former colleagues will continue imposing restrictions on the ATF in the name of gun rights. Information the ATF develops from tracing weapons can be shared, on an individual basis, with state and local law-enforcement authorities, but it cannot be released to the public or used in civil litigation. Since 2005, the federal Protection of Lawful Commerce in Arms Act has prevented firearms manufacturers and dealers from being held liable for crimes committed with guns they make or sell, unless they violated laws themselves.

The NRA and Cox's rhetoric in fund-raising has overtones of the debates in the founders' time about the danger of federal tyranny, but those debates were about the dangers to the states of overwhelming federal power. Most Americans today are grateful to those in uniform for defending them against terrorists around the world, but two centuries ago a standing army was seen as the worst possible threat of tyranny. Patrick Henry warned the Virginia convention considering ratification of the Constitution, "My great objection to this Government is, that it does not leave us the means of defending our rights; or, of waging war against tyrants. . . . Have we the means of resisting disciplined armies, when our only defence, the militia, is put into the hands of Congress?"[8] He was talking then about the rights of the Commonwealth of Virginia, not individual rights, but Cox used the same rhetoric to try to convince gun owners that gun control threatens their personal liberty: *"And you and I must never forget that ANY battle we lose brings our nation one step closer to the day when only the police and the military are allowed to possess guns— the day when ALL our freedoms will be as good as gone,"* he wrote in one appeal for contributions to the NRA's lobbying arm, the Institute for Legislative Action. He urged gun owners to "keep watch on every single anti-gun scheme that's proposed in Congress and the state legislatures—hundreds of bills in all—and implement the grassroots battle plan that will be needed to defeat all of them."[9] For the NRA, scaring people is how to raise money.

The Second Amendment has never barred reasonable local, state, or federal regulations designed to ensure that only law-abiding citizens and adults can legally get their hands on guns, and that they may be used only for lawful purposes. True conservatives have always recognized this. In a *Reader's Digest* article in 1975, Senator Barry Goldwater of Arizona wrote that he thought a lot of gun-control laws were "unconstitutional in intent," but then he added:

> Well then, I'm often asked, what kind of gun laws *are* you for? I reply that I am for laws of common sense. I am for laws that prohibit citizen access to machine guns, bazookas and other military devices. I am for laws that are educational in nature. I believe that before a person is permitted to buy a weapon he should be required to take a course that will teach him how to use it, to handle it safely and keep it safely about the house.[10]

Weapons kept unsafely around the house accounted for most of the sixty-five deaths of children younger than fifteen because of accidental discharge of firearms that were recorded by the Centers for Disease Control in 2007. But this is one area in which gun-fatality statistics show encouraging news—and surely an important reason is that laws in twenty-six states and the District of Columbia make gun owners criminally liable for leaving weapons loaded or unlocked and accessible to children. Gun owners have been paying more attention to keeping and storing arms safely, locked and unloaded, and keeping them away from children, since the 1990s, when the CDC figures showed an average of 166 children every year being killed accidentally when guns went off in their or a playmate's or friend's hands, or when guns were dropped or fell on the floor, or whatever. Access to weapons that children shouldn't have still accounted for fifty-three suicides by minors using firearms in 2007, and for many of the 201 minors murdered with guns in the same year. But again, those numbers are sharply down, by more than half, from the 1990s.[11]

For those on the gun-rights side of the culture war, cracking down on criminals is the key, as Barry Goldwater thought nearly forty years ago: "We have a crime problem in this country, not a gun problem," he wrote, and if prosecutors and judges would insist on heavy sentences for criminals convicted of gun violence, that would go a long way toward turning the tide against the crime wave. Today Wayne LaPierre, the NRA's chief executive officer, calls for "laws in every American city under which every time a drug dealer or a gang member or a felon touches a gun, you prosecute the criminals 100 percent of the time and take them off the street and put them in jail. And that's the only thing that works." In 2010, according to the *New York Times,* the New York City police seized 5,318 illegal firearms— including 2,984 pistols, 1,402 revolvers, 403 rifles, and 349 shotguns—guns that lacked the necessary permits, in other words. Many, perhaps most, of these guns were found at crime scenes or taken from people arrested for violent crimes. Those 37,000 New Yorkers who are legally in possession of handguns, according to the *Times,* which obtained the records through the Freedom of Information Act and a lawsuit, include "dozens of boldface names and public figures: prominent business leaders, elected officials, celebrities, journalists, judges and lawyers," but the *Times* disclosed only a few of them. There are also 14,602 retired police officers licensed to have weapons.[12]

But New York City gun laws make it far more difficult for gun owners to comply with the regulations than it is for criminals to ignore them. Even people who live elsewhere in the state and have pistol licenses cannot bring their guns legally into the five boroughs of the city unless they get their permit validated there first, and good luck with that. If you live in another state, fuhgeddaboudit. Periodically, some out-of-state gun owner ignorant of the city's rules flies in, declares a gun stowed in a piece of luggage, is arrested for illegal possession, and then becomes a poster boy for outraged gun-rights supporters. It happened to Mark J. Meckler, a cofounder of the Tea Party Patriots, when he presented a locked gun box with the Glock pistol he has a permit to carry in California at a boarding gate for a flight to Detroit at La Guardia Airport in Queens in December 2011. Legal in California, not legal in New York City, his gun got him placed under arrest for illegal "possession of a weapon in the second degree." Like most such unintentional violators, he was allowed to plead to a lesser charge—disorderly conduct, a misdemeanor—but the embarrassment remained.

Some try to embarrass the law instead. The right-leaning *New York Post* took up the case of Ryan Jerome, an ex-marine from Indiana who came to New York City with his legally registered .45 Ruger in September 2011 because he was expecting to be transporting gold jewelry. He had misread the New York City regulations, and when he tried to check his gun in before going up to the observation deck of the Empire State Building, he was clocked in by the police instead. Websites and Facebook pages defending Jerome carped that "Semper Fi" apparently didn't mean much in Gotham, but prosecutors countered that this Leatherneck's military service had ended with an "other than honorable" discharge. Eventually he pleaded to a misdemeanor and paid a $1,000 fine instead of risking a three-and-a-half-year jail sentence for a conviction on the gun charge. Meredith Graves, a thirty-nine-year-old Tennessee woman who saw a "No Guns Allowed" sign at the World Trade Center Memorial site when she visited just before Christmas in 2011 and asked police there where she could check the loaded .32-caliber pistol she was carrying, was promptly arrested for illegal possession. She, too, eventually took a plea to a misdemeanor charge and was let off without punishment.[13]

Any New Yorker who thinks she has a right to have a handgun at home for self-protection can apply for a premises permit, but a lot of good that will do her, because hardly any are ever granted. An application alone requires payment of a fee of $340, plus $94.25 for fingerprinting. After these are paid, the permit can be denied for a multitude of state, local, and federal reasons, including a lack of "character and fitness for a license or permit." If, exceptionally, a permit is approved, the next step is a handgun purchase authorization, itself valid for thirty days. Once bought, the gun has to be registered within seventy-two hours at the One Police Plaza headquarters.

A handgun can be taken to and from an approved firing range, but only unloaded, in a locked container inaccessible during transit and separate from ammunition. Also, a New York City premises permit for a pistol is not valid in any county outside the five boroughs without a state permit valid there.

City clerks look at applications so skeptically that some people conclude they are under instructions to discourage people from applying. A friend of mine was told he needed a New Jersey permit, as well as New York and Connecticut papers, to take his rifle to Connecticut to hunt, because, the clerk explained, "You can't go between New York and Connecticut without going through New Jersey." The geography-challenged clerk was eventually set right by a superior.

The city regulations make permits to carry a handgun out on the street all but impossible for any ordinary resident to get. "We have had guys coming in here with bullet holes in them, and we don't give them carry permits," a permit office clerk with the New York City Police Department (NYPD) told a graduate student, now a Columbia University professor I know, when he tried to apply for one some years back. He wasn't perforated, but he might have come close.

"I was coming home from the library, carrying books, and went into my apartment building and pushed the button for my floor," he told me. "At that point a guy who had come in with me grabbed me by the throat with one hand, keeping the other in the front pocket of his sweatshirt, and said, 'I have a gun—give me your money.' I gave it to him, and he said, 'Now go into your apartment.' I refused, afraid that if I did he would kill me. He then took his hands out of the front pocket of his sweatshirt and I saw that he actually didn't have a gun, and I went after him. I chased him through the streets and finally he threw the money at me and yelled, 'I'm going to get you.'"

Back at the apartment building, the police had arrived, and they cruised around the neighborhood with the victim until they spotted the man who had tried to rob him, then arrested him. He turned out to be a violent felon on work release with a long record of criminal violence and ended up with a long jail term.

From prison, sometime later, the convict sent a letter to the soon-to-be professor, by name, at home, with this chilling message: "Do you remember me? You are dead." He went to the police in something of a panic, wondering what to do about a threat that seemed only too credible. The cops were sympathetic, agreeing informally that the best thing he could do would be to get a carry permit for a pistol. That was when he went to apply and was told by the clerk that he wasn't going to get one. He went ahead anyway and paid the fee, and in due course, eleven months later, his application was rejected. Eventually, he did succeed in getting a premises permit for a pistol—after paying the fee for that and waiting another six months, of course.

The object of gun-control laws ought to be more to try to keep illegal guns off the streets than to discourage legal ownership. The NYPD uses many different tactics to try to keep the number of illegal guns down. Voluntary programs offer $1,000 for information leading to the arrest of someone on grounds of criminal possession of a firearm. The police also offer occasional buyback programs, giving $200 bank cards to people in high-crime neighborhoods who turn in illegal guns, with no questions asked (the guns have to be in working order, though), and they bring in perhaps a couple of thousand illegal guns a year this way.

More intrusive police methods in New York City have been less effective, at least on illegal guns—tactics like stopping and frisking people on the street for suspicious behavior, furtiveness, closeness to a crime scene, or other reasons, for example. A study of the results of 2,805,721 stops like this all over the city from 2004 to 2009 found that only 1.5 guns were turned up in every thousand stops—about nine hundred guns a year. The study found that blacks were far more likely to be stopped and frisked than whites (the relatively few who were stopped at all), but far less likely to be carrying weapons than the whites who were stopped had on them. In the mostly black Brownsville section of Brooklyn, in 52,000 random stops between January 2006 and March 2010, the police found only twenty-five guns. People in such neighborhoods fear the gun glut, but they also resent being stopped for no other reason that they can see beyond "being black." Peter F. Vallone Jr., chairman of the New York City Council's Public Safety Committee, said that these stops were "the best way to get guns off our streets," but his assertion is simply not borne out, not even by the police department's own statistics.[14]

"The buy-back program gets more guns off the streets than stop-and-frisk," New York City councilman Jumaane Williams told me. "Stop-and-frisk, the way it's being applied, just doesn't work." His

Brooklyn district includes East Flatbush, where for years African American residents have been frequently stopped and frisked, yet gun violence in the Sixty-seventh Precinct there was the second-worst in all of New York City in 2011. "The shootings are increasing at the same time as stop-and-frisks are increasing. It's a good tool for police to have, but it's being abused in communities like mine," Williams said. The overwhelming majority of those stopped and questioned this way in 2011 in the city as a whole, 87 percent, were black or Latino, according to official statistics obtained by the New York Civil Liberties Union from the City Council.[15]

In early 2012, Police Commissioner Raymond W. Kelly raised the possibility of using electronic scanners rather than stop-and-frisk to find people carrying illegal guns, but complained that critics of the tactic offered few alternatives. Later, he and Mayor Bloomberg agreed to a proposal made by Governor Andrew M. Cuomo to elim-inate a side effect of the policy that those stopped and frisked had found one of the most objectionable. Usually they were ordered to empty their pockets, and if they then ended up holding small amounts of marijuana in their hands, the police would arrest them for the crime of open possession. Most of the 50,000 such arrests in the city in 2011 were of black or Hispanic people, while white tokers were seldom stopped, frisked, or prosecuted. Cuomo unsuccessfully proposed to the state legislature that open possession of twenty-five grams of pot or less be decriminalized and made a "violation," with a maximum fine of $100 for first offenders. Commissioner Kelly en-dorsed the idea as a good way to eliminate "confusion" about a policy he continued to justify as a way to protect "people of color," who are 96 percent of the victims of gun violence in the city.[16]

Indeed, bullets do take the lives of African Americans nationwide at a disproportionately high rate. Blacks, 10 percent of the popula-tion, suffer one-fourth of the total firearms deaths and suicides in

America, year after year. And most of the bullets that kill them in street crime come from illegal guns, acquired from "informal swaps, trades and purchases among family members, friends, acquaintances, and street and black-market sources," as one scholar associated with gun rights, James D. Wright, put it.[17] Peter Diaczuk, the director of forensics science training at John Jay College of Criminal Justice, a part of the City University of New York, agreed with this viewpoint: "Legally bought guns are not the crime guns. The bad guys get their guns in a black-market way, like drugs," he told me. Every year, according to FBI statistics, more than 150,000 legally registered firearms are stolen, and most are never recovered—and many end up on the streets. Criminals also acquire some through straw purchasers—people who buy guns not for themselves but for others not legally entitled to buy them—or they get them on the international black market.

In Williams's view, the most important thing that could be done to reduce this kind of gun violence would be to convince the young people on the streets that going for a gun for any reason is almost always a terrible idea. "We need to be talking about the root causes of why people are making these terrible and poor decisions," he said— the decisions that lead people to pick up guns to settle disputes or matters of honor, avenge insults, or acquire things they cannot afford. "What's happening now to black and brown (usually) young men here is not new," Williams said. "When the complexion was different, fifty, sixty, or seventy years ago, in pockets of poverty in areas where people felt disenfranchised, there was violence then, but it's different now because the influx of the guns is amazing."

Williams is cochairman of the City Council gun violence task force. From his experience there, the main thing he learned was how little city-state-federal coordination there was in dealing with illegal guns. Even at the city level, he complained, "We're passing the city budget, and we're cutting all of the youth programs, and all the after-school programs, and we're cutting the scholarships to go to college. You can't do all those things and then act surprised when the violence increases. You should sit down with the police department and everyone else and say, 'What effect is this going to have on the crime mission?'" Crime is down in New York City as a whole, but, Williams pointed out, "That's not in all neighborhoods, and it's a problem."[18] (The NYPD suffered a severe blow to its credibility on the need to strengthen federal gun-control laws to stop interstate gun traffic in late 2011, when five active-duty officers and three retired colleagues were arrested and charged in federal court with conspiring to take money from an FBI informant to transport stolen goods, including "assault" rifles and handguns—many with serial numbers made illegible so they couldn't be traced—across the state line from New Jersey, in exchange for money. Four of them later pleaded guilty.)[19]

Cathy Lanier, the District of Columbia police chief, told *Fox TV News* in 2009 that a 23 percent decline in the murder rate there from 2008 to 2009 (from 186 to 144, down to only about one-third of the number of murders there a decade earlier) was due partly to a change in her department's focus. "It's a small number of people who consistently carry guns and engage in repeat violent gun offenses," she said. "If you can focus on those people and get them off the street that is the number one key ingredient," but she added that the police could not produce results without seeking cooperation from the community.

I f the objective of controlling violence is seen as a kind of disease-prevention measure, people on either side of the gun-war cultural divide should be able to talk to each other across it. A good example is a law-enforcement program in Virginia with an emphasis on community outreach that began in Richmond as "Project Exile" in 1997, after a spike in gun violence in 1996 that gave that city the second-highest per capita murder rate in the country—140 murders, 122 of them committed with firearms, with a shooting or a shooting death every two days.[20] The average criminal, former US attorney James Comey told a police symposium later, "put on pants, shirt, socks, and gun with equal reflection. In a city where everyone on the street saw a gun as a 'necessary article of clothing,' firearms were used to settle everything from a minor spat over a girl to a major dispute over a drug deal."[21]

Local police authorities, the FBI, and federal prosecutors at first worked out a plan to prosecute criminal use of guns under federal rather than state law, because the federal laws carried higher punishments. Reaching out to local community leaders appalled by the violence, state and local leaders explained that they hoped to deter it with stiff penalties for using firearms to commit crimes: Anyone convicted of doing that would be sent away, not to a local prison but to a faraway federal one (hence the name Project Exile) for at least five years.

The word soon got around, with television and radio commercials, billboards, and city buses emblazoned with the slogan, "An illegal gun gets you 5 years in federal prison." By 2001, the murder rate was half what it had been five years earlier. But federal judges objected that the program overburdened courts and jails that should not be saddled with problems the state judicial system should handle, and the law was changed. People found guilty by state courts of possessing firearms after previous convictions for violent felonies now go to Virginia prisons, not federal ones, for a minimum of five years.

But of course hardened criminals are not the only perpetrators of gun violence. Young people, young men especially, in troubled, drug-ridden neighborhoods, who look to guns for security, self-protection, and self-esteem can fall into a self-destructive vicious circle. Breaking that pattern takes more than just tough law enforcement.

Programs in Boston, Chicago, New York City, and many other cities also approach gun violence as a sociological problem that law enforcement alone is not enough to solve.

The Chicago program began in the mid-1990s with the Chicago Project for Violence Prevention, founded by an epidemiologist, Gary Slutkin, who had been treating and figuring out how to prevent tuberculosis, AIDS, and other infectious diseases in Africa for twenty years before returning to his hometown in 1995. There he found another kind of epidemic: "I listened to hundreds of stories about ten-year-olds shooting twelve-year-olds, and about how incredibly unsafe American cities were becoming. I had heard nothing like that overseas—except for war zones," Slutkin recalled later. "There were all kinds of programs and projects, but I didn't see a city that really had a strategy for reducing violent behavior—certainly not one that made any sense."

The strategy that Slutkin devised for what he called CeaseFire in Chicago was inspired by what he had learned as a doctor. Running the anti-tuberculosis program in San Francisco, where the disease was spreading among Southeast Asian immigrants in the early 1980s, he concentrated on the most highly infectious patients and got fellow immigrants they trusted to make them follow their treatment. That kept them from spreading the infection to others, and gradually the number of new TB cases declined.

Slutkin explained in an op-ed essay in the *Chicago Tribune* in 2011, a few days after the Chicago Police Department announced that the 435 murders in the city in 2010 were the least since 1965, half as many as in the 1970s (though they spiked again in 2012):

The important stories behind the data are the homicides that didn't happen.

Consider the homicide that didn't happen a year ago on Chicago Avenue in the Austin neighborhood. At the time, two warring gangs were enforcing a boundary line between their respective territories. People who lived nearby knew not to cross that line without the very real threat of getting shot.

One day, a 14-year-old boy was walking to school when he accidentally crossed that line. The price for his mistake was a bullet to his back. The shooting wasn't fatal, but he was paralyzed from the waist down. What happened next would determine whether more lives were destroyed.

There was immediately a move to retaliate. The days that followed saw threats and counterthreats by gang members with the means and motive to back them up. The invisible boundary line wouldn't hold for long.

When two trained violence interrupters with histories in those two gangs caught wind of the escalating danger, they intervened and were able to calm the situation, and after a month even persuaded the rival factions to sit down. They eventually negotiated a peace treaty, and today the boundary line is gone. More important, there hasn't been a single shooting related to that conflict since.[22]

"Violence interrupters" in similar programs in other cities that have adopted and support this approach are people who have been themselves involved in gangs or violent behavior in the past but—because they are now older and wiser—have completed their prison sentences, or realized that they survived to middle age only by pure luck, and have decided to turn the page. CeaseFire programs, supported by city funds, employ the interrupters to use their influence and street credibility on younger people like themselves to talk them out of the idea that getting hold of a gun is the best way to avenge an insult, or even a killing—to bring down the level of gun violence by changing the behavior patterns that lead to it.[23]

The Chicago Public Schools have developed another approach to the problem of gun deaths of school-age children in the city, using a study of five hundred shooting victims over a two-year period to produce a profile of other students who might be at high risk of suffering the same fate. Most were black, poor, and male, with poor attendance and academic records, and had been frequently in detention for serious misconduct. The $20 million program has paid adult mentors to try to influence the behavior of 1,700 teenagers, in school and in the streets, to encourage them to be better students and show self-control, less likely to go get a gun when challenged or infuriated, or to be shot by somebody who did, according to a report on National Public Radio's *Weekend Edition Sunday*.[24]

The Boston Operation Ceasefire program also began in the mid-1990s, with a multiagency law-enforcement task force, in cooperation with social scientists, that succeeded in reducing homicides after a murder spike in 1990 that had left many feeling that the city was out of control. Putting unrelenting law-enforcement pressure on street gangs in chronically violent black neighborhoods, together with intense efforts to reach out to gang members, their families, and their friends, worked, after gang members became persuaded that the pressure would let up only if the killings stopped and illegal firearms were surrendered.

The approach also led to some new insights in Boston about ATF tracing data. Some stereotypical law-enforcement assumptions had been wrong—the idea that youth gangs favored older guns taken from adult relatives or stolen guns, for example (as 80 percent of convicted older criminals had told researchers for the Justice Department they had gotten theirs; only 14 percent of convicts interviewed in prisons for one study in 1997[25] said they had bought them from dealers, at gun shows, or from pawnshops). In Boston's street gangs, 33 percent of the guns turned out to have been sold less than two years before being used in crimes, and semiautomatic pistols were even newer than that: "In all probability, these guns had been deliberately diverted from gun stores into young people's hands," the academic participants in Operation Ceasefire noted in 2001.

Finally, nearly 20 percent of all guns recovered from youths had obliterated serial numbers—a marker of illicit firearms trafficking. Analysis disproved the belief, on the other hand, that all youth crime guns in Boston were coming from southern States. More than 33 percent of traceable guns had first been sold at retail in Massachusetts; the next largest source state was Georgia, at only 8 percent. Guns originating in all southern States combined equaled a volume slightly below that of Massachusetts. Contrary to the expectations of the entire law enforcement community, Boston had a large problem essentially in its own back yard.

But the combination of outreach and toughness produced, in the words of the social scientists who participated in the beginning of the study, "the extraordinary picture . . . of young gang members turning over their guns to the police—literally walking up to the . . . Warren Street headquarters [of the Boston Police Department's Youth Violence Strike Force] with paper bags full of guns and dropping them off."

The study's authors made no exaggerated claims for this unusual experiment in gun control, which it was, among other things. "It is impossible to say with certainty what caused the falloff in youth homicide in Boston or exactly what part Operation Ceasefire played," they conceded. "Because Ceasefire was conceived as an intervention aimed at interrupting the overall dynamic of violence in which all Boston gangs and gang members were involved, the operation could not be set up as a controlled experiment, with certain gangs or neighborhoods excluded for purposes of comparison. Some things are clear, however. Youth homicide in the city declined abruptly following the first gang forum in May 1996, and this low level continued through 1998 and 1999."[26]

A decade later, Boston's mayor, Thomas M. Menino, and New York's Michael R. Bloomberg, as cochairmen of the activist coalition Mayors Against Illegal Guns, issued a report in September 2010—"Trace the Guns"—using ATF data that they said showed that disproportionately high numbers of guns used in crimes nationwide had originally been sold in states with lax gun laws. Controlling for population, the report said, Mississippi, Virginia, Kentucky, Alaska, Alabama, South Carolina, Indiana, Nevada, and Georgia "exported" up to ten times as many crime guns per 100,000 population as, for example, Massachusetts or New York, concluding: "The wide range in export rates suggests that criminals and gun traffickers may favor certain states as the sources of guns."

The NRA criticized the report for, among other things, failing to take into account the fact that a short time between a gun's original, traceable legal sale and the commission of a crime with it is the most reliable indicator that it has been trafficked—sold to somebody else illegally, or stolen—along the way. In fact, the report found that more than 24 percent of the crime guns that had originated in the top ten "high-export" states (in 2009, Georgia, Florida, Virginia, Texas, Indiana, Ohio, Pennsylvania, North Carolina, California, and Arizona) had been sold less than two years before being used in crimes, compared to 13.8 percent of those from the bottom ten (Michigan, Illinois, Rhode Island, Minnesota, California, Massachusetts, New Jersey, New York, Hawaii, and the District of Columbia). In New

York City, of guns that had been used in crime and could be traced by the ATF in 2009, only about 15 percent had been originally sold in New York state. Virginia alone was the source of almost as many.[27]

So, after fifty-two shootings and thirteen deaths during the 2011 Labor Day weekend in New York City, it was hardly surprising that Mayor Bloomberg called on the federal government to take more effective action to control illegal gun traffic, or that he did it again after eight NYPD officers were shot in the first four months of 2012. "All the shootings have a disgraceful fact in common: all were committed with illegal guns that came from out of state," he said. "And that is the case with nearly every shooting in our city."[28]

"Straw purchasers" are a major problem for police departments nationwide, and mayors like Bloomberg insist that the federal government should tighten the laws and close the loophole in the NICS system that absolves private sellers from verifying that their buyers qualify. The NRA has fought against this tooth and nail, and calls Mayors Against Illegal Guns "the greatest organized threat to our Second Amendment rights." To be sure, the mayors' "Trace the Guns" study has its flaws—for one thing, California, because of its huge population, is also year after year one of the top ten "exporters" of guns later used in crimes, despite its stringent gun laws. But that shouldn't absolve federally licensed dealers of responsibility to do all they can do to ensure that the only people they sell guns to are those who are legally entitled to buy them.

Federal law makes straw purchasing of guns or providing false information for the required federal background check punishable by up to ten years in jail and a $250,000 fine. But, the mayors' report showed, states with laws providing also for state and local prosecution of people who do those things—and of licensed dealers who fail to carry out the checking procedure, a misdemeanor punishable under federal law by up to a year and a $100,000 fine—were less likely to be sources of trafficked guns used in crimes. The logical conclusion is that if states make it harder for criminals to buy guns illegally from straw purchasers, it will be harder for criminals to use guns to commit crimes. Does that translate into lower crime rates? Maybe it does, but even so, criminals have access to about 500,000 guns stolen from private homes every year.

The mayors' group recommended adoption of other measures, all regarded by gun-rights groups as anathema. These included purchase permits for all handgun sales, discretion for local law-enforcement authorities to approve or deny concealed-carry permits (the kind of discretion New York City exercises in deciding who actually "needs" them, which, as has been shown, can be arbitrary), and local control of firearms regulations (as cities are more apt to want stricter controls than rural counties, and gun-rights supporters prefer looser ones to be statewide).

The mayors' group also regularly calls for closing the loophole that allows private purchasers of weapons at gun shows to avoid the background check. After a rash of shootings, New York City sent investigators posing as gun purchasers to a Crossroads of the West gun show in Phoenix in early 2011, where one of them bought a Sig Sauer semiautomatic 9-mm pistol for $500 from a private seller after this exchange:

> INVESTIGATOR: So, you're not one of those, you know, dealer guys, right?
>
> SELLER: No. No tax, no form, you don't have to do transfers or nothing.
>
> INVESTIGATOR: Yeah, yeah.
>
> SELLER: Just see an Arizona ID and that's it with me.
>
> INVESTIGATOR: So no background check?
>
> SELLER: No.
>
> INVESTIGATOR: That's good, because I probably couldn't pass one, you know what I mean?[29]

Mayor Bloomberg made a big deal of this "sting," variations on which have been played out by gun-control advocates again and again over the years to dramatize the need to close the loophole that exempts private sellers at gun shows from checking their buyers with the national database. The mayors' group did not point out that the "gotcha" came only after numerous other prospective sellers had turned the investigator away, saying they couldn't legally sell to him.

But the "gun show" loophole goes far beyond gun shows, because only 3 to 8 percent of all private gun sales take place there.[30] That leaves more than 90 percent of them exempt from the federal background check requirement, and as for state controls, as of 2010, only sixteen states[31] and the District of Columbia required background checks before private handgun sales at gun shows; four of those[32] did not require checks for private sales outside of shows. All the rest left private individuals free to buy or sell without background checks for handguns or any other kind of firearms.[33] But this does not mean that all of them are willing to sell to people who admit to being, or appear to be, unentitled legally to buy guns.

Requiring private sellers of arms to get their buyers to fill out paperwork and then to put in a call to the national instant background check number would not seem such an unpardonable imposition if coupled with other measures that would save lives, such as making sure all states submit to the background check database the names of people who should be denied the right to purchase firearms for mental health reasons.

Mayors Against Illegal Guns has been pressing for years for other measures to make it easier for law-enforcement authorities to trace crime guns back to criminals—by making it harder for people who commit crimes to erase or obliterate the manufacturers' serial numbers, for example. "Violent criminals, including the perpetrator of the shootings at Virginia Tech, have attempted to obliterate those marks on thousands of guns recovered in crimes each year," the mayors said in a 2009 report, "A Blueprint for Action on Illegal Guns," calling for regulations requiring gun makers to imprint all weapons with hidden, tamper-proof sets of identifying information.

Some makers take this concern seriously—being part of the problem doesn't mean they can't also be part of the solution. Some might ask, which one is Tom Deeb? His company, Hi-Point Firearms, in Mansfield, Ohio, makes guns that are cheap, reliable, and easy to buy. His intended market, he says, is ordinary folk who don't have a lot of money but want guns for sport or self-protection, but he is well aware that criminals and young gang members, among others, are also drawn to Hi-Point guns because they don't cost much.

One of the three guns used in the massacre at Columbine High School near Denver, Colorado, in 1999 by Eric Harris and Dylan Klebold was a Hi-Point carbine with a ten-round magazine. A female friend, a fellow senior who was old enough (over eighteen) to buy it legally, got it for him at a Colorado gun show, along with two shotguns Harris and Klebold then sawed short (illegally). The two youths had planned to kill as many as five hundred people in and around Columbine with their guns and bombs they had made, but after killing twelve students and a teacher, they found themselves cornered and killed themselves.

Hi-Point and Tom Deeb bore no responsibility for the horrors at Columbine, but he said he felt terrible about what happened anyway. "I'm a small manufacturer. I don't have the millions of dollars for litigation fees, and I don't have insurance," Deeb told the *Denver Post* a few months later, facing seventeen lawsuits by major cities trying to hold gun makers like him responsible for crimes that had been committed with weapons they made. "You consider yourself a good American," Deeb said. "Then all of a sudden, in the space of six months, you have cities looking at me like I'm a criminal. And one of my guns gets used in a heinous crime. Damn, I'm cast in a bad lot. We're just ordinary people."[34]

Deeb deliberately makes it easy for law-enforcement authorities to trace bullets and shell casings back to Hi-Point guns, and he has his defenders. His detractors say he should be ashamed of himself for making weapons that turn up so often in the wrong hands, but Peter Diaczuk of John Jay College of Criminal Justice says that he believes Deeb is "addressing the criminal use of guns" in the manufacturing process—by having his employees use a tiny belt sander on the breech face of his firearms before they're sold. It's a step that marks cartridge casings and bullets in a way that is unique to that gun.

As much as the mayors and police on one side of the cultural war over guns emphasize the importance of tracing, those on the "Tiahrt" side do their best to resist and discredit the practice. Licensed firearms dealers are caught in the crossfire—at least, conscientious dealers who have not exposed themselves to it by reckless behavior that itself seems criminal. The *Washington Post,* in a series of articles called *The Hidden Life of Guns* in the fall of 2010, found that since 1998, of 6,800 guns originally sold in Virginia and later seized in connection with crimes, 60 percent were traced to only 40 of the state's 3,400 dealers (a pattern that has been found repeatedly, over many years, in other states). Those 40, including "mom-and-pop gun shops, inner-city pawn dealers and suburban sporting-goods outlets," were relatively high-volume stores, but even so, accounted for only 30 percent of the gun sales volume in the state, not 60 percent, the *Post* said. So the question—one the *Post* could not definitively answer—was whether some of these dealers either paid less attention to carrying out background checks on purchasers than they should have, or deliberately turned a blind eye to signs that the guns were being purchased for illegal purposes. One article quoted James Cavanaugh, a retired ATF special agent, telling police chiefs: "I can tell you that most of the gun dealers are not bad gun dealers—they help us get the traffickers. But to really put this in perspective, a bad gun dealer is like a bad cop. He can really hurt us because he can really pump the guns out."[35]

Is this what happened with a Hi-Point 9-mm semiautomatic pistol, serial number 502139, a Saturday night special that was used in a drive-by street-gang shooting of a promising high school basketball star, Daniel Williams, in August 2003 in Buffalo, New York? Williams was shooting baskets in front of a neighbor's house at the time. The gang member who shot him later said that the shooting was a mistake; he thought Williams was somebody else, his intended victim. According to evidence presented in court, the shooter got the gun illegally from a Buffalo convict and gun trafficker, James Nigel Bostic. In Ohio, Bostic had been able to use straw men without criminal records (mostly women, actually) to buy guns for him that he could then take back to Buffalo to resell illegally to members of street gangs and others. The one that sent a bullet through Williams's stomach was just one of eighty-seven handguns that one such fraudulent buyer, Kimberly Upshaw, had bought in early October 2000 at a gun show in Dayton, Ohio, from Charles Brown, the owner of a Dayton company that was Hi-Point's exclusive distributor, MKS Supply, Inc. Bostic was at the gun show with Upshaw and picked out the guns he wanted; Upshaw, who had made multiple gun purchases from the dealer previously, filled out the paperwork and paid for them with several thousand dollars in cash, and then allegedly resold them for profit, illegally, to others; eventually, this particular gun came into the hands of the gang member who fired it at Williams.

All these allegations were made by the victim and his father, supported by the Brady Campaign Against Gun Violence, in a lawsuit in 2005 in New York state court in Buffalo seeking damages from everybody involved, from Deeb, the Hi-Point owner, to the shooter. Bostic, the lawyers' brief for the Williamses said, could never have presided over an extensive gun-running operation in Buffalo for which he was later tried, convicted, and imprisoned if Hi-Point and its exclusive dealer Charles Brown had not both irresponsibly turned a blind eye to straw purchases. A collector might buy eighty-seven guns at a gun show, but collectors do not find Hi-Point guns worth collecting, the lawsuit said; the suit charged that both Brown and Deeb knew that Hi-Point pistols were disproportionately used by criminals, but that neither they nor the operator of the gun show had taken any steps to tighten procedures to screen out straw buyers.

Federal law requires licensed dealers to report multiple sales to the ATF, so it is hard to see how Upshaw could do what he did with Brown's knowledge. Brown's lawyer argued that he, as distributor of Hi-Point weapons, could have no way of knowing that Upshaw was not legitimately buying handguns for himself. Although Brown was in contact with Deeb almost daily, Deeb, the manufacturer, maintained that Hi-Point had no direct knowledge of this particular sale. Risible though Brown's defense sounds, federal law since 2005—when the NRA and other lobbies persuaded congressional legislators that pressuring firearms dealers to conform to the law was an attack on gun rights—has barred most civil lawsuits seeking to hold firearms dealers or manufacturers responsible for crimes committed with weapons they made or sold. Dealers who knowingly sell to people on the prohibited list or conspire with them to falsify information to qualify them as purchasers are excepted. The Williamses' case was dismissed by the state court in 2010. They have appealed.[36]

More members of Congress listen to the NRA than listen to the ATF. The result, as the *Washington Post* found in its series of articles in the fall of 2010 about the problems of separating criminals from guns in greater Washington, is that legislators have been persuaded to hogtie the ATF so thoroughly that it is hampered in doing the most important part of its job, preventing and deterring gun crime and the criminals who commit it.

After the rise of the Tea Party in the 2010 elections, it seems unlikely that Congress will be disposed to lift restrictions on a government agency that millions of gun owners are being encouraged by the most powerful lobby in Washington to think of as an example of the federal tyranny the founders feared. The Tea Party and the NRA speak much the same language, and though there are distortions that reverberate down through two centuries, there are echoes in it of Samuel Adams and Patrick Henry. This can be puzzling to Americans, but it is even more puzzling to outsiders. An astute observer of America who came from the Soviet Union and now teaches at the University of Minnesota, Melor Sturua, shakes his head about the American fascination with firearms. "The Second Amendment is for a country that was—what?—two or three million people?" he said, "and now you have 300 million, and so many guns." So different, yet so much the same. Uncomfortable as it may make some Americans, Patrick Henry and Samuel Adams would still feel very much at home here today.

Seung-Hui Cho would not have been prevented from killing thirty-two other people at Virginia Tech in 2007 even if the Assault Weapons Ban's ban on large-capacity magazines had not been allowed to expire three years earlier. Because it had, and because Virginia had no state ban, either, he had no trouble buying such a magazine for one of the handguns he used, a Glock 9-mm semi-automatic, but that didn't increase his firepower much, as it held only five more rounds than an ordinary magazine.

After the massacre, there were the inevitable calls for remedial measures such as reinstating the ban, but they missed the most crucial lapse: Cho should never have been able to go out and buy the Glock and its magazine, or the Walther .22 pistol he also purchased, under provisions of the Brady Handgun Violence Prevention Act that were in effect at the time and still are. Their aim is not to ban weapons but to keep people who should not ever have access to weapons from acquiring them. If the provisions were effectively enforced, Cho could never have gotten those guns, at least not legally.

Why the fatal omission? As a review panel reported to Virginia's governor Tim Kaine after the tragedy: "Virginia is one of only 22 states that report any information about mental health to a federal database used to conduct background checks on would-be gun purchasers. But Virginia law did not clearly require that persons such as Cho—who had been ordered into out-patient treatment but not committed to an institution—be reported to the database." Had that information been in the database, he would not have passed the background checks required before he could buy the guns. Virginia later tightened up its laws, and twelve other states that had not been supplying information to the national database about people disqualified from gun purchases because of mental problems began doing so. In addition, six states that had provided some names submitted many more.

One of those states was Arizona, but the list of names it provided did not include Jared Loughner, a mentally troubled twenty-two-year-old in Tucson, who at the start of 2011 set off with a Glock pistol he had acquired at a sporting goods store to shoot Representative Gabrielle Giffords, who was meeting with constituents outside a Safeway supermarket. Inserted in the Glock was a large-capacity extended magazine that would allow him to fire off more than thirty rounds, one after another at the touch of his trigger finger, before reloading.

If Loughner's name had been in the database, the store would not have sold him the gun. He had been suspended from Pima Community College and told he could not return until he had a mental-health examination finding that he would not be a danger to himself or others, but that was not part of any formal record. Neither the college, nor the US Army, which had rejected him for drug use, nor anybody else had been required to report any of this troubled background to the background-check database. After shooting Giffords in the head, he kept firing into the crowd, killing six people, including a judge and a nine-year-old girl, and wounding twelve others besides, before finally running out of bullets. A sixty-one-year-old woman then knocked away the magazine when he was trying to reload. Other bystanders—one of them a man who was carrying a gun himself, as Arizona law allows, and was ready to use it against the shooter but wasn't sure who it was—rushed up and kept Loughner from continuing the slaughter. Fortunately for the injured victims, he was not using self-defense rounds that expand on impact to create maximum damage as they tear through flesh and bone, as Cho had used at Virginia Tech, but full-metal-jacket rounds, one of which passed clear through Giffords's skull instead of destroying her brain.

There was much anguished self-examination, in Tucson, in Congress, and across the country after that atrocity, about whether inflammatory right-wing rhetoric on radio talk shows and Fox Television (and its inflammatory left-wing counterparts on MSNBC and elsewhere) had created a political climate that fostered such violence. But the anguish, and some of the cheap-shot publicity stunts that followed, missed the point—that gun-control legislation already on the books could have been tightened in a way that would have kept Loughner from acquiring his lethal weapons.

Liberals wondered after Tucson why the United States could not become more like Japan or Europe, where guns are strictly controlled in most countries. Yet no American gun massacre has yet taken as many lives as the sixty-nine, mostly high school students, who were shot to death at a lakeside summer camp in Norway in mid-2011 by a single gunman, an anti-Islamic extremist named Anders Behring Breivik (who also set off bombs that killed another eight people in Oslo the same day). Great Britain has been a less violent society than the United States over most of its modern history by all measures, but despite tough firearms laws that were tightened in 1996 after a gun massacre in Dunblane, Scotland, in mid-2010, Derrick Bird, a fifty-two-year-old taxi driver in the Lake District of England, went berserk and killed twelve people and then himself with a shotgun and a .22-caliber rifle with sniper scope that he had inherited from his father. In Germany, gun control has been strict since 1972, in the wake of the massacre at the Munich Olympics and the activities of the Baader-Meinhof and other radical-leftist terrorist groups. Yet in April 2002, Robert Steinhäuser, a nineteen-year-old who had been expelled from the Gutenberg Gymnasium in Erfurt, went back to the school, packing a pump-action shotgun and a 9-mm semiautomatic Glock pistol that he was able to purchase legally with falsified application forms, with five hundred rounds of ammunition. He killed thirteen teachers and two students and then shot himself to death. Germany later raised the legal age for purchasing weapons like shotguns to twenty-one, but that did not prevent another German school massacre in March 2009 that took sixteen lives and ended in a shootout with police miles away. Again, the shooter was the last to die, at his own hand—Tim Kretschmer, a mentally disturbed seventeen-year-old who used the one unsecured gun (out of fifteen) that his father, who belonged to a shooting club and had legal ownership of the weapons, had left in his bedroom. All this in a country of 80 million people where only 30,000 (besides police) can legally carry guns and an average of only 200 people a year die in homicides involving firearms.

Subsequent atrocities in Brazil, the Netherlands, and the one in Norway showed that the United States does not have the patent on mass killings. In China, where it is virtually impossible for anybody to own a gun, there has been a rash of school massacres, but in these the deadliest weapons available to the perpetrators were knives. Five slashing assaults by deranged adults on schoolchildren between March and May 2010 killed seventeen people and wounded nearly one hundred others. When people, insanely or otherwise, become bent on murder, they will find the means to accomplish it whether or not they can get hold of guns. What guns do is make it less likely that the attempt will fail, and they also sharply increase the probability of serious injury.

But strict gun control alone cannot solve our gun problems. It is not guns that cause those problems, but human behavior, and influencing that in communities troubled by gun violence is just as important as cutting down the number of illegal guns available there. Hard as it is for many liberals to accept, what the gun-rights activists say is mostly true—guns don't kill people; people do.

CHAPTER SEVEN

THE THINKING BEHIND GUN RIGHTS

*As long as they insist on restricting me because of what thugs
are doing, I am not going to put up with that.*
JOSEPH E. OLSON, MINNEAPOLIS, 2010

I t should be possible for Americans to agree on ways of ensuring
that people who clearly should not have guns can be denied access
to them—minors, criminals, those with mental disorders, drug addicts, and so on. But it cannot happen without some constructive
engagement between two forces that are now at each other's throats.
So, as someone trying to write a book that would encourage that
kind of dialogue, I went to Minneapolis in early 2010 to meet one
of Minnesota's leading gun-rights advocates, Professor Joseph Edward Olson of Hamline University School of Law in St. Paul.

It was sort of like walking straight into the "gun lobby," so dubbed
by what one of its best-known leaders, the NRA's Wayne LaPierre,

denounces as "gun banners" and "enemies of freedom." But, once inside, I found Olson open-minded and willing to engage.

For people like him, the counterintuitive solution to gun violence
is more guns, not fewer, in more people's hands. Guns do not commit crimes, they argue; criminals do. If more law-abiding people
carry weapons, criminals will think twice before committing crimes
with guns. Mass shooters might be stopped more quickly if their potential victims carried weapons of their own and could shoot back.
As it is, defenseless people in mass shootings can only wait like sheep
to be slaughtered, as Olson sees it. At Virginia Tech, he believes, if
more people at the school—not necessarily students—had been carrying arms, someone might have been able to stop the carnage. Even
just firing at the ceiling, Olson told me, "would have changed the dy-
namics and would not have added to the overall danger. The
shooter would have stopped just firing at people and would have had
to think about defending himself. A gun carrier in the crowd would
have had a chance to shoot at him again." But, of course, the shooter
would also have had a chance to bring down the gun carrier and then
carry on the slaughter. "There's no guarantee that you'll win," Olson
conceded.

Later, thinking about what he said, I found the logic that being
armed might just give a chance of success in mass-shooting situations like these to be seductive, but flawed. There have been so many
gun massacres since 1966, when Charles Whitman shocked the
country by killing fourteen people and wounding thirty-two others
with a rifle from a tower at the University of Texas in Austin, that
these things have almost come to seem inevitable. In Utah, students
over twenty-one who have concealed-carry permits for handguns
can carry them on campus, and after the Giffords shooting in Tucson
in 2011, legislators in Arizona and Texas debated whether to allow
pistol-packing students on campuses there as well.[1] Someone like

Olson, who is an expert marksman with almost a lifetime of experience using firearms, might easily imagine himself reacting calmly in a scenario like Virginia Tech—if he had the gun at the ready, was not confused in the chaos, knew who was doing the shooting, and had a clear shot, anyway. But how likely would that be in a crowd of gun carriers who never even had to go to a firing range or demonstrate that they knew how to hold, aim, or shoot a gun? In Arizona, gun owners can now carry concealed weapons without a permit—without doing any of those things, if they choose not to. How would people like that react under the incredible stress of a mass murderer systematically gunning down everybody in sight? Some might just duck under a desk and hope not to be seen, some might fire back, some might fire wildly. The police, who normally can concentrate on finding and stopping the shooter in scenarios like Virginia Tech, would now face an enormously more confusing situation.

The University of Arizona's police chief, asked by the *New York Times* what he thought of letting students carry guns there, said, "his officers would be at a loss if they arrived at a shooting scene in a lecture hall holding hundreds of students and found scores of people pointing, and possibly shooting, weapons at one another."[2] He and his colleagues from Arizona State University and Northern Arizona University pleaded with legislators to defeat a bill that as originally drafted would allow carrying of guns anywhere on campus, including in classrooms. "Law enforcement intervention should be done by law enforcement personnel who have been specifically selected and trained to perform these duties, not by individuals who may have marginally completed an eight-hour course years ago or other marginal training and possibly have not practiced with the firearm they are now carrying," they said. The Arizona legislature finally passed a measure that would allow guns only on "a public right of way" on campuses, but Governor Jan Brewer, a strong supporter of gun rights, found that language unclear and vetoed it in April 2011. Supporters there vowed to try again.[3]

At Fort Hood, Texas, on November 5, 2009, Major Nidal Hasan pulled out a semiautomatic pistol, shouted "Allahu Akbar!" and began shooting. Olson argued that some of the twelve fellow soldiers (and a civilian) he killed and the twenty-nine he wounded might have been able to stop him if they had been allowed to carry arms in the Soldier Readiness Center, where he started his rampage, but the center is a medical treatment facility where weapons are barred. "The room was full of men who had advanced infantry training and could have stopped Major Hasan if they had been allowed to carry their weapons into that facility," Olson said. "Every death after the first in that incident was the result of gun control." Fort Hood did not change its weapons policy after Hasan's rampage.

Proposals to control gun violence might have more chance of grudging acceptance by gun owners if supporters of gun laws, and those laws themselves, made it clearer that what they aim to change is not the common-law right of most people to own and use firearms, but the misuse of firearms, especially by the tiny minority of people who under common law can and should be denied that right. Too often, proposals to reduce gun crime are couched in language that seems to treat anybody who wants to own a gun as potentially criminal. That is not the case with the provisions of existing federal law that deny the right to drug users, people committed to mental institutions, those convicted of domestic violence crimes, people who have renounced American citizenship, and felons, for example.

Federal appeals courts have upheld such provisions since the *Heller* and *McDonald* decisions. In one case, a man named James Barton, who had prior convictions for cocaine possession with intent to distribute and for receipt of a stolen firearm, was indicted in Pennsylvania on charges of violating federal law by owning seven pistols, five rifles, three shotguns, and various kinds of ammunition, and tried unsuccessfully to get the indictment dismissed after the *Heller* decision. Then he made a conditional plea of guilty, but appealed the fifty-one-month sentence he received, on the grounds that he had the constitutional right, affirmed by *Heller,* to "use arms in defense of hearth and home." A panel of three judges for the Third Circuit Court of Appeals found against him in March 2011 and let his sentence stand. "*Heller* requires that we 'presume,' under most circumstances, that felon dispossession statutes regulate conduct which is unprotected by the Second Amendment," they ruled.[4]

Some years ago, Olson founded a group called the Gun Owners Civil Rights Alliance, which he was running with David Feinwachs and David M. Gross when I talked with them in 2010. Feinwachs told me, "Most people agree that a convicted felon may not own a firearm." It is restrictions that seem to have the aim of making gun ownership as burdensome as possible for people who don't have criminal records or mental-health problems, he said, that they object to—"the same strategy as with tobacco."

I met Olson and his colleagues through Robert R. Buck, a mutual friend I had come to know years earlier. Buck's views about judges and elected or appointed government officials who give less than totally unqualified support to constitutional rights, to bear arms or anything else, are totally uncompromising—he believes in the Second Amendment and the rest of the Bill of Rights almost as strongly as he believes in the Bible, he says, and he has invented and applied for a patent for a reticle aiming device for precision long-range shooting. He's a serious gun expert, and he took me with him to hook up with Olson at a gun show at the Minnesota State Fair Coliseum in St. Paul.

Before we went in, Olson was carrying a pistol, as he said he usually does; he declared and surrendered it for safekeeping at the entrance, as all carrying gun owners were required to do before going in. The coliseum was packed with mostly white, middle-aged men, though there were a few women, a few African Americans, and even a young family with a small child in a stroller wandering through the displays of pistols, hunting rifles, and curiosities such as a lethal-looking ArmaLite AR-50A1 .50-caliber rifle. "I've taken it out and shot it at a range," Olson told me. "It's like owning a Porsche that will go 275 kilometers an hour that you can't drive on any highway." Feinwachs was there to buy a pistol from one of the licensed dealers at the show, finding one for $650. Another buyer had no objection to letting me watch him buy a Glock from another dealer—showing a permit from his police chief to buy, filling out the required Federal Bureau of Alcohol, Tobacco and Firearms Form 4473 for the dealer to call in to the NICS instant background check, certifying that he was buying the gun for himself, was not a convicted felon or illegal drug user, had not been adjudged mentally defective or otherwise disqualified as a purchaser, and then, after the ATF gave the dealer the go-ahead to sell to him, swiping his credit card for $539.95. "I could sell him a pistol here at the show without asking for a permit, but if he gets in trouble in the next year I'm on the hook," the dealer said—"that's only here in Minnesota."

Olson, a "short, balding tax attorney," as he once unflatteringly described himself, grew up without guns in an air force family in Europe and later in Texas. He says he has been able to understand why people come to think they need guns for personal protection ever since he first felt that need himself, in the civil rights struggle of the summer of 1967, when he was working as a community organizer in rural North Carolina before starting law school at Duke University.

"I discovered that there were people in bedsheets that wanted to kill me," he told the *St. Paul Pioneer Press* in 2003. "There you are driving your car with Missouri license plates down lonely country roads in rural North Carolina.... And remember, [Michael] Schwerner and [Andrew] Goodman and [James] Chaney were killed in Mississippi just three years before. All of us knew their names and what had happened to them." As he recalled in an interview with me seven years later, "One day a pickup comes up and bangs the rear bumper of my Buick Skylark. It just kept at me, but eventually I got away, and when I went to work I told the story, and one of the guys said I needed a gun. They got me a Colt .38, and I dropped it in my coat pocket." Later, he replaced it with one of his own. The closest he ever came to actually using it was when the same thing happened again, twice, with a truck pulling up within a few feet of his back bumper and turning on the high-beam headlights. "All I had to do was take it out and wave it, pointing up, in front of my rearview mirror," he said. "The lights would turn off and the pickup would drop back right away, and then take off." But, he told the *Pioneer Press*, it was not until 1981, when the federal court challenge to the effective gun ban in Morton Grove, Illinois, was in the news, that he really became a convert to the gun-rights cause—again, in his car, listening to the radio on the way from Wayzata to Minneapolis. "I thought to myself, 'That's unconstitutional. I'm an American. I'm entitled to own and possess firearms,'" Olson said. He dates that as the beginning of a new phase of his legal career, as a defender of and lobbyist for that right.

Olson is no friend of gun-control laws. He was an author of amicus briefs urging the Supreme Court to declare handgun bans unconstitutional in both the *Heller* and *McDonald* cases. He views gun controls as restrictions imposed on people who obey the law because of the actions of thugs who violate it. "As long as they insist on restricting me because of what thugs are doing, I am not going to put up with that," he says.

Olson was instrumental in negotiating passage of a must-issue concealed-carry law in Minnesota in 2003 to allow gun owners to carry concealed guns for self-defense, as he does. Forty states have either no restrictions or have passed laws like Minnesota's that deny law-enforcement officials the kind of discretion they have in such states as New York and California to decide who really "needs" a permit to carry a concealed weapon, but even there, some people can. Only Illinois and the District of Columbia flatly do not allow concealed carrying.

The way the Minnesota law came to be, and how its provisions were negotiated, gives some insight into how to find out what kind of regulation both gun owners and supporters of gun control can find acceptable. Called the Minnesota Citizens' Personal Protection Act, it obligates law-enforcement authorities to issue a carry permit to any adult applicant legally permitted to own a handgun who meets the requirements, or to refuse to issue one if there is "real evidence" that granting it would be "dangerous." No applicant can get a carry permit without training in how to fire a pistol and use it safely. More than 75,000 people now have permits in Minnesota, where there are 5 million people, and perhaps as many guns. (Florida, which has had a must-issue carry law since 1987, has granted almost 770,000 permits.)

In a monograph about the legislative history of the Minnesota law, Olson wrote that the initial impetus came from two women— a lawyer and an executive—who testified at a hearing in 1996 against a bill to amend Minnesota laws to make unlicensed carrying of a pistol a felony. They argued that they needed permits to carry handguns for personal protection but had not been able to convince the police that they did. One police chief "would only issue permits to security guards protecting large amounts of money," Olson wrote, and the other "didn't think she needed it 'enough.'" At the hearing, a former commissioner of public safety acknowledged that there were problems with the way the police exercised their discretion.[5]

The Minnesota law frames the issue in a way the United States Supreme Court did not catch up with until *Heller* in 2008: "The legislature of the state of Minnesota recognizes and declares that the Second Amendment of the United States Constitution guarantees the fundamental, individual right to keep and bear arms," it says. The legislation was delivered by the Republican-controlled House to the Senate as an amendment to an unrelated Department of Natural Resources bill in 2003, and bypassing standard procedure was part of its sponsors' strategy to get it through the Senate, Olson told Minnesota Public Radio; Governor Tim Pawlenty then signed it into law. "I've been sort of struck by the screaming and whining from the other side," Olson said at the time; "I mean, playing by the rules is playing by the rules." Nevertheless, state courts later struck down the law on the grounds that the Minnesota constitution required it to stand on its own, not as part of unrelated legislation, and it had to be reenacted. It was, with no trouble and a few mostly minor changes, in 2005.

Olson is a feisty and combative but also professorially engaging man—wiry and wily, with a hint of the sardonic in his smile. He has also been president of the American Association of Certified Firearms Instructors, which his biography describes as "an organization dedicated to training civilians not only on the law and technicalities of carrying a handgun for personal protection, but on strategies and tactics for avoiding any necessity of the use of a handgun for personal protection." His understanding of the need to balance gun rights with public safety is that of a gun-rights advocate, and it is reflected in the text of the Minnesota handgun law he helped draft. It acknowledges that the state has a "compelling interest" in regulating those rights to ensure public safety but asserts that courts interpreting the regulations must follow the rules of strict scrutiny, which demand that regulations be narrowly, not broadly, drawn.

The main objection he and many other gun owners had to the Minnesota law that was in force when debate about replacing it began in the mid-1990s was its arbitrariness. Although it provided that carry permits could be issued to applicants at least eighteen years old who had no record of criminal, mental health, or addiction problems and had passed a test or otherwise shown they knew how to use a pistol safely, it also required applicants to demonstrate a special need or a "personal safety hazard." What that might be was left to the judgment of the police chief or other official who decided on the application, and as Olson wrote, "there was no requirement that a permit actually be issued" to a person who did meet the criteria.[6] Police chiefs gave permits and denied them based on their gut feelings and personal inclinations, a state of affairs that supporters of a new law believed amounted to "trivialization" of their right to personal safety.

Supporters believed, as many gun owners in America do, that a nondiscretionary carry-permit system would have some of the same effects on violent crime as hiring more police and prosecutors would, and would cost less besides. If criminals aren't sure whether their intended victims might be armed, the theory goes, they will be less likely to try to attack them. Its backers say the theory is supported by statistics that show that crime rates fall in states with nondiscretionary, must-issue systems, now forty in all. But statistics are suspect when it comes to showing cause and effect; crime rates have been falling generally all over the United States, for many and varied reasons.[7]

After the initial hearings in 1996, backers of a nondiscretionary Minnesota carry law and police chiefs and sheriffs who opposed it squared off for several years, but Dennis Delmont, the head of the

Minnesota Police Chiefs Association, made clear its view of the main obstacle to the proposals the proponents had made: it did not give the chiefs authority to deny permits to applicants they considered untrustworthy—people involved with criminal gangs, people who drank heavily, people who were mentally unstable. Police authorities boycotted all negotiations and legislative hearings in 2001; still, the bill was reworked into a form that passed the House but fell two votes short of a majority in the Senate.

In the summer of 2001, the Minnesota Sheriffs Association—the eighty-seven county sheriffs are elected officials—left the boycott and started talking with supporters of a bill. The sheriffs' legislative affairs committee issued a statement accepting the principle of a nondiscretionary, must-issue permit system, but they wanted to en-sure that authorities could turn down an application if they could show clear and convincing evidence that granting it would create a threat to public safety. The sponsors of the bill soon recognized that they could have their must-issue carry law if they agreed to this con-dition, and they were ready to do that, but only if elected sheriffs, not appointed police chiefs, would have the authority to issue or deny permits. "The issue became how to define the few persons who might be objectively qualified but whom the sheriff was unwilling to trust carrying a pistol in public," Olson wrote. Ensuing negotia-tions cleared the way for passage of the law in early 2003.[8]

What these agitators for broader gun-rights activists and these of-ficers enforcing regulations for public safety were finally able to agree on was a law that required county sheriffs to issue state carry permits to all US citizens or permanent residents who qualified. It actually *raised* the minimum age for a permit, from eighteen to twenty-one. Applicants had to show proof of "training in the safe use of a pistol" by a certified instructor within a year of submitting the application, including "successful completion of an actual shooting qualification exercise" and "instruction in the fundamental legal aspects of pistol possession, carry, and use, including self-defense and the restrictions on the use of deadly force," about eight hours of instruction in all. The statute as originally enacted spelled out the professional or law-enforcement organizations that can certify instructors, and the NRA was one of them. But in 2005, the amended law specified "an orga-nization or government entity that has been approved by the De-partment of Public Safety in accordance with the department's standards"; the American Association of Certified Firearms Instruc-tors, including Joe Olson, is among them.

The law also disqualifies applicants listed in the Minnesota crim-inal gang investigative data system as possible gang members. Sher-iffs may also deny permits to a person if they believe it is substantially likely or highly probable that the person would pose a danger to him- or herself, or to others carrying a pistol in a public place. A sheriff can show this "substantial likelihood" with "clear and convincing ev-idence," but it cannot include "incidents of alleged criminal miscon-duct that are not investigated and documented."

"The concession by proponents allowing inclusion of a straight 'dangerousness' ground for denial of a permit was the most impor-tant act in eliminating active opposition by official representatives of the sheriffs and police chiefs," Olson explained. "As long as the sheriff has real evidence, the sheriff can deny anyone a carry permit regardless of lack of a conviction, lack of a judicial commitment, lack of a hospitalization, etc. The testimony of a spouse or neighbor can be sufficient."[9] Sheriffs have thirty days to issue or deny permits, and denials, which must be detailed and in writing, can be appealed to district courts, where the burden of proof rests on the sheriffs.

Olson likes to say that the law was written to address behavior and character, not geography, though the law provides that people can prohibit firearms from being brought into their private residences and that operators of offices, restaurants, and bars can post conspicuous signs at every entrance identifying themselves as banning guns in their establishments—"conspicuous" being at least eleven by seventeen inches with bold black Arial typeface lettering 1.5 inches high. "This allows the carry permit holder to act 'Minnesota nice' and politely take their business elsewhere, secure the firearm in their vehicle, or request the owner's permission to enter with their firearm," Olson wrote; anyone carrying a firearm into such an establishment and then refusing to leave after being personally asked to do so is guilty of a petty misdemeanor offense. The sign has to be "within four feet 'laterally of the entrance' and at eye level," in Olson's words. "It cannot be hidden behind a potted palm nor posted on the door. The proponents knew that doors are often propped open (so the sign would be edgewise and not easily visible) and that vision is often blocked by persons entering or exiting through the door."[10]

So the "proponents" were wary and protective of their rights in negotiating the terms of the law but also took into account the rights of Minnesotans who do not carry or want guns around them. The underlying assumption of the law is clearly and consistently about individual responsibility, and about the presumption of good behavior. A gun-control law that bars people from carrying weapons into places where alcohol is served is based on a different assumption—that human beings don't always do what's right. Pistol-packing patrons might take a drink even though they know they shouldn't, and after that, well, guns and alcohol don't mix. The Minnesota law assumes what gun-rights advocates wanted it to assume—that people punctilious enough to get carry permits know that guns and alcohol don't mix, and therefore won't imbibe. It assumes a certain amount of maturity, with the minimum age for a permit being twenty-one. So the law allows people legally carrying pistols to take them into bars and other places that serve alcohol, unless they have signs saying weapons are banned on the premises. But if permit holders do take even a single drink or otherwise put themselves under the influence of alcohol or drugs while carrying a weapon, they can be arrested and their permits can be suspended or revoked, whether they're civilians or law-enforcement officers. Guns or replicas that look like guns are off-limits in schools, except in carefully restricted cases (marksmanship courses, and so on). Public and private universities and colleges can make their own rules, but no criminal sanctions apply to violators.

How well does it work in practice? In 2009, 22,378 applications were filed, and 374 were denied; twenty permits were revoked or rejected. There were three instances of "lawful and justifiable use of firearms by permit holders." As for unlawful or unjustifiable use of firearms by permit holders since 2003, as of 2009 forty of these Minnesotans had been convicted of carrying a pistol while under the influence; thirty-four had been convicted of assault (but only six used a pistol to do it); two were convicted of murder or manslaughter, but only one of the two cases involved use of a pistol. There were twenty-two convictions of people licensed to carry for "terroristic threats," three involving a pistol; and so on—but of 598 various crimes in all, only fifty-five were known to have involved use of a pistol.[11]

All in all, the violations rate seems statistically insignificant in Minnesota, unlike Texas, where studies have shown that thousands of concealed-carry license holders have been arrested for violent crimes or found to be mentally unstable. Minnesota is not Texas, and it is not the District of Columbia—its rate of violent crimes in 2007 was 289 per 100,000 of population, compared to 1,414 in DC (414 in New York, 730 in Louisiana, 661 in Alaska, and 118 in Maine), according to Census Bureau and FBI figures in the Statistical Abstract of the United States. Figures compiled by the Disaster Center from official reports show that rates of all violent crimes, and, separately, murder, were lower in Minnesota in 2009 than they had been in 2003, when the carry law went into effect, despite a spike in 2006.

The fact that there is less crime now in Minnesota than there was before the law was enacted proves, for people like Joe Olson, that the law itself is an important reason for the decline. I'm not convinced. About all the figures really prove, to me, is that allowing 70,000 people to carry concealed firearms did not result in an increase in violent crime in Minnesota. Without a scientifically accurate study of data, it is not possible to say precisely what effects concealed-carry laws actually have on crime rates. Some studies have been done on other states that have concealed-carry laws, but none with conclusive results on that question.[12]

Olson counters that no gun-control regulation has ever been shown to reduce the crime rate. At the time we talked, Olson and his gun-owners' group were concentrating their fire on a bill proposed in the state legislature by Representative Michael Paymar, a St. Paul Democrat, to close the gun-show loophole. Most outrageous to them was a provision that would make it a misdemeanor punishable by a $3,000 fine and up to a year in jail to find a buyer at a gun show after the loophole was closed, and then complete the sale later somewhere else to avoid the need to go through the background check. All that and the rest of the bill would do, they said in one of many denunciatory press releases, was "impose unnecessary deprivation of liberty, hassle, delay and cost on Minnesota's 1.5 million legitimate gun owners," as straw-man buyers at gun shows accounted for only a small percentage of weapons acquired by gangs and criminals.

Paymar's bill died in committee.

"It makes no sense to have regulations that have no positive effect, and it's immoral for a society to remove from me my ability to protect myself when it cannot protect me," Olson said. "Our whole system is messed up because it's focused on things, when the problem is people."

Indisputably, whatever the facts may be, concealed carry has been carrying the day in Washington. In mid-November of 2011, the US House of Representatives voted, 272 to 154, to approve a bill that would require all forty-nine states that permit concealed carry to recognize permits granted by other states. If it became law, visitors from any of the forty-nine could bring their guns with them almost anywhere except Illinois and the District of Columbia, as long as they had their permits handy, provided that local laws and regulations allowed concealed carrying. A bill to do the same was introduced in the Senate a few months later.

If it became law, it would still not allow anyone to carry a concealed weapon through an airport security checkpoint onto an airplane. Nor would it mean that New York City, with its strict gun-control laws, would have to allow out-of-state visitors to stroll through Times Square packing pistols, though they would be free to carry guns in many other parts of New York state where concealed carrying is permitted.

But imagine, for a minute, that New York City had to recognize out-of-state concealed-carry permits. Would that really make violent crime worse there? Ask yourself how many criminals who come gun-toting to Gotham with mayhem on their minds are likely to have taken the trouble to get concealed-carry permits first, and you may have the answer.

More problematic is the risk of abuse of stand-your-ground legislation like the law in Florida that came under fire after Trayvon Martin was shot to death there in February 2012. Shortly after that, Minnesota's governor, Mark Dayton, a Democrat, vetoed a shoot-first measure that had been passed by the state legislature, citing opposition to it by police and sheriffs' groups and objecting to a provision that would require Minnesota to recognize carry permits issued by states under looser requirements than the law Olson helped draft. Still, Olson said, according to the *Minneapolis Star Tribune:* "In each state, the police organizations ran around in circles screaming and shouting the sky is falling. It hasn't fallen in any state. It wouldn't have fallen in Minnesota." Its supporters in the Republican-controlled legislature said the legislation would be back.[13]

I don't doubt it, with sophisticated and skilled advocates such as Joe Olson. But at least he's willing to try to convince people on the other side with calm and reasoned argument instead of fear-mongering. That is hardly the case with the NRA.

CHAPTER EIGHT

WHAT CAN
BE DONE

*Like most rights, the right secured by the Second Amendment
is not unlimited.*

JUSTICE ANTONIN SCALIA, MAJORITY OPINION,
DISTRICT OF COLUMBIA V. HELLER, 2008

"For too long, most members of the legal academy have treated the Second Amendment as the equivalent of an embarrassing relative, whose mention brings a quick change of subject to other, more respectable, family members," Professor Sanford Levinson wrote in his 1989 *Yale Law Journal* article arguing that one purpose of the Second Amendment was to protect the right of individuals to defend themselves against attack.

That will no longer do. It is time for the Second Amendment to enter full scale into the consciousness of the legal academy.... Perhaps "we" might be led to stop referring casually to "gun nuts" just as, maybe, members of the NRA could be brought to understand the real fear that the currently almost uncontrolled system of gun ownership sparks in the minds of many whom they casually dismiss as "bleeding-heart liberals." Is not, after all, the possibility of serious, engaged discussion about political issues at the heart of what is most attractive in both liberal and republican versions of politics?[1]

More than two decades later, the "embarrassing relative" has been fully rehabilitated by the Supreme Court, yet the NRA still acts and sounds as if the Court might any day change its mind about *Heller* and *McDonald*; as if the federal government might any day surreptitiously mobilize to launch a wholesale seizure of private firearms: as if, in sum, the NRA didn't realize that it hadn't *lost* the cultural war about gun rights; it had *won*. The "engaged discussion" about "real fear," entirely justified by so many needless deaths day after day, year after year, that Professor Levinson called for in 1989 has yet to begin. President Obama tried to start one in the spring of 2011, calling on gun-control advocates and the gun lobby to join "a new discussion on how we can keep America safe for all our people," but the NRA saw only a public relations ploy or a trap: "Why should I or the NRA go sit down with a group of people that have spent a lifetime trying to destroy the Second Amendment in the United States?" Wayne LaPierre responded.[2] In the writing of this book, I had no better luck than the president did; I asked LaPierre for a discussion about some of the ideas in this chapter, but I could not even get him to respond. Stephen L. Sanetti, the president and chief executive officer of the firearms industry's trade association, the National Shooting Sports Foundation, Inc. (NSSF), was, in contrast, willing to talk with me, openly and frankly, though I am not suggesting he agrees with my proposals.

It is long past time for a cease-fire in the cultural gun wars. Perhaps, after the 2012 elections, there will be a chance for a fresh start in thinking about how to control gun violence. Republicans could be successful with a constructive new approach if they were so inclined. Once electoral passions are cooled, Democrats could try again, more seriously this time. Regardless, the national discussion about guns will get nowhere without constructive participation by the NRA, which would be a true service to the national interest and civic health of the country and to the constitutional right the NRA professes to defend so vigorously. I can still remember the days when the NRA was mostly known for education and training, particularly of young people—and I have a marksmanship certificate that was awarded to my son from an NRA qualification course at his summer camp in Maine in 1987. Theodore Roosevelt IV says he wishes the group would change its focus from self-defense and remember the interests of the many Americans who use guns for hunting or shooting sports. "It should help Americans to recognize and revitalize the value of public lands—help people understand that hunting is a valuable activity," he said. The NRA was founded in 1871, as Adam Winkler points out, by two Civil War veterans—William C. Church, a former reporter for the *New York Times,* and George W. Wingate, who had been appalled by the lack of marksmanship skills they had observed in their fellow soldiers then and wanted to create an organization to "promote and encourage rifle shooting on a scientific basis," to train Americans in a skill they would need when the country went to war again.[3]

The NRA still does training, to be sure, but on the whole, I agree with Saul Cornell, a leading constitutional law scholar who is an expert on the Second Amendment, that its focus is more selfish than patriotic: "Gun rights ideology has fostered an anticivic vision, not a vision of civic-mindedness," he wrote in his book *A Well-Regulated Militia* in 2006. "In this ideology guns are primarily viewed as a means of repulsing government or other citizens, not a means for creating a common civic culture." But he also faulted those on the other side for short-sightedness: "Modern gun control ideology has also failed to create a positive constitutional vision in which the Second Amendment is more than a vestigial part of our legal culture. . . ."[4]

Effective gun regulation, regulation that has a chance of actually reducing gun violence and crime, has to begin with positive recognition by all Americans who want to achieve it that the right to keep and bear arms is an individual right, and that law-abiding individuals should be able to exercise that right without being made to feel as if they were criminals. But those who value the right must also recognize that it is not absolute, and that it comes, as all rights do, with responsibilities. In the beginning, two centuries ago, it was connected with a civic duty: militia service in the defense of community and freedom. Today, gun owners should be encouraged to recognize their civic duty to do what they can to make the free use of firearms safer than it is today—not just for themselves but for all of us.

Stephen Sanetti, of the industry trade association, as a trained lawyer, thought I was confusing civic duty with individual responsibility. "If you're a gun owner, of course you have a constant responsibility to handle firearms safely and use them wisely," he told me.[5]

In the light of the *Heller* and *McDonald* Supreme Court decisions, NRA warnings that all proposals to make gun use safer are simply stealth threats to individual liberty, and that only total mobilization against them can save the right to keep and bear arms, make no sense, effective though they may be in fund-raising. The Supreme Court has pronounced the right to keep and bear arms a protected individual right, an indisputable conclusion, even if the reasoning that brought the Court to that view is disputable, as this book has tried to show. Gun-control advocates have to recognize the reality that Americans have had an individual common-law right to own guns since Jamestown and Plymouth Rock. This book makes clear, I hope, that there is no way any combination of Supreme Court justices is going to be able to reverse that reality.

But gun-rights advocates also have to recognize that the Second Amendment does not make gun owners a law unto themselves. The NRA would have them believe that they are. It's not enough for the organization to encourage people to own guns—it has succeeded in getting state legislatures in two dozen states to pass stand-your-ground laws like the one in Florida that initially discouraged the police from arresting George Zimmerman, the neighborhood watch volunteer who killed seventeen-year-old Trayvon Martin, because Zimmerman told them the boy had attacked him and he had shot in self-defense. Stand-your-ground and castle-doctrine laws make it explicitly defensible for gun owners to shoot first in confrontations with attackers, rather than as a last resort. A person in one of these states who "reasonably believes" himself or herself to be in danger of death or great bodily harm can pull the trigger without worrying unduly about having to prove that to a jury in a murder trial, or about being sued afterward by relatives of the deceased. Castle-doctrine laws give the same latitude to people in their homes to shoot intruders intent on violence or robbery.

But how often, before these laws started sprouting in so many states, have people who had to shoot attackers in self-defense actually been convicted of murder or manslaughter? Americans have always had the right to defend themselves, and the duty to retreat from confrontation only applies if retreat can be done in safety. Are stand-your-ground laws really necessary to ensure that you have that right? Is it really a good idea to make it easier to justify killing people? Even supporters of laws like these have to concede that they can be abused, for example, by a person who commits murder and then claims self-defense, as the special prosecutor in Florida finally accused George Zimmerman of doing. Under its stand-your-ground law, as Adam Winkler has pointed out, defendants like Zimmerman have the right to a pre-trial hearing to challenge their indictment. At a pre-trial hearing, a judge could rely on a "preponderance of the evidence" and rule that an accused murderer had acted in self-defense and drop the murder charge. But if the case went to trial, the jury would have to be convinced "beyond a reasonable doubt," a much stronger standard. Zimmerman's defense will now have to meet that standard if he goes to trial on charges of second-degree murder.[6] Florida's stand-your-ground law, the prosecutor had argued, in effect puts the police in the position of having to prove that a killer did not act in self-defense before they can make an arrest.

In Alaska, where debate on a stand-your-ground law was under way when the Florida case broke, James Fayette, an assistant district attorney in Anchorage, told the *Anchorage Daily News,* "I talk to families of homicide victims all the time. Please don't make me explain to them that the one thing the Alaska Legislature accomplished in 2012 was the ability to make it easier to kill people."[7] Why should anybody have an interest in making it easier for criminals to get off scot-free with laws that weren't intended to benefit them but that make it easier for them to use self-defense to beat a murder rap? State legislators should stop and think again about the effect of stand-your-ground and castle-doctrine laws. Florida set a good example with the task force it set up after the Trayvon Martin case. But other states with stand-your-ground laws should do the same.

Nothing in the Constitution says that the right to bear arms is an absolute right, and nothing in the Second Amendment prevents reasonable regulation of the right. Some regulations are clearly unreasonable: outlawing handguns, or making them almost impossible for anyone to acquire, is not reasonable regulation. However, devising and enforcing better ways of ensuring that people whose age or behavior everybody agrees should make them ineligible to buy handguns—minors, criminals, those with mental disorders, drug addicts, people subject to restraining orders—is an entirely reasonable aim. Regulations to make firearms themselves safer to keep and use should be acceptable and even welcome, if drafted in the right spirit.

Below are some suggestions for measures that could help make us all safer, offered with no illusions about how easily or quickly any of them will ever become reality, so long as the cultural wars are raging and deficits are considered to be public enemy number one. Mayors Against Illegal Guns has offered some proposals that go beyond these, eliciting hostile reactions from gun-rights supporters. Legal Community Against Violence, a national public-interest law center in San Francisco that was founded after a gun massacre in law offices at 101 California Street there in 1993, has exhaustively studied federal, state, and some city gun laws in all fifty states and the District of Columbia and made comprehensive recommendations for changes in its study, "Regulating Guns in America," published in 2006 and updated in 2008.[8] *Private Guns, Public Health*, the groundbreaking study by David Hemenway published by the University of Michigan Press in Ann Arbor in 2004 and updated since, has made numerous recommendations for gun laws that in Hemenway's judgment would be "acceptable to the large majority of Americans," though many of them would not be acceptable to the NRA or to the legislators who pay attention to what the NRA says, and they are legion.

Some of the ideas below may have the same problem, but some, I hope, will not. Authorization by legislation, after exhaustive public debate and consideration, is preferable to executive or agency fiat or decree in every case. "Are you for or against the Second Amendment?" is a question I am frequently asked. I am for it, as I am for the First or the Fifth Amendments, but it's a meaningless question. Constructive consideration of the following suggestions might move the stalemated debate about guns in America in a more constructive and meaningful direction.

Fill in holes in the national instant background check database by requiring states to report in timely fashion the names of people found to be drug abusers, psychiatrically disturbed, or otherwise disqualified as gun purchasers under federal law.

This alone might have prevented the Virginia Tech and Tucson gun rampages, as discussed in Chapter 6. The burden of entering into the NICS database the names of people who have been adjudicated as mentally defective or have committed serious criminal acts or otherwise been disqualified from buying firearms from federally licensed firearms dealers falls mainly on the states, which have been under tremendous financial pressure since the Great Recession began in 2008. Federal law does not now prohibit people who are voluntarily committed to a mental hospital from owning firearms, but some state laws do. The FBI told Mayors Against Illegal Guns in 2008 that there were 5,411,470 names of "prohibited persons" in the federal database, 584,985 of them for reasons connected with mental illness. The fifty states and the District of Columbia provided 469,000 of those names and federal agencies provided the rest, but because states are not required to specify reasons for putting people on the forbidden list, and some states keep mental health records from law-enforcement agencies to protect individual privacy, the number of people who *should* be on the forbidden list because of mental-health issues is certainly much higher than the number who are actually on it. Most of the mental-health names that were provided came from only a few states—California alone accounted for 216,853, followed by Virginia with nearly 100,000, Michigan with more than 78,000, and all but a few of the rest from Missouri, Florida, Ohio, and Connecticut. As of 2008, New York had reported a grand total of five people who should not be allowed to buy firearms because of mental illness, and New Jersey had reported none.[9]

State budgets for treating mental illness (like budgets for everything else, including law enforcement) are under strain because of the current political fixation on reducing government spending to cut deficits. More effective treatment of people with mental disorders would arguably do more to prevent horrors like Virginia Tech than any number of gun-control measures, but that doesn't seem to be in the cards.

A more important obstacle is the obvious conflict between the public interest in being safe from violence committed by mentally disturbed individuals and those individuals' right to privacy. In the course of a lifetime, we all know friends or relatives who suffer from delusions or psychotic episodes that could be deadly if these people ever had a weapon in their hands, but if they haven't been adjudicated as mentally ill or been involuntarily committed to an institution, should their names be entered on a government-run database that deprives them of their right to own a gun? Should being entered on the list once mean being listed forever?

That last question shaped the last important compromise federal gun legislation, the NICS Improvement Amendments Act of 2007, passed after the Virginia Tech massacre and signed into law by President Bush at the start of 2008. Representative Carolyn McCarthy of New York, a Democratic legislator whose husband was killed and whose son was badly wounded by a deranged shooter on a commuter train in Long Island in 1993, co-sponsored the legislation with Senators Charles E. Schumer of New York and Edward M. Kennedy of Massachusetts. The law provides for financial assistance to states to provide the records of people adjudicated as mentally ill to the NICS database, and financial penalties if they fail to do so. The NRA had long supported closing what Wayne LaPierre himself in 1999 called "the Hinckley loophole" because the mental illness treatment records of John Hinckley, the man who shot President Reagan, had been inaccessible to the NICS system.[10] But the NRA insisted on a provision that allows people denied gun ownership because of mental disability to petition for removal of their names from the NICS list—"relief from disabilities"—if they no longer suffer from the condition that originally barred them. How to decide whether petitioners have overcome their disabilities was left up to the states.

And there's the rub, as Michael Luo reported in the *New York Times* in 2011: "States have mostly entrusted these decisions to judges, who are often ill-equipped to conduct investigations from the bench. Many seemed willing to simply give petitioners the benefit of the doubt. The results often seem haphazard." That is, when there were any results at all. Of twenty-two states that applied for financial assistance for complying with the mental-illness reporting system in 2009 and 2010, only nine had gotten any, the *Times* found, and most of the rest had been denied it because they did not have certified programs in place for the "relief" procedure. Virginia passed a new law allowing judges to restore firearms rights to petitioners they deemed "not likely" to "act in a manner dangerous to public safety" if "the granting of the relief would not be contrary to the public interest," providing no guidance on how to make such determinations. Judges found twenty-five people out of forty they considered in 2010 qualified for relief, including fourteen who had been involuntarily committed to mental-health treatment. One case in Amherst General District Court in early 2009 took only eight minutes to restore to David Neal Moon gun rights he had lost after his involuntary commitment in 1995 because of schizoaffective bipolar disorder. A month after he got his guns back, his ex-wife obtained a protective order against him because he had been making "veiled threats by phone and telling his children about demons in the walls," the *Times* reported.[11]

Convicted felons and those indicted for felonies, people under domestic violence restraining orders or convicted of domestic violence crimes, fugitives from justice, illegal aliens, users of illegal drugs, people who have been dishonorably discharged from the armed forces, and those who have renounced American citizenship are also all supposed to be included in the NICS database, but states all too often do not report their names, or report them only after long delays.

And, as Luo also reported in the *Times*, some states—notably, Minnesota, Ohio, Virginia, and Washington—allow felons, even those convicted of violent crimes, to apply for restoration of their gun rights after they have served their sentences. Charles Hairston served eighteen years for killing a man with a shotgun in North Carolina, and after moving to Ohio, eventually had his right to own a firearm restored after he told a judge there, "I am in a situation now where if, God forbid, if someone was to come into my home and attack me, my wife, there isn't a lot I could say about it, there isn't a lot I could do." Eventually, four decades after the original fatal shooting, he was able to go out and buy himself a 9-mm handgun again. Washington, Luo reported, bars people convicted of Class A felonies, the most violent crimes, from applying for restoration of their gun rights. But Luo's analysis of the cases of more than four hundred ex-felons there who succeeded in getting their right back and later committed crimes found more than seventy who went on to commit Class A or B felonies. State laws like these were passed with the urging of gun-rights lobbies that have been unable to get Congress to enact similar federal legislation. The NRA and other gun-rights groups have always supported get-tough laws for criminals using guns, and rehabilitation is a desirable goal, but Luo's reporting showed that closer study might have led state laws to have, at the very least, long waiting periods before restoration of gun rights for criminals, as a hedge against recidivism. As things are, judges often make the decision with little real information to go on.[12]

On the other side of the scales, Senator Schumer and eleven members of Congress, supported by Mayors Against Illegal Guns, introduced a "Fix Gun Checks" bill in early 2011. The proposal would cut federal grants to states for improvements in their handling of violent crimes by up to 25 percent unless they supplied 90 percent of the records they had on individuals who should not be allowed for any reason to buy arms. Federal agencies and the military would be required to certify their own compliance to the Justice Department, twice a year. "This legislation does nothing to impinge upon gun owners' rights, but it does provide greater incentive for reporting individuals who should not have access to guns to a national do-not-sell list, helping better protect innocent Americans from senseless gun violence," Schumer said.

The NICS database also has built-in holes that the states themselves should take initiatives to remedy. Misdemeanor convictions (except for domestic violence) do not disqualify would-be gun purchasers under federal law, though as of 2008, twenty-three states and the District of Columbia have their own laws that do disqualify people with misdemeanor records.[13] Still, state and federal laws now leave people free to buy guns if they wish, even if convicted of, among other things, publicly displaying a firearm in a threatening manner; possession of equipment for illegal drug use; assault and battery not involving a lethal weapon or serious injury; drunk and disorderly conduct; or carrying concealed firearms without a permit where a permit is required.[14]

Should names on various terrorist watch lists, no-fly lists, and so on be entered into the NICS database? Just after Faisal Shahzad, an immigrant from Pakistan who was a naturalized US citizen, almost succeeded in blowing up Times Square with a terrorist truck bomb in May 2010, he was found and pulled off a plane to the Middle East at John F. Kennedy Airport. Shahzad had earlier been on a no-fly list, but he had no trouble two months before his arrest buying a Kel-Tec Sub-2000 rifle for $400 from Valley Firearms in Shelton, Connecticut, passing the NICS check and even a state-imposed waiting period. New York City police commissioner Kelly and Mayor Bloomberg cited Shahzad as an example of why Congress should "make it harder for terrorists to buy guns." That seems like a no-brainer at first, but it's harder than it seems. Almost all of the names on the government's terrorist watch lists are foreigners living in deserts or mountain wilderness caves and warrens nowhere near the United States, but some Americans have found their names on no-fly lists for no good reason other than confusion or rumor, placed there without formal judicial review. Thus, "making it harder for terrorists to buy guns" by putting the watch list into the NICS database is more problematical than it seems, on due-process and other constitutional grounds that go far beyond the Second Amendment. Look how hard it has been for some of the people who landed on no-fly lists for no justifiable reason, or through confusion, to get their names removed.

But in any case, entering names on a list is just the beginning. Gun owners who were able to buy firearms legally and later commit felonies or otherwise fall into a disqualified category should not be able to keep their weapons, but many do. Roy Perez, for example, in Baldwin Park, California, bought a Glock 9-mm handgun in 2004, but his name was later placed on California's computerized Armed

Prohibited Persons System when he showed signs of dangerous mental instability. The list has 18,000 names on it, and agents of California's state firearms bureau set a date in March 2008 to confiscate Perez's weapon. Two weeks before that date, Perez fired sixteen shots at his mother in their home, killing her, and then went next door and shot and killed a neighbor and her four-year-old daughter. An article in the *New York Times* in early 2011 about the problems California and other states have had in following up on lists of prohibited gun purchasers in this and similar cases reported that many local law-enforcement authorities either did not know about the existence of the Armed Prohibited Persons System, did not know how to access its data, or didn't have enough time or personnel to keep current and follow up on names in their jurisdiction. Dr. Garen J. Wintemute, who helped set up California's program (which had NRA support when it was legally established in 2002), told the newspaper that there could be 180,000 disqualified gun owners like Perez, with guns still in their hands, in the United States as a whole.[15]

Increase state penalties for crimes committed with guns, or prosecute the criminals in federal courts when federal penalties are heavier than they are under state law.

Laws like Virginia's, discussed in Chapter 6, that bring the law down hard on criminals with guns make a lot more sense than measures like the so-called Rockefeller drug laws passed in the 1970s that imposed draconian sentences on anyone convicted of possessing even small quantities of certain drugs. And Virginia's example shows that the entire burden does not automatically have to fall on the federal judicial system. The NRA will have no problem with harsher prosecution of gun-toting criminals.

Close the loophole that exempts private sellers of arms, at gun shows or anywhere else, and online, from the requirement to clear buyers with the NICS database. Ignore NRA protests that this is an inconvenient im-position or intrusion on privacy.

Gun owners are grown-ups; this requirement won't kill them, but the lack of it can kill people by allowing criminals to acquire guns. Right now, in many states, a convicted murderer could buy a hand-gun from a private seller—many advertise online—without any kind of background check. One gun enthusiast told me that he could see some benefit in making it possible for owners who sell guns to pri-vate individuals to voluntarily submit the name of buyers to an NICS check—if only so as to be immune from civil liability if a gun they sold turned out later to have been used in the commission of a crime. In Delaware, Nevada, and Oregon, private sellers have the option of requesting background checks of purchasers (and Oregon requires it if the sale takes place at a gun show).

It's just not that onerous a procedure, so what's wrong with mak-ing it mandatory, not only at gun shows but anywhere? Only Califor-nia, Rhode Island, and the District of Columbia required background checks for purchasers in private sales of all types of firearms as of 2008; Maryland required it for handguns and "assault" weapons, and Pennsylvania and Connecticut did for handgun purchasers.[16]

Some states that require a license or permit to buy firearms re-quire all purchasers to pass background checks first. Background checks of buyers in all firearms sales, not just those by federally li-censed dealers, ought to be mandatory, at least for handguns, in all fifty states. The irritating inconvenience to law-abiding gun owners who just want to sell a gun to a friend is a small price to pay for safety. Millions of Americans put up with airport security screening mea-sures every year, though 30,000 people a year never died as a result of airplane hijackings, even in 2001, the year of the 9/11 atrocity. How unconstitutional can it be to ask gun owners to do the same, to try to save lives? Yet opposition from the NRA and other lobbies to legislation that would do that has been so strong that Senator Schumer of New York has rated the odds of getting it done as "not high."[17] Gun ownership in this country has always had a connection to civic duty. How are gun owners fulfilling civic duty by refusing to do something that could save lives?

Crack down on straw purchasers, and on firearms dealers who knowingly sell to them or to disqualified buyers.

Yeah
definitely

There is no federal firearms trafficking statute. There ought to be a law! Because there is none, a Justice Department inspector general report found in late 2010, "ATF must use a wide variety of other statutes to combat firearms trafficking." Purchasers of guns from federally licensed firearms dealers have to fill out a Firearms Transaction Record, ATF Form 4473, for the background check, and making a false statement on the form is a crime punishable by up to ten years' imprisonment and a $250,000 fine. "However, cases brought under these statutes are difficult to prove and do not carry stringent penalties—particularly for straw purchasers of guns," the report found; "Federal Sentencing Guidelines categorize straw-purchasing related offenses as lesser crimes."[18] Often, straw purchasers who are tracked down are let off the hook in plea bargains by prosecutors who get them to testify against the criminals for whom they bought the guns.

They shouldn't be let off scot-free, and neither should it be considered a lesser crime for a federally licensed firearms dealer to sell knowingly to a straw buyer. The NRA reflexively defends gun dealers, questioning the use of ATF trace data in criminal prosecutions, but it should rethink its position and, instead of trying to systematically thwart the ATF, encourage the government to make ATF operations aimed against criminals more effective. Almost all the handguns traced from crimes and found to have been sold less than three years earlier—the ones most likely to have been trafficked—come originally from a small fraction of dealers, only 7 percent of the total number in the country, as a study done in 2000 for the National Association for the Advancement of Colored People found; ATF tracing data from about the same time showed that 389 dealers—less than 0.5 percent—accounted for more than half of all crime guns traced in 1996–1998.[19] Yes, there are mitigating factors—for one thing, for the ATF, all guns traced from crimes are "crime guns," even if they turn out to have been stolen from owners who bought them perfectly legally from dealers, who in such cases feel unjustly stigmatized. For another thing, a high-volume gun shop in an area or a city with high crime rates is frequently going to turn out to be the original source of a gun used in a crime, no matter how carefully it tries to comply with the law. But high volume does not explain everything. Dealers who turn up on the most-traced lists year after year, as some of them do, should be subject to rigorous supervision, and those taking shortcuts or ignoring the requirements of the law should be prosecuted and shut down for good.

Running a gun shop is serious business, and it can be tricky, as my Minnesota friend Robert R. Buck, who once worked at a gun store in Michigan, recalled: "I more than once had to tell people to please leave the store; I wasn't going to sell them any kind of gun," he said—"somebody with beer on his breath, another person who said he was going to get a sword to cut people up. I once had to pull a gun on a guy who I thought was about to shoot me." Stephen Sanetti, the head of the gun industry trade association, the NSSF, had a similar experience—not in a gun store but in a liquor store in Woodbury, Long Island, where he had grown up and was working summers back in the early 1970s to earn money to help pay for law school in Virginia, before going on active duty in the US Army as a Judge Advocate General's Corps officer. "I was held up by a guy with a doubtless illegally owned revolver," Sanetti told me. He had been fascinated by firearms since he was a boy, going on hunting trips in upstate New York with his father and, prior to the liquor store robbery, had applied for a handgun permit to practice marksmanship because he expected the army to send him to Vietnam. "I couldn't get a permit because I was going to law school in Virginia and New York didn't issue permits to people who live out of state," he said, laughing. "Pretty ironic."

Sanetti made it into the army with no further holdups, and years later went to work as a lawyer for a well-known gun maker in Southport, Connecticut, Sturm, Ruger & Co. This was a way to combine his hobby with his professional legal skills. He became a close associate of William B. Ruger, the president, and after his death, served in that position himself from 2003 to 2008, when he went to the industry's trade association as its president.

"For all the ATF's faults," he told me, "we work closely with them. When I first started with Ruger in 1980, that wasn't the case. It's much more of a give-and-take today." One of the collaborative efforts is a trade association program, supported by both the ATF and a $2.15 million grant from the Justice Department, to educate dealers on how to spot and turn down would-be straw purchasers. A video called *Don't Lie for the Other Guy* (on www.dontlie.org) shows dealers in a number of uncomfortable confrontations with people trying to buy guns for friends or relatives, or for people legally barred from buying them. If two people come into a gun store together and the one who wants to buy the gun lets the other one ask all the questions, or seems to know nothing about guns, it's probably a straw purchase, the narrator says. If someone tries to buy a gun and can't pass the NICS background check, and then someone else with the same name or address comes in later and tries to buy the same gun, dealers are told to politely refuse to make the sale.

Realistically, the video shows that a dealer behaving this way can provoke hostile reactions. In fact, if I were an arms dealer who wasn't armed myself, I wouldn't want to be telling some of these characters they weren't going to walk out of the store with the weapons they came in determined to buy. But the video encourages dealers to stick to their guns, as it were, and says they can and should legally deny any sale to a prospective buyer who makes them feel suspicious.

But how many do that? Mayors Against Illegal Guns has chapter and verse on "easy" dealers in several states with a reputation among traffickers for selling guns no questions asked. One straw in Georgia told investigators that "each time he went in, the same two employees were in the store and treated him like a VIP. They gave him their 'undivided attention' and knew he would be buying multiple guns, the trafficker said. The store gave him a free gun with every four he purchased." Many of these later turned up in New York, according to the report, "Inside Straw Purchasing: How Criminals Get Guns Illegally," published in 2008.

Virginia passed a law in 1993 limiting handgun purchases to one per month, after an ATF report showed that 40 percent of guns found at crime scenes in New York had originally been bought in Virginia. The law had little obvious effect on gun crimes in New York, and at the end of February 2012, it was repealed.

Gun dealers cannot catch every would-be purchaser who lies, of course. The *Washington Post's Hidden Life of Guns* series in the fall of 2010 reported that Robert Marcus, the owner of Bob's Gun Shop in Norfolk, Virginia, which had sold more than 32,000 guns since 1998, said his employees were under instructions to be "vigilant in looking for telltale signs of a straw purchase, such as one person asking all the questions but another person filling out the paperwork." About once a day, Marcus said, the staff turned a would-be buyer away for one reason or another, kept close track of inventory, and had surveillance cameras in operation. Yet his store was "one of the leading sources of crime guns in Virginia," the *Post* said. Marcus gave Norfolk's demographics and his high volume as the most likely explanation.[20]

Unlike Marcus, another dealer in nearby Virginia Beach was repeatedly caught by ATF inspectors selling firearms to straw purchasers, and when warned, "questioned the impact that straw purchases have on crime," the inspectors reported. The dealer, Norman Gladden, later had his license revoked, for recordkeeping violations and selling to straw purchasers. But he is still selling guns. He simply transferred a license he had for a store in another location to the one in Virginia Beach, the *Post* reported.

Dealers who deliberately flout the law or disregard it should be prosecutable. Dealers who strictly observe it, and they are the vast majority, should support strict enforcement. The laws governing businesses that sell firearms have been astonishingly lax. Getting a federal firearms dealer license was as simple as chewing gum in 1968, when the system was first established. Until 1993, all it took to meet the federal requirements was to be over twenty-one and pay a $10 fee, and more than 284,000 people had licenses by 1992. When the Brady Act went into effect in 1994, the fee increased to $200 for three years, and $90 for each following three-year period, and shortly after that, licensees had to submit photographs and fingerprints and certify that they were complying with state and local laws; the number of license holders then dropped, to just under 103,000 in 2001. Numerous state laws also apply, but only Connecticut, Pennsylvania, and the District of Columbia, as of 2008, and New York City and a few other cities have laws holding dealers criminally or civilly responsible for gun crimes committed by purchasers who should have been turned away.[21]

Encourage all fifty states to pass legislation requiring state or local licenses to own a gun, mandate training in the use and storage of firearms, and institute state registration.

State registration of devices that can kill people is already commonplace and generally accepted: take a look at the license plate on your car. But as of 2008, absurdly, seven states actually had laws *prohibiting* registration, a long reach away from the colonial-era laws that *required* it in one form or another. California and Pennsylvania prohibit registration of long guns; Delaware, Florida, Georgia, Idaho, Rhode Island, South Dakota, and Vermont either do not require gun registration or prohibit it generally. Congress has forbidden the use of ATF tracing data in any way, shape, or fashion that could lead to establishment of a national registry. This was at the insistence of the NRA, but the gun lobby's opposition to a national gun registry is not absurd; it is entirely rooted in Second Amendment history. A national registration system like Canada's would be impossible here even if it didn't cost a billion dollars, as the Canadian system did. But the framers of the Constitution and the Bill of Rights would be astounded to learn that so many *states* have banned registration—the original thirteen couldn't have had effective militias if they had no idea who had working firearms. As of 2006, only Hawaii and the District of Columbia required registration for all firearms. A few cities, such as Chicago, Cleveland, New York City, and Omaha, also require licenses for owners or purchasers of firearms, and registration.

Nothing in the Constitution or the Second Amendment requires a ban on state registration and licensing of guns. It ought to be required in all fifty.

A license to own firearms, like a driver's license, should be issued to anyone legally entitled to own a gun (passing the NICS check and whatever other requirements states or municipalities impose), but gun owners, just like drivers, should also be required to demonstrate competency, on a firing range and in an examination on the laws governing firearms. Ideally, the competency requirements should be no more onerous than they are for driving licenses. In all cases, the standards to be met should be reasonable ones by the standards of the issuing jurisdiction, not obstacle courses that enable the authorities to deny as many licenses as possible or to grant them only to people who have shown a "need" for them.

The underlying criteria need not and should not be the same everywhere, nor the same for most long guns and for handguns, as is now the case in many places. Stuart Krone, who does firearms instruction in Phoenix, said, "Here, I think the licensing standards are very good, the training is excellent and readily available, and it is not too expensive. Speaking as one who does training, and has for years, I support training, but not the government deciding the standards—they will set the standards impossibly high." Krone believes sensible people who acquire firearms will, in the best of all possible worlds, seek out training voluntarily.

Training should not be left to chance, but it should also not be left up to law-enforcement authorities or state and local government bureaucrats. The standards can and should be worked out with the NRA or the NSSF, the firearms industry's trade association, both of which already write and disseminate training standards. NRA instructors across the country certify training for many kinds of firearms, and for licenses to carry.

The interest of government should not be to fail as many people as possible—"keeping me from having a gun to keep criminals from having them," as Stephen Sanetti puts it—but to make sure applicants know how to use and store guns safely, can shoot straight, and know what state and local laws say about carrying and using a weapon in self-defense. There is no reason that getting a firearms license should be any more difficult in this respect, or any less, than getting a driver's license—or any more expensive. "The question is what kind of regulations can you have, requiring people to have training without making it too expensive for poor people to afford," Krone said.

Better training of gun owners in how to safely store guns is a no-brainer. The NRA has supported safety courses for decades and says it has more than 55,000 certified instructors who train about 750,000 gun owners a year. In 2000, Wayne LaPierre told Katie Couric on NBC's *Today* show: "We have always felt, and I feel, that owning a gun is a responsibility. And the fact that you have young children in the house, you'd better lock up your guns, and you'd better make them inaccessible. And if you're criminally negligent, you should be charged and we support that. . . . In fact, we've supported trigger locks for years."[22]

The Supreme Court's *Heller* decision in 2008 said that the District of Columbia could not require handguns in the home to be bound by a trigger lock at all times—that would make them useless for self-defense in case of sudden intrusion—but federal law requires dealers and manufacturers to provide safe storage or other safety devices with guns they sell. Some states—mainly the ones that have already established safety standards—have their own requirements. Whether people who buy guns actually use any of the devices is left up to them, except in Massachusetts, where even after *Heller* and *McDonald*, state law continued to require trigger locks on guns kept in the home.

Federal law does not require firearms dealers to warn or give written warnings to customers that the guns they buy should be stored in a safe way completely inaccessible to children, but since 1999 the trade association, the NSSF, in cooperation with the ATF and, during the Bush administration, with support from Justice Department grants, has distributed safety guidelines to gun owners as part of a program called Project ChildSafe. They include admonitions like these:

If you must have quick access to a loaded firearm in your home, you need to take special safety measures. Keeping a gun to defend your family makes no sense if that same gun puts your family members or visitors to your home at risk. Many home firearms accidents occur when unauthorized individuals, often visitors, discover loaded firearms that were carelessly left out in the open.

If you choose to keep a firearm for home security, your objective should be to create a situation in which the firearm is readily available to you, yet inaccessible or inoperative to others. Special lockable cases that can be quickly opened only by authorized individuals are options to consider.

You must exercise full control and supervision over a loaded gun at all times. This means the gun must be unloaded and placed in secure storage whenever you leave the gun in your home or elsewhere. Secure ammunition separately.

Your most important responsibility is ensuring that unsupervised children cannot encounter loaded firearms. The precautions you take must be completely effective. Anything less invites tragedy and is a serious violation of your responsibility as a gun owner.[23]

But, as of 2008, only eleven states required such warnings, and twenty-six states, as discussed previously, make gun owners criminally responsible if they don't keep their firearms safe from children. These state laws are not identical or uniform. They are enforceable only after the fact of some horrible crime or school shooting or accident, and most effective as deterrents. Even the age of a "child" varies from state to state, from under eighteen to only under fourteen (as in Illinois, Iowa, Virginia, and Wisconsin).[24]

Still, school shootings, assaults, and adolescent suicides might all be far less frequent if all fifty states had laws making gun owners responsible criminally and in civil suits for deaths and injuries inflicted by minors with guns they were able to get hold of because they had been left loaded and unlocked, or otherwise negligently stored. Federal law since 2005 has exempted handgun owners from civil liability suits if "at the time the handgun was accessed it had been made inoperable by the use of a secure gun storage or safety device."[25]

Some regulations are better left to cities and towns than imposed by statewide fiat. The criteria for issuing firearms licenses should be locally determined, especially in cities where people, particularly those who live in crime-ridden neighborhoods, feel especially threatened by illegal guns. Gun-rights supporters disagree violently with this, because local ordinances are often far more strict than state or federal ones, and as a result of their resistance, most states now have laws restricting what controls over firearms towns and cities can impose. In Florida, the state can fine local authorities that try to impose tougher regulations that go beyond the state's—up to $100,000—and can fine and remove the local officials who did it.

Where public safety and law enforcement are concerned, I do not see how state legislators or executives can possibly know better than the people who live in cities and towns what kind of gun laws are best for them, especially laws on handguns. Since the seventeenth century, from east to west, American towns and cities have had their own rules about where guns may be carried, when they must be unloaded, and how they should be stored when not in use. There is no one size that fits all. I have argued earlier in this book that those local rules are sometimes unreasonably strict, but the way to change them is not by state fiat.

Safety standards for firearms—not their operators, but the guns themselves—are, on the other hand, something the national government should oversee.

Authorize national operational safety standards, or guidelines for state safety standards, for all firearms—not behavioral safety standards for gun owners, but standards for the mechanical safety of the guns themselves.

The federal Consumer Products Safety Commission (CPSC) has no authority over firearms—in fact, it is specifically prevented from regulating them, by federal law. Gun-control groups such as the Violence Policy Center in Washington and such public-health experts as David Hemenway have called for the creation of a new federal agency to regulate firearms as a consumer product. No regulation at all certainly serves the profit motive of gun manufacturers, but how does it serve the interests of gun owners? Libertarians may resist the imposition of safety requirements, much as some motorcyclists resent being required to wear safety helmets. But a gun that goes off accidentally does not endanger only its owner. The industry counters that firearms accidents are at an all-time low, less than one-half of 1 percent of all fatal accidents.

The best way to achieve sensible standards that ensure that firearms are made safer to operate, not that as many as possible are removed from the market, is to try to enlist the industry's cooperation in writing the rules. Who better? The leading firearms companies set up the Sporting Arms and Ammunition Manufacturers' Institute, Inc., in 1926 to set up voluntary safety and performance standards. But the industry is wary, as Stephen Sanetti put it, that "the CPSC opens the door to a lot of mischief." The concern the industry had when Congress was persuaded to bar the agency from having jurisdiction over firearms, he said, was that it could be used to implement unreasonable gun control, a concern that seemed to be borne out by attempts to get the CPSC to ban all handgun ammunition as a "hazardous substance." As Sanetti said, "You can't design all the danger out of a gun."

If guns didn't shoot, of course, they wouldn't be dangerous. But they should be manufactured so as not to fire accidentally if dropped on a hard surface. Releasing a safety should take more pressure or require more dexterity than a toddler can bring to bear, and so should triggers. The industry itself, Sanetti said, had been voluntarily including locking devices with firearms since the early 1980s. Only eight states, as of 2008, had laws requiring safety standards, devised to drive handguns of poor quality, often used in crime-ridden neighborhoods, out of circulation. According to Legal Community Against Violence, California, Massachusetts, and New York require testing of handguns made, sold, or owned in those states to make sure that they would not fire if dropped on the floor or on the ground, or misfire or blow up if fired many times in succession rapidly. Melting-point tests are also required in Hawaii, Illinois, Massachusetts, Minnesota, New York, and South Carolina, to show that the working parts of handguns will not melt (and make them likely to fail structurally or explode) when fired. California, Massachusetts, and New York require handguns to have safety devices to prevent unintentional firing, or show clearly that a cartridge is in the firing chamber, or prevent a semiautomatic pistol with a detachable magazine from firing when a magazine is not inserted. Massachusetts also requires handguns to be operable only by the owner.[26]

Whether a national or a coordinated system of state firearms safety agencies is entrusted with applying nationwide regulations, collection of data on things that go wrong should be part of the job. David Hemenway has suggested "a national violent death data system (a surveillance system) that provides information on the circumstances and weapon for every fatality, along with a sample of nonfatal firearm injuries." The data would be used the way the National Transportation Safety Board uses the data it collects from investigations of the cause of airplane crashes to determine what is preventable.[27]

Require everyone who owns firearms to report firearms losses, or thefts, to local law-enforcement authorities within forty-eight hours of the time of discovery.

Licensed firearms dealers already have to report guns missing from inventory to the ATF within this short time period, but owners don't. Firearms theft should be prosecuted more vigorously, as the law permits: theft of weapons that have been imported, or shipped in interstate commerce, is punishable by up to ten years' federal imprisonment. But "lost" firearms are also a major factor in gun crimes. A Centers for Disease Control study of school shootings between 1992 and 1999 found that "the majority of the firearms came from the perpetrators' homes or from friends and relatives."[28] A Dade County grand jury investigation report in Florida in 1997 said, "We have reached one inescapable and shameful conclusion. When we legally arm ourselves for our own protection, we may be inadvertently arming the very persons we are seeking to protect ourselves against. The statistics from the Metro-Dade Police Department prove that a substantial number of stolen firearms come from our homes, our cars, and our businesses. . . ."[29] Only seven states[30] and the District of Columbia require registered firearms owners to report the loss or theft of a gun to law enforcement. Chicago, Cleveland, Columbus, Hartford, Los Angeles, New York City, and San Francisco also have their own such laws.[31] Stolen guns are illegal guns, and illegal guns are the criminals' favorite weapons.

Gun owners are rightly wary of being prosecuted as criminals themselves for crimes committed with weapons that are stolen from them. The aim should not be making owners of stolen guns liable to prosecution as accessories to crimes they did not commit, but giving law enforcement at least a possibility of finding stolen weapons before that happens, and going after the criminals who stole them. It should be clear that reporting within forty-eight hours of the time theft is *discovered* is what is required.

"Fingerprint" bullets and shell casings, to make it easier to trace guns used in crimes.

The NRA fights every attempt to make manufacturers do this, on the grounds that criminals who know their way around firearms can easily subvert the mechanisms that accomplish it and that it would add unnecessarily to the cost of ammunition. This strikes me as similar to arguing that seat belts should not be required in cars because people can leave them unfastened and because they make cars cost more.

Focus the ATF on criminals. Then get Congress off its back.

It often seems that the ATF can't win. Like the Internal Revenue Service, which it was part of until 1972, its task is partly law enforcement and partly tax collection—a combination that wins few friends. It stayed in the Treasury Department until 2003, when as the Bureau of Alcohol, Tobacco, Firearms and Explosives it became part of the Justice Department. Its budget in 2010 was almost $1.21 billion, for a staff of 5,145. Of those, 2,485 were special agents, the personnel who investigate violations of federal firearms and explosive laws. The bureau wanted a 3.8 percent increase in funds for the 2011 fiscal year, mostly to pay for twenty-five agents to intensify operations along the border in the Southwest against gunrunners who it said had smuggled tens of thousands of weapons to the brutally violent and increasingly powerful drug cartels in Mexico. "The violence, and associated trafficking, will take significant efforts to quell," the bureau said in explaining its request for the operation, Project Gunrunner.

Gunrunner was not the first attempt by the ATF to try to get a handle on smuggling across the border. A predecessor operation called Wide Receiver, carried out during the administration of George W. Bush by the ATF's Tucson office in 2006 and 2007, had also allowed guns to "walk" in an attempt to identify smugglers, apparently with meager results. A review by the Justice Department's Office of the Inspector General in late 2010 also found serious shortcomings in the Gunrunner project. "ATF's focus remains largely on inspections of gun dealers and investigations of straw purchasers, rather than on higher-level traffickers, smugglers, and the ultimate recipients of the trafficked guns," it said. "For example, we found that 68 percent of Project Gunrunner cases are single-defendant cases, and some ATF managers discourage field personnel from conducting the types of complex conspiracy investigations that target higher-level members of trafficking rings. Federal prosecutors told us that directing the efforts of Project Gunrunner toward building larger, multi-defendant conspiracy cases would better disrupt trafficking organizations." The ATF did not play well with others, the report added, not coordinating well with Mexican authorities or with other US task forces working against drug smuggling. Nevertheless: "We also found that while reports of multiple sales of handguns produce timely, actionable investigative leads for ATF, the lack of a reporting requirement for multiple sales of long guns—which have become the cartels' weapons of choice—hinders ATF's ability to disrupt the flow of illegal weapons into Mexico."[32]

Early in 2011, the ATF asked the White House for "emergency" approval to use "demand letters" to require reports from firearms dealers in Arizona, California, New Mexico, and Texas—8,500 of them, according to the NRA—on any customers who bought within five days two or more semiautomatic rifles bigger than .22 caliber that were capable of accepting detachable magazines. These are the kinds of guns frequently smuggled into Mexico by the drug cartels, and efficient law enforcement could use the information to head off at least some of them before they crossed the border. But for the NRA, the request was just another attempt to blame American gun purchasers for illegal shipments of weapons to Mexico that were more often the work of international smuggling rings. It was, the NRA said, a way "for the Obama administration to impose new restrictions on gun owners and the gun industry, without bothering to go to Congress."[33] Federally licensed firearms dealers have to file such reports for multiple handgun sales, but long guns have been exempted by law because they are not so often used in crimes—it's mostly hunters and target shooters who have them. After many Democrats joined Republicans in the House of Representatives in a vote to prohibit the use of federal funds for collection of the information (not included in the final passage of the legislation it was attached to), the Obama administration decided in early February 2011 that the ATF should not proceed immediately by fiat, but should use standard procedure—a three-month review period, with public hearings—before trying to impose a new requirement.

But, for a Democratic administration in the middle of a twenty-first-century Tea Party, getting the cooperation of the gun lobby or its many sympathizers in Congress was doomed to failure. The ATF's congressional critics, led by Senator Charles Grassley, the Iowa Republican, had been hearing for weeks that the agency had been deliberately letting suspected straw purchasers buy assault weapons. Soon there were leaks to newspapers and to *CBS News,* which reported that seven arms dealers in and around Phoenix had actually volunteered information to ATF agents in late 2009 about multiple buys of large numbers of semiautomatic, military-style "assault" weapons, supposedly for personal use, by obvious gunrunners who paid with cash from paper bags. The dealers didn't want to keep making these sales; that's why they reported their suspicions. But instead of cracking down on suspect buyers, the ATF encouraged some dealers to keep selling the guns to them, in hopes of getting a better track on how they found their way to Mexico, and on who the Mexican recipients were. Some 2,020 weapons were knowingly sold this way to straw buyers, and many probably ended up in the hands of the drug cartels across the border—but the ATF lost track of them.

This, called Operation Fast and Furious, blew up in the agency's face after two of the weapons were found at the scene of a shootout with Border Patrol agents near the Mexican border in Arizona on December 14, 2010, in which one of the agents had been killed.[34]

For the ATF's critics, in the NRA and in Congress, the death of the agent made the whole project a demonstration of misplaced priorities, if not incompetence—and a golden opportunity to blame it all on the Obama administration and its nefarious plans to undermine Americans' own gun rights. President Obama called the operation a "serious mistake," but it was worse than that—it left the ATF's credibility on other matters in shreds. If the bureau couldn't manage its leads better than that, the NRA's chief Washington lobbyist, Chris W. Cox, wrote, "how would mandating thousands of additional reports be useful?"[35] Or what would they be useful for, besides keeping tabs on Americans who own guns so that the government would know which people to take them away from when it did away with the Second Amendment?

Congressional hearings in mid-2011 made the Justice Department and ATF officials who testified look like fools. The NRA called for the removal of Attorney General Eric Holder after Senator Grassley asked him how a rifle that had been "walked" out of a gun shop as part of Operation Fast and Furious could end up at the scene of the murder of a Border Patrol agent, and the attorney general answered, "I frankly don't know." The Justice Department said in July 2011 that it would go ahead anyway with the multiple-rifle-purchase reporting requirement for licensed dealers in the four Southwest border states, and two senators, a Republican and a Democrat, introduced a bill to cut off funding to enforce it. But a month later, the ATF's acting director, Kenneth E. Melson, was replaced in that job by B. Todd Jones, the US attorney in Minnesota, amid calls from all sides for investigations. (The bureau had not had a permanent director since 2006, in President George W. Bush's second term; Republicans in Congress, in full cry, rejected any comparison between Fast and Furious and the earlier gun-walking operation carried out by the ATF's Tucson office during his watch in 2006 and 2007.)

Interference is not unusual for Congress where the ATF is concerned, but little wonder, given the bureau's record. The fiasco of the ATF raid on the militia compound of the lunatic Branch Davidian sect in Waco, Texas, in 1993, which ended after a long siege by the FBI with a conflagration that killed seventy-six people, is perhaps the worst example. Largely because Congress has kept it on a short budget leash, the ATF has the same number of ATF special agents— 2,500, more or less—as it had in 1972, according to the *Washington Post*'s *Hidden Life of Guns* series in fall 2010.

The bureau's success in bringing about federal prosecution of dealers for breaking the law is limited: thirty-six prosecutions in 2000, twenty-five in 2001, twenty-seven in 2002; an average of only fifteen a year at the end of that decade, though the number has been rising more recently because of Project Gunrunner activity. "The firearms bureau inspects only a fraction of the nation's 60,000 retail gun dealers, taking as much as eight years between visits to stores," the *Post* reported. "By law, the ATF cannot require dealers to conduct a physical inventory to determine whether any guns have been lost or stolen. The ATF is supposed to regulate the gun industry, but many within the bureau say it is the industry that dominates the agency."[36]

Nevertheless, another report by the Justice Department's Office of the Inspector General, in 2004, had found that "resource shortfalls" were not the only reason for weaknesses in the ATF's inspection system. Another was that "the ATF manipulates the criteria it uses to target FFLs [federal firearms licensees] for inspections so that it only identifies as many such FFLs as it has the resources to inspect. Therefore, the ATF has not applied its established indicators of potential trafficking to objectively identify the full universe of potential traffickers."

"Although we recognize that the ATF's resources are limited, we concluded that the ATF's lack of standardized inspection procedures results in inconsistent inspections of FFLs and significant variation in the implementation of the inspection program by Field Divisions," that report found. "The most recent performance data available show that ATF's Field Divisions took from 24.5 hours to as much as 90 hours per compliance inspection. Further, we found little or no correlation between longer inspection times and outcomes such as criminal referrals and adverse actions taken. We concluded that the ATF needs a more standardized and efficient inspection regimen."[37] According to the *Post,* revised procedures now permit 11,000 inspections a year, but that still leaves most dealers unaudited for ten years at a stretch.

The *Post* went on to report that there were eighty-seven lines of congressional direction in the ATF's appropriations bill, one of them the requirement that information from the NICS database be released only to law-enforcement agencies pursuing specific investigations. Another prohibits the records from being searchable electronically by firearm or by firearm owner—they cannot be used, in other words, to become a federal gun registry. As the founders feared a standing army as an instrument of federal tyranny, so do modern-day defenders of the Second Amendment fan the flames of fear of a federal gun registry. This is all the more reason to leave registration and licensing to the states, as argued above.

A congressional amendment tacked on in 2003 is what prohibits the ATF from requiring dealers to take inventories. This is an outrageous act of legislative meddling. The DC snipers, John Allen Muhammad and Lee Boyd Malvo, who killed ten people in unprovoked attacks in the Washington area in 2002, had among other weapons a .223-caliber Bushmaster rifle that had disappeared from Bull's Eye Shooter Supply in Tacoma, Washington. The shop had been unable to account for 150 guns in an ATF audit two years previously and had been punished by nothing more than a warning from the agency. Since 2005, at least 113,000 guns are known to have un-accountably disappeared from dealerships. The pathetic justification given by the NRA for its opposition to mandatory inventories for gun dealers is that the inconvenience could lead to increases in the price of firearms. Gun dealers will point out, as John R. Hansen, who sells antique, used, and new guns in Southport, Connecticut, did to me, that most of them do conduct inventories themselves, and that they are required to maintain records of all firearms received and sold, and to report missing guns to the ATF within twenty-four to forty-eight hours. When the ATF audits manufacturers' inventories, Sanetti says, "missing" guns often turn out to be imperfect guns that were destroyed, or guns destroyed before being sold, or nothing more than a list of prospective serial numbers that were never ap-plied to guns. The trade association has begun a campaign to remind retailers that taking stock of inventory is good business practice.[38]

But hamstringing the ATF in ways that make it difficult for the agency to identify and go after those few dealers who are negligent about keeping track of their stocks or either careless or criminally contemptuous about the NICS checks amounts to protecting crim-inals. It may be popular in the modern Tea Party era to villainize gov-ernment bureaucracies, but government law-enforcement agencies tasked with uncovering criminal activities should not be hampered in the performance of those duties. If the bureau's focus were more clearly centered on criminals themselves, perhaps its antagonists in the NRA would redirect their fire, as well. For the NSSF trade group, the ATF, for all its flaws, is preferable to the possible alternative of turning over its functions to the FBI, Stephen Sanetti told me. It has brought on many of its problems with Congress by arbitrary rulings and enforcement of bureaucratic technicalities that sometimes leave you scratching your head and wondering what they have to do with going after gun crime.

On July 13, 2005, for instance, the ATF issued an open letter that announced a new interpretation of a provision of the 1968 Gun Control Act, which generally prohibited the import of firearms from foreign countries, except for four categories, including one exempting guns that are particularly suitable or readily adaptable for "sporting purposes" such as hunting, skeet shooting, or trap shooting.

> The Bureau of Alcohol, Tobacco, Firearms and Explosives (ATF) has determined that the language of 18 U.S.C. § 925(d)(3) permits no exceptions that would allow frames, receivers or barrels for otherwise non-importable firearms to be imported into the United States. Accordingly, ATF will no longer approve ATF Form 6 applications for importation of any frames, receivers, or barrels for firearms that would be prohibited from importation if assembled. No exceptions to the statutory language, for example for "repair or replacement" of existing firearms, will be allowed.
>
> ATF recognizes that importers have, in the past, obtained import permits authorizing the importation of barrels and receivers for non-importable firearms for "repair or replacement" and may have entered into contracts in reliance upon such authorizations. In order to mitigate the impact of ATF's change in import policy and to allow importers a reasonable period to come into compliance, ATF will forgo enforcement of this import restriction for 60 calendar days and allow importers holding existing permits to continue to import barrels and receivers for a period of 60 calendar days. ATF believes this time period is adequate for importers who have entered into binding contracts for the sale and shipment of such barrels and receivers to complete the process of importing the items into the United States. ATF will advise Customs and Border Protection that in no event should these permits be accepted to release these items for entry into the United States after September 10, 2005.

What this meant in practice was that parts for weapons that could be imported in the past (and those weapons were "grandfathered," by law, during the 1994–2004 "assault weapons" ban), like semiautomatic rifles derived from the AK-47, can no longer be imported. Semiautomatic AK-47s can be manufactured in the United States, though, and sold to gun enthusiasts in states that permit them. So anyone who has one that was imported can no longer get parts, nor can someone who wants to "build" an AK-47 with foreign parts do that.

I can attest that AK-47 "assault weapons" are great fun to shoot at a firing range. How useful they are for self-defense, for most Americans in most situations, is harder to see, but it is self-evident that in the hands of a lunatic or a terrorist in a crowd of innocent people, a rifle based on a design intended to make it possible to kill as many enemy soldiers as possible in combat can be far more dangerous and lethal than an ordinary semiautomatic pistol or a hunting rifle of approximately the same caliber.

But if the purpose of the new regulation was to keep terrorists or criminals from acquiring "assault weapons" assembled with imported parts, why was there an exemption for so long in the first place? And why the sixty-day delay in implementing this new ban on parts? Little wonder that reaction to the regulation among gun enthusiasts was uniformly negative. This comment from a conservative website, Free Republic, was typical: "This is one more example of arbitrary abrogation of the supposed 'supreme law of the land' by unelected bureaucrats who are killing our nation by slow regulatory strangulation."

Gun owners frequently complain about administrative rulings interpreting existing laws that have the same effect as changing those laws. "If ATF had played by the rules, it would have published a notice in the Federal Register citing legal authority by which the rule was proposed and presented the basics of the proposed rule," an article on one such change in a gun magazine published by the gun-rights activist Second Amendment Foundation complained. "ATF obviously did not want to do this as it would have given the interested parties, i.e., importers, gunsmiths and gun shop owners an opportunity to participate in the rule making process. The Administrative Procedures Act mandates that the federal agency proposing the rule concisely summarize the basis and purpose of the rule making such as the purpose of the rule and the rationale for its adoption."[39]

Forty-three years after the Gun Control Act, at the start of 2011, the ATF got around to taking aim at imported shotguns, with a study concluding that characteristics like folding, collapsible, or telescoping stocks; flash suppressors; and large-capacity magazines on shotguns were useful for military or law-enforcement purposes but not for sport, as the laws defined shooting sports, and that importing shotguns with such features should therefore not be allowed.[40]

The study did not say that there was any special reason to single out shotguns for more scrutiny after so much time; it just said the bureau hadn't gotten around until 2011 to examining whether shooting shotguns was really sport. The public was invited to comment, and the NRA's comment was that it was time for Congress to do away with the "sporting purposes" test, because it had been imposed at "a time when the right to self-defense with a firearm was not as widely respected by the courts as it is today. Clearly, the main reason to change the law is that the Second Amendment—as the Supreme Court said in *District of Columbia v. Heller*—protects our right to keep and bear arms for defense, not for sports," the NRA asserted.[41]

In fact, *Heller* said the Second Amendment protects the right to keep and use handguns specifically, and guns generally, for self-defense in the home; it didn't say "not for sports" at all. Justice Scalia also wrote in that opinion: "Like most rights, the right secured by the Second Amendment is not unlimited"; it was always understood that it is "not a right to keep and carry any weapon whatsoever in any manner whatsoever and for whatever purpose." The prohibition of sales to criminals and mental cases, the regulations outlawing machine guns and other weapons that are "dangerous and unusual" and do not qualify as being "in common use" by civilians, even if they may actually be in common use nowadays in the armed forces, should not be considered as thrown into doubt, Scalia wrote; nor should "laws imposing conditions and qualifications on the commercial sale of arms" or "laws forbidding the carrying of firearms in sensitive places such as schools and government buildings."[42]

The justices repeated these qualifications in the *McDonald* case: Justice Alito said that incorporating the Second Amendment right to keep and bear arms into the Fourteenth Amendment applying to all the states "does not imperil every law regulating firearms."[43]

As noted earlier in this book, the Court did not say much about which of the many thousands and thousands of other federal, state, and local gun laws and regulations were not imperiled. Some saw in this omission an invitation for thousands and thousands of lawsuits challenging these regulations, and there have been several hundred since the *Heller* decision in 2008. But in most cases, courts have upheld the regulations.

American history shows that gun-control laws have always been with us, and that reasonable ones will continue to be. Gun-control laws barred Anne Hutchinson and her followers in the early seventeenth century from having guns. Other laws confiscated the weapons of loyalists during the Revolutionary War. There were all those towns in the Wild West in the nineteenth century that barred itinerant gunslingers from bearing arms within city limits. Reasonable gun control is not unconstitutional—but gun control can be unreasonable. Clearly, outright bans of handguns in big cities are beyond the pale. What is reasonable elsewhere ought to be able to be worked out, city by city, county by county, state by state, as it always has been.

It will not be easy to end the cultural wars about guns. The battle lines have been drawn hard and fast, and traces may endure for as long as the European trenches from World War I have, still visible today. Cynics may say that compromise on any of the issues is impossible for the NRA because compromise would not be good for fund-raising. Richard Feldman, who once worked for the NRA, argued in an article in the *Washington Post* in 2007: "Safeguarding the rights of gun owners has become secondary to keeping the fund-raising machinery well greased and the group's senior staff handsomely compensated."[44]

Some of the reasons the NRA asks its members for money do seem to support this view. "For more than a dozen years, your NRA has been fighting one of the most important battles for freedom that will take place in our entire lifetimes—or perhaps in the entire history of our nation," Wayne LaPierre said in an appeal to members in late 2011. "I'm talking about the ongoing effort at the United Nations to pass an Arms Trade Treaty that could all but ban civilian ownership of firearms worldwide . . . A treaty that, without even a full vote from Congress, could force YOU and every American gun owner to comply with dozens of U.N. restrictions—to register your guns, store your firearms locked and unloaded, and obtain a government license before you're allowed to purchase a firearm or even a box of ammunition." Donations to the NRA's lobbying arm would help stop it.

LaPierre's premise was condescending nonsense. It counted on NRA members' knowing nothing about how the UN works or what the treaty its members were trying to work out would actually do. The UN General Assembly did, in 2009, after the Obama administration dropped its predecessor's opposition to the idea, set up a negotiation process to draft an arms trade treaty to regulate the import, export, and transfer of conventional arms in international trade. But the parameters, established earlier by an international group of governmental experts, included this one: "Exclusively internal transfers or national ownership provisions, including national constitutional protections on private ownership within that State's territory, should not fall under an arms trade treaty."[45] A conference at UN headquarters in New York City convened in the summer of 2012 to work out the terms—with the NRA denouncing them all the while—but fell short of full agreement and adjourned until later.

The agenda was not insidious UN world government, nor you or me selling our guns to a dealer abroad, but a far broader one—the trade not just in small arms but in military weapons, machine guns, bazookas, grenades, even tanks and missiles and aircraft—and the aim was to do a better job of keeping weapons out of the hands of terrorist organizations and repressive regimes. And no treaty could emerge except by unanimous agreement of all countries participating; constitutionally, no treaty can ever bind the United States unless two-thirds of the members of the US Senate vote to ratify it. What is the likelihood that a treaty restricting individual Americans' gun rights would ever find the support of sixty-seven US senators? Less than zero. NRA members would have done better to save their money and spend it on guns and ammunition rather than throw their dollars away as LaPierre asked them to do, to stop something that had no chance of ever happening.

Instead of fighting chimerical battles, American gun-rights and gun-control enthusiasts should be talking to each other about what can be done in the United States itself to reduce gun violence, particularly by addressing the criminal and psychopathological behavior patterns that cause it. There are plenty of laws on the books that can be more vigorously enforced, as the NRA keeps saying, against felons who use guns. Perhaps, after the Tea Party is over, Americans will see that absolutist demands and positions have never been the American Way. Reasonable compromise has made the United States the great country that it is.

Again, acknowledging that Americans do have an individual right, recognized in the Constitution, to keep and bear arms does not mean that those who own a gun have a right to be a law unto themselves. The misconstruction of the Second Amendment as an unlimited right not connected with any responsibility or civic duty has cost many more American lives than terrorism has. All of us have the right to keep and bear arms, but also the right to life, liberty, and the pursuit of happiness—the right to live in safety. The NRA is at the forefront of a self-declared battle to give gun owners in all states the right to carry guns concealed and has flogged state legislatures into passing castle-doctrine and stand-your-ground laws that make it less risky for gun owners to use their guns in self-defense when threatened. But the NRA ought to be encouraged to train gun owners to recognize that such laws do not give a green light to wielding a weapon anytime, anywhere. Even if Congress passes a nationwide right-to-carry law, state laws on the use of firearms should continue to apply.

The Second Amendment does not condemn us to unending gun violence. What does is our obstinate refusal to engage with each other about constitutional ways to control it. The founders would be astonished by the ideological rigidity that has led to so much tragedy, and they would say we should be ashamed of ourselves for not finding a way to prevent so many deaths. We should work to be worthy of the heritage they left us.

I really appreciated his consise statements about what we should do and his conclusion was very powerful

ACKNOWLEDGMENTS

Why write a book about guns if you've never owned a gun? Maybe it's in the genes—Eli Whitney, one of the first assembly-line producers of guns, was a nephew of one of my direct ancestors, and besides, he was born in Westborough, Massachusetts, where I grew up.

Thanks first of all to Wendy Strothman of the Strothman Agency for her encouragement and constructive criticism of the manuscript of this book at an early stage. She has an interest in its success as my agent, of course, but as a former publisher herself, she knows what makes a book good. She pushed me as hard as she could to try to make this one worthy. Grant Ujifusa, another former editor and a classmate at Harvard many years ago, also read the manuscript at an earlier stage and, with pointed constructive criticism, urged me on.

Brandon Proia, my editor at PublicAffairs, cut me no slack, with insightful questions and suggestions that exposed lapses in logic and other faults and allowed me to correct (I hope) most of them. I thank Susan Weinberg, the publisher of PublicAffairs, for wanting the book, and Peter Osnos, founder and editor-at-large of the house and a lifelong friend, for encouraging me to submit it to her. Collin Tracy, the project editor for *Living with Guns* at Perseus Books, and Michele Wynn, the meticulous and insightful copy editor, turned the manuscript into the finished book, for which I thank them; and thanks to Tessa Shanks, Lisa Kaufman, and Jaime Leifer at PublicAffairs for promoting and publicizing.

Part of the reward of doing the historical research at the New York Public Library was the pleasure of seeing, for the first time, I am abashed to admit, the splendid main reading room of the library's main branch on Fifth Avenue, the Beaux Arts building now named for Stephen A. Schwarzman. The lions outside are one thing; the coffered ceiling of this enormous space is something else—one of the glories of American architecture and cultural life. I didn't do my research in that room, though;

thanks to David Offensend, the library's chief operating officer and a neighbor in Brooklyn, for introducing me to Jay Barksdale, the study rooms liaison librarian, who assigned me a place in the Wertheim Study. This is a small room where researchers can keep rare volumes on a shelf of their own and read and take notes in a quiet setting. Mr. Barksdale, on occasional afternoons, even served tea. The library's support for scholars and authors is an invaluable resource.

I thank Robert R. Buck for introducing me to Professor Joseph E. Olson, and Joe Olson for letting me spend most of a day with him, Buck, David Feinwachs, and David M. Gross during a gun show in St. Paul, when they were graciously willing to answer all questions I put to them. Justin Whitney, my nephew, was just as hospitable, and his friends in Phoenix, particularly Stuart Krone, equally willing to help me understand their reasons for wanting to own and carry guns, and even to understand the fun of shooting, by taking me to a range and letting me use some of their guns. Peter Diaczuk, the director of forensics science training at John Jay College of Criminal Justice in New York City, also shared some of his expertise about tracing firearms used in crimes. Terence Nelan, the son of a former Moscow colleague, who now lives in New Hampshire, was good enough to share well-thought-out views about gun control. Henry L. Hokans, who taught me how to play the pipe organ back in the 1950s, and his wife, Louise, warmly welcomed my wife, Heidi, and me to their home in Maine while Hank told me about his lifelong interest in firearms. *Guns 'n' Organs* would make a great title for a book someday.

Closer to home, very close in fact, Ted and Connie Roosevelt shared some of their hunting experiences with me, and Dwight Demeritt not only acquainted me with the craftsmanship of early gun makers in Maine, on which he is an expert, but with John R. Hansen, founder of the Hansen and Hansen Arms and Antiquities shop in Southport, Connecticut. I owe Jay Hansen the privilege of a lunch and interview with Stephen L. Sanetti, the president and chief executive officer of the National Shooting Sports Foundation, the firearms industry trade association. Thanks to all of these for helping me try to be gun literate; if I have failed, in places, it's not their fault; and I do not mean to imply that any of them agrees with my conclusions.

Thanks as well to those who told me their stories but preferred not to be named. And thanks to Adam Winkler, a professor of constitutional law at the University of California, Los Angeles, who wrote the excellent book *Gunfight: The Battle over the Right to Bear Arms in America,* for reading my manuscript.

I am also grateful to the National Rifle Association for the subscription to their monthly newsletter that comes with membership. I would never have believed half the things the media say the NRA has said if I hadn't read them in the magazine. I think the NRA could contribute enormously to a better understanding of gun rights if it chose to, and perhaps someday it will.

Finally, once again, thanks to Heidi Whitney for putting up with it all.

CHAPTER 1

1. Louis Armstrong, *Satchmo: My Life in New Orleans* (New York: Prentice-Hall, 1954, and Da Capo Press, 1986), p. 33: "As a matter of fact that is what taught me how to play the trumpet."

2. Figures cited in Don B. Kates Jr., "Handgun Prohibition and the Original Meaning of the Second Amendment," *Michigan Law Review,* vol. 82, no. 2 (November 1983), p. 263.

3. Franklin E. Zimring, "Firearms and Federal Law: The Gun Control Act of 1968," *Journal of Legal Studies* (1975), p. 148.

4. Alexander DeConde, *Gun Violence in America: The Struggle for Control* (Boston: Northeastern University Press, 2001), p. 173.

5. Adam Winkler, *Gunfight: The Battle over the Right to Bear Arms in America* (New York: W. W. Norton and Company, 2011), p. 243.

6. Reva B. Siegel, "Dead or Alive: Originalism as Popular Constitutionalism in Heller" (Cambridge: Harvard Law Review Association, Harvard Law Review, 2008), 122 *Harv. L. Rev.* 191, p. 7.

7. "Pro–Gun Control Statement Endorsed by Charlton Heston," Violence Policy Center, at www.vpc.org/nrainfo/memo.htm.

8. "U.S. Panel Urges Handgun Seizure to Curb Violence," *New York Times,* July 29, 1969.

9. David Brooks, "Children of the '70s," *New York Times,* May 18, 2010.

10. Winkler, *Gunfight,* p. 19.

11. Ibid., p. 256.

12. Siegel, "Dead or Alive," p. 10.

13. In 1990, Congress passed the Gun-Free School Zones Act, which made it a federal crime for anyone to bring a firearm knowingly into a school zone—which was already a state crime almost everywhere. The

federal law was declared unconstitutional by the Supreme Court in 1995, on the grounds that it breached the separation of powers, in *United States v. Lopez,* a decision written for the majority by Chief Justice William Rehnquist. He ruled that government arguments that the law promoted interstate commerce because of its potential to reduce violent crime were a reach too far for the Constitution's commerce clause, which gives Congress the power to regulate commerce among the several states.

14. Christopher S. Koper, principal investigator, Report to the National Institute of Justice, Department of Justice, "Updated Assessment of the Federal Assault Weapons Ban: Impacts on Gun Markets and Gun Violence, 1994–2003" (Philadelphia: Jerry Lee Center of Criminology, University of Pennsylvania, June 2004, "Key Findings and Conclusions").

15. David Hemenway, *Private Guns, Public Health* (Ann Arbor: University of Michigan Press, 2004, rev. 2007), p. 220.

16. In 2011, seventy-one police officers nationwide were killed by firearms, up from fifty-nine in 2010 and about as many as in 2001, when there were seventy-two, according to the National Law Enforcement Officers Memorial Fund. Police spokesmen quoted on national television made it sound as if the 20 percent rise from 2010 were due to the lapsing of the assault ban.

17. *Printz v. United States* (95–1478), 521 U.S. 898 (1997).

18. See http://concordlive.wordpress.com/2008/04/11/charlton -heston-on-political-correctness-1997-address-to-the-free-congress- foundation/ or www.americancivilrightsreview.com/docs-folder-guns- heston.html.

19. "Record-Low 26% in U.S. Favor Handgun Ban," October 26, 2011, at www.gallup.com/poll/150341/Record-Low-Favor-Handgun-Ban.aspx.

20. "Protester Busts Out the Big Gun for Obama Rally," *New York Post,* August 18, 2009, and Tim Vetscher, "Tempe Pastor Reiterates Wish for President Obama's Death," *Southeast Valley News,* August 31, 2009.

21. Interview with Theodore Roosevelt IV, New York City, January 16, 2010.

22. "Fearing Obama Agenda, States Push to Loosen Gun Laws," *New York Times,* February 23, 2010.

23. "President Obama: We Must Seek Agreement on Gun Reforms," special to the *Arizona Daily Star,* March 13, 2011.

24. Chris W. Cox, "'Castle Doctrine' Legislation: Protecting Your Right to Protect Yourself," *American Rifleman* (April 2012), pp. 17–18.

25. Florida Statutes, Title XLVI, Chapter 776.013.

26. The applicable subparagraph of the statute says: "A person who is not engaged in an unlawful activity and who is attacked in any other place where he or she has a right to be has no duty to retreat and has the right to stand his or her ground and meet force with force, including deadly force if he or she reasonably believes it is necessary to do so to prevent death or great bodily harm to himself or herself or another or to prevent the commission of a forcible felony."

27. The White House, Remarks by the President for the Nomination of Dr. Jim Kim for World Bank President, March 23, 2012.

28. Ralph Blumenthal, "Bull's-Eyes of Texas: Getting a Gun License," *New York Times,* July 14, 2006.

29. Excerpts from Constance Rogers, "Elk in the Bitterroots," *Gray's Sporting Journal* (May 1996).

30. Dwight B. Demeritt Jr., *Maine Made Guns and Their Makers* (Augusta: Friends of the Maine State Museum, 1997).

CHAPTER 2

1. David A. Price, *Love and Hate in Jamestown* (New York: Vintage Books/Random House, 2005), p. 10, quoting a tract by Robert Johnson, "Nova Britannia," from 1609.

2. Ibid., pp. 31–43.

3. Ibid., pp. 104–106.

4. Ibid., p. 192.

5. Ibid., pp. 220–221.

6. Duane A. Cline, "The Pilgrims and Plymouth Colony: 1620," at www.rootsweb.ancestry.com/~mosmd/.

7. James Ciment, ed., *Colonial America: An Encyclopedia of Social, Political, Cultural and Economic History* (Armonk, NY: M. E. Sharpe, Sharpe Reference, 2006), p. 888.

8. Demeritt Jr., *Maine Made Guns,* p. 1.

9. Nathaniel B. Shurtleff, ed., *Records of the Governor and Company of the Massachusetts Bay in New England,* vol. 1, *1628–1641* (Boston: William White, 1853), pp. 26, 76, 84.

10. Ibid., pp. 190–210.

11. Ibid., pp. 211–212.

12. Shurtleff, ed., *Records,* vol. 2, *1642–1649,* p. 24.

13. Ibid., p. 119.

14. Robert J. Spitzer, *The Right to Bear Arms: Rights and Liberties Under the Law* (Santa Barbara, Denver, Oxford: ABC Clio, 2001), pp. 17–19.

15. Ibid., p. 14.

16. See Amy Cope, *People of the First Light* (Wordclay, 2006), and also http://militaryhistory.about.com/od/battleswars16011800/p/King -Philips-War-1675-1676.htm.

17. See Robert S. Grumet, *First Manhattans: A History of the Indians of Greater New York* (Norman: University of Oklahoma Press, 2011), pp. 5, 17, 37, and passim.

18. Daniel J. Boorstin, *The Americans: The Colonial Experience* (New York: Random House, 1958), p. 353.

19. Demeritt, *Maine Made Guns,* p. 21.

20. Boorstin, *The Americans,* p. 350.

21. Stephen P. Halbrook, *The Founders' Second Amendment: Origins of the Right to Bear Arms* (Chicago: Ivan R. Dee, 2008, published in association with the Independent Institute, Oakland, CA), pp. 340–341, and Breyer, J., dissenting opinion in *District of Columbia v. Heller,* 554 U.S. 07 –290 (2008), p. 5.

22. DeConde, *Gun Violence in America,* pp. 22–23.

23. Boorstin, *The Americans,* pp. 364–365.

24. Halbrook, *The Founders' Second Amendment,* pp. 9–11.

25. Oliver Morton Dickerson, ed., *Boston Under Military Rule, 1768– 1769, as revealed in A Journal of the Times* (Boston: Chapman and Grimes, 1936), February 6, 1769.

26. Halbrook, *The Founders' Second Amendment,* pp. 20–21; Leonard W. Levy, *Origins of the Bill of Rights* (New Haven: Yale University Press, 1999), pp. 140–141; Mark V. Tushnet, *Out of Range: Why the Constitution Can't End the Battle over Guns* (Oxford: Oxford University Press, 2007), pp. 17–18.

27. William Blackstone, "Commentaries on the Laws of England," cited in Joyce Lee Malcolm, *To Keep and Bear Arms: The Origins of an Anglo- American Right* (Cambridge: Harvard University Press, 1994), p. 130.

28. Halbrook, *The Founders' Second Amendment,* p. 252.

29. Harry Alonzo Cushing, ed., *The Writings of Samuel Adams,* collected and edited by Harry Alonzo Cushing, vol. 1, *1764–1769* (New York: Octagon Books, 1968), pp. 264–265, 299, 317–318.

30. Frederic Kidder, *History of the Boston Massacre, March 5, 1770; Consisting of the Narrative of the Town, the Trial of the Soldiers: and a Historical*

Introduction, Containing Unpublished Documents of John Adams, and Explanatory Notes (Albany: Joel Munsell, 1870), p. 237.

31. Halbrook, *The Founders' Second Amendment*, pp. 44–49.

32. John Adams, *The Works of John Adams, Second President of the United States: with a Life of the Author, Notes and Illustrations, by his Grandson Charles Francis Adams, Vol. IV., the whole published 1850–56* (Freeport, NY: reprinted by Books for Libraries Press, 1969), p. 39.

33. Robert A. Gross, *The Minutemen and Their World* (New York: Hill and Wang, 1976 and 2001), p. 59.

34. Ibid., p. 60.

35. Ibid., p. 69.

36. Boorstin, *The Americans*, p. 351.

37. Charles Winthrop Sawyer, *Our Rifles* (Boston: Williams Book Store, 1946, originally published 1920), pp. 12–13.

38. Timothy Dwight, *Travels in New-England and New-York,* vol. 1 (London: Wm Baynes and Son, and Ogle, Duncan and Company, 1827), pp. 351–352; Halbrook, *The Founders' Second Amendment*, p. 79; Gross, *The Minutemen and Their World*, p. 117.

39. Gross, *The Minutemen and Their World*, p. 125.

40. Dwight, *Travels in New-England and New-York,* vol. 1, p. 352.

41. Boorstin, *The Americans*, p. 351.

42. Colin Gordon Calloway, *The American Revolution in Indian Country: Crisis and Diversity in Native American Communities* (Cambridge: Cambridge University Press, 1995), p. 35.

43. Richard Frothingham, *History of the Siege of Boston* (1851), p. 95; Halbrook, *The Founders' Second Amendment*, pp. 83–95.

44. Halbrook, *The Founders' Second Amendment*, p. 97.

45. Robert Middlekauff, *The Glorious Cause: The American Revolution, 1763–1789* (Oxford/New York: Oxford University Press, 2005), pp. 563–569.

46. Richard Berleth, *Bloody Mohawk: The French and Indian War and American Revolution on New York's Frontier* (Hensonville, NY: Black Dome Press Corp., 2010), p. 232.

47. Ibid., p. 315.

CHAPTER 3

1. Adams, *Works,* vol. 4, p. 199.

2. Ibid., vol. 6, p. 197.

3. An early version, perhaps, of "If guns are outlawed, only outlaws will have guns."

4. J. Jefferson Looney, ed., *The Papers of Thomas Jefferson: Retirement Series*, vol. 1 (Princeton: Princeton University Press, 2004–), pp. 344, 353, 363.

5. Saul Cornell, *A Well-Regulated Militia: The Founding Fathers and the Origins of Gun Control in America* (Oxford/New York: Oxford University Press, 2006), p. 18; the document cited is a draft resolution by Mason for the Fairfax County Committee of Safety on January 17, 1775.

6. Cornell, *Well-Regulated Militia*, p. 21, and Halbrook, *The Founders' Second Amendment*, p. 138.

7. Brett F. Woods, ed. and annotator, *Letters from France: The Private Diplomatic Correspondence of Benjamin Franklin, 1776–1785* (New York: Algora Publishing, 2006), p. 25.

8. Adams, *Works*, vol. 4, pp. 220–227.

9. Ibid., p. 454.

10. Oscar and Mary Handlin, eds., *The Popular Sources of Political Authority: Documents on the Massachusetts Constitution of 1780* (Cambridge: Belknap Press of Harvard University Press, 1966), pp. 574 and 624.

11. Roy G. Weatherup, "Standing Armies and Armed Citizens: An Historical Analysis of the Second Amendment," *Hastings Constitutional Law Quarterly* (1975), pp. 979–980.

12. Tushnet, *Out of Range*, p. 35.

13. David McCullough, *1776* (New York: Simon and Schuster Paperbacks, 2006), pp. 31, 37–38.

14. Ron Chernow, *Washington: A Life* (New York: Penguin Press, 2010), pp. 373, 375, 389, and passim.

15. Washington's speech in "Rediscovering George Washington," The Claremont Institute, 2002, on PBS.org at www.pbs.org/georgewashington/milestones/newburgh_read.html.

16. Bradford K. Peirce and Charles Hale, eds., *Debates and Proceedings in the Convention of the Commonwealth of Massachusetts held in the year 1788, and which finally ratified the Constitution of the United States* (Boston: William White, 1856), p. 239.

17. Jonathan Elliot, *The Debates in the several State Conventions on the adoption of the Federal Constitution, as recommended by the General Convention at Philadelphia, in 1787, in Five Volumes*, vol. 5 (Philadelphia: J. B. Lippincott and Co., 1861), pp. 440–443.

18. Ibid., p. 465.

19. Ibid., pp. 552–553.

20. Ian Shapiro, ed., *The Federalist Papers: Alexander Hamilton, James Madison, John Jay* (New Haven: Yale University Press, 2009), p. 243.

21. Ibid., pp. 141–143.

22. Ralph Ketcham, ed., *The Anti-Federalist Papers and the Constitutional Convention Debates* (New York: Penguin Putnam, Signet Classic, 2003), pp. 288–292.

23. Ibid., p. 240.

24. Ibid., p. 255.

25. Ibid., text of the Pennsylvania Minority, pp. 237–257.

26. Peirce and Hale, eds., *Debates and Proceedings in the Convention*, pp. 86–87 and 266. See also Pauline Maier, *Ratification: The People Debate the Constitution, 1787–1788* (New York: Simon and Schuster, 2010), pp. 204–205.

27. Ketcham, *The Anti-Federalist Papers*, p. 202.

28. Ibid., pp. 214–215.

29. Halbrook, *The Founders' Second Amendment*, p. 231.

30. For a full discussion of the ratification debate, see Jack N. Rakove, "The Second Amendment: The Highest Stage of Originalism," in *The Second Amendment in Law and History*, ed. Carl T. Bogus (New York: New Press, 2000), pp. 74–116.

31. Levy, *Origins of the Bill of Rights*, p. 282.

32. Ibid., p. 288.

33. Tushnet, *Out of Range*, p. 24.

34. See, for example, Malcolm, *To Keep and Bear Arms*, pp. 159–164.

35. Halbrook, *The Founders' Second Amendment*, p. 259.

36. Ibid., p. 190.

37. Spitzer, *The Right to Bear Arms*, pp. 160–161.

38. Halbrook, *The Founders' Second Amendment*, p. 303.

39. St. George Tucker, *Blackstone's Commentaries: with Notes of Reference, to the Constitution and Laws of the Federal Government of the United States, and of the Commonwealth of Virginia* (Philadelphia: William Young Birch and Abraham Small, 1803), book 1, appendix, p. 273.

40. Saul Cornell, *Whose Right to Bear Arms Did the Second Amendment Protect?* (Boston/New York: Bedford/St. Martin's Press, 2000), p. 82, and DeConde, *Gun Violence in America*, p. 41.

41. Seth Lipsky, *The Citizen's Constitution: An Annotated Guide* (New York: Basic Books, 2009), pp. 74–75.

42. Sawyer, *Our Rifles*, p. 10.

43. William H. Sumner, *An Inquiry into the Importance of the Militia to a Free Commonwealth* (Boston: Cummings and Hilliard, 1823).

44. Joseph Story, *Commentaries on the Constitution of the United States,* vol. 2 (New York: Da Capo Press, 1970), pp. 746–747.

CHAPTER 4

1. Dwight, *Travels in New-England and New-York,* vol. 1, preface, pp. xiv-xv.

2. Ron Chernow, *Alexander Hamilton* (London: Penguin Books, 2004), p. 683.

3. Ibid., pp. 701–718, and Thomas Fleming, *Duel: Alexander Hamilton, Aaron Burr, and the Future of America* (New York: Basic Books, 1999), pp. 314–355.

4. Boorstin, *The Americans,* pp. 208–210.

5. Clayton E. Cramer, *Concealed Weapon Laws of the Early Republic: Dueling, Southern Violence, and Moral Reform* (Westport, CT: Praeger Publishers, 1999), pp. 56, 62–63, and 139–140.

6. Alexis de Tocqueville, *Journey to America,* ed. J. P. Mayer, trans. George Lawrence (New Haven: Yale University Press, 1960), Non-Alphabetic Notebooks 2 and 3, pp. 107–108.

7. Sidney George Fisher, diary entry, quoted in DeConde, *Gun Violence in America,* p. 57.

8. *Aymette v. the State,* 2 Humphreys 154 (Tenn. 1840), and cited in John F. Dillon and S. D. Thompson, eds., *The Central Law Journal* (St. Louis: Soule, Thomas and Wentworth, 1874), vol. 1, p. 273.

9. DeConde, *Gun Violence in America,* p. 52.

10. See Eugene Volokh, "State Constitutional Right to Keep and Bear Arms Provisions, by Date," at www2.law.ucla.edu/volokh/beararms /statedat.htm.

11. *State v. Chandler,* 5 La. Ann. 489, 52 Am. Dec. 599 (1850).

12. *Nunn v. State,* 1 Ga. (1 Kel.) 243 (1846).

13. *English v. State,* 35 Tex. 473, 14 Am. Rep. 374 (1872).

14. Victoria Post Ranney, ed., *The Papers of Frederick Law Olmsted,* vol. 5, *The California Frontier, 1863–65* (Baltimore: Johns Hopkins University Press, 1990), pp. 628–630, 686–687.

15. Winkler, *Gunfight,* pp. 171–172.

16. *State v. Newsom*, 27 N.C. (5 Ired.) 250 (1844).

17. Witold Rybczynski, *A Clearing in the Distance: Frederick Law Olmsted and America in the Nineteenth Century* (New York: Scribner, 1999), p. 139.

18. Quoted by Justice Scalia in Opinion of the Court, *District of Columbia v. Heller,* 554 U.S. 07-290 (2008), pp. 36–37.

19. Eric Foner, *Reconstruction: America's Unfinished Revolution, 1863–1877* (New York: Perennial Classics, HarperCollins, 2002), p. 48.

20. Cornell, *Well-Regulated Militia,* pp. 169–171.

21. See Opinion of the Court in *McDonald et al. v. City of Chicago, Illinois, et al.,* 561 U.S. 08-1521 (2010), pp. 24–25.

22. Cornell, *Well-Regulated Militia,* p. 169.

23. Cited by Justice Scalia in *Heller,* Opinion of the Court, p. 42.

24. Cornell, *Well-Regulated Militia,* p. 174.

25. Foner, *Reconstruction,* pp. 438–439.

CHAPTER 5

1. John Forrest Dillon, "The Right to Keep and Bear Arms for Private and Public Defence," *Central Law Journal,* vol. 1, citations from p. 296 and p. 287.

2. Foner, *Reconstruction,* p. 437.

3. *U.S. v. Cruikshank,* 92 U.S. 542 (1875).

4. *Presser v. State of Illinois,* 116 U.S. 252 (1886).

5. "Mrs. Hetty Green, Menaced, Arms Herself," *New York Times,* May 9, 1902.

6. *United States v. Miller,* 307 U.S. 174 (1939).

7. *Heller,* Stevens, J., dissenting, pp. 2–3.

8. *Lewis v. United States,* 445 U.S. 55, 65 no. 8, 66 (1980).

9. *Quilici v. Village of Morton Grove,* 695 F.2d 261 (7th Cir. 1982), *cert. denied,* 464 U.S. 863 (1983).

10. Stuart R. Hays, "The Right to Bear Arms: A Study in Judicial Misinterpretation," *William and Mary Law Review,* vol. 2, no. 2 (1960), pp. 381–406.

11. Don B. Kates Jr., "Handgun Prohibition and the Original Meaning of the Second Amendment," *Michigan Law Review,* vol. 82, no. 2 (November 1983), pp. 217–225.

12. Ibid., pp. 265–266.

13. Winkler, *Gunfight,* p. 105.

14. Sanford Levinson, "The Embarrassing Second Amendment," *Yale Law Journal,* vol. 99 [99 *Yale L.J.* 661 (1989)], as transcribed in http://www.firearmsandliberty.com/embar.html.

15. Robert J. Spitzer, "Heller's Manufactured Gun Rights Can Be Traced to a Flawed Law Review Article" (2008), George Mason University, History News Network, at http://hnn.us/articles/51600.html.

16. Glenn Harlan Reynolds, "A Critical Guide to the Second Amendment," *Tennessee Law Review,* vol. 62 (1995), pp. 461–511.

17. See also Adam Liptak, "A Liberal Case for the Individual Right to Own Guns Helps Sway the Federal Judiciary," *New York Times,* May 6, 2007.

18. *U.S. v. Emerson,* 270 F.3d 203, pp. 72–73. See http://www.caselaw.findlaw.com/us-5th-circuit/1332436.html.

19. Office of Legal Counsel, Department of Justice, "Whether the Constitution Secures an Individual Right," Memorandum for the Attorney General, August 24, 2004, at www.justice.gov/olc/secondamendment2.pdf, and Joseph Story, *A Familiar Exposition of the Constitution of the United States* (New York: Harper and Brothers, 1865), p. 264.

20. 15 U.S.C. 7901 (a)(2).

21. Linda Greenhouse, "Case Touches a 2nd Amendment Nerve," *New York Times,* November 13, 2007.

22. *Shelly Parker, et al., v. District of Columbia,* U.S. Court of Appeals for the District of Columbia Circuit, No. 04-7041, decided March 9, 2007.

23. John Smilie, Pennsylvania Ratifying Convention, November 28, 1787, in *The Founders' Constitution,* chap. 8, document 16, at http://www.press pubs.uchicago.edu/founders/documents/v1ch8s16.html.

24. Letters from the Federal Farmer to the Republican, III, October 10, 1787: as reproduced in infoplease, Anti-Federalist Writings, at www.infoplease.com/t/hist/antifederalist/.

25. Letters from the Federal Farmer XVIII, January 25, 1788.

26. *District of Columbia v. Heller,* Opinion of the Court, p. 19.

27. Ibid., p. 22.

28. Ibid., p. 26.

29. Ibid., pp. 4, 63.

30. J. Harvie Wilkinson III, *Cosmic Constitutional Theory: Why Americans Are Losing Their Inalienable Right to Self-Governance* (Oxford/New York: Oxford University Press, 2012), p. 58.

31. Josh Horwitz, "Dick Heller: In His Own Words," at www.huffing tonpost.com, September 23, 2008.

32. *Dick Anthony Heller, et al., v. District of Columbia, et al.,* U.S. Court of Appeals for the District of Columbia Circuit, No. 10-7036, decided October 4, 2011.

33. *McDonald v. Chicago,* Opinion of the Court, p. 1.

34. Ibid., opinion of Alito, J., p. 36.

35. Ibid., Breyer, J., dissenting, pp. 36 and 31.

36. Wilkinson, *Cosmic Constitutional Theory,* p. 58.

37. *McDonald v. Chicago,* Breyer, J., dissenting, p. 20.

38. "State Gun-Carry Law Unconstitutional, Federal Judge Rules," *Baltimore Sun,* at www.baltimoresun.com, March 5, 2012.

CHAPTER 6

1. Hemenway, *Private Guns, Public Health,* pp. 2–3.

2. U.S. Census Bureau, 2011 Statistical Abstract, Crime Rates by State, 2007 and 2008, and by type, 2008, table 304.

3. *Heller,* Breyer's dissent, p. 21.

4. Jo Craven McGinty, "The Rich, the Famous, the Armed," *New York Times,* February 18, 2011.

5. Figures from "National Crime Victimization Survey," Bureau of Justice Statistics, Department of Justice, Special Report, 2003; Annual Report, 2008; Federal Bureau of Investigation, 2008, "Crime in the United States." And in Hemenway, *Private Guns, Public Health,* p. 114.

6. The National Opinion Research Center at the University of Chicago has conducted a General Social Survey since 1972 that asks the question: "Do you happen to have in your home (if house: or garage) any guns or revolvers?" Since 1980, those who answer that they do have been asked, "Do any of these guns personally belong to you?" The decline, citing the GSS, was reported by the Violence Policy Center in 2010.

7. "Deaths: Final Data for 2007," Department of Health and Human Services, Centers for Disease Control and Prevention, National Vital Statistics Reports. FBI figures from FBI Uniform Crime Reports 2010, at www .fbi.gov/about-us/cjis/ucr/crime-in-the-u.s/2010/crime-in-the-u.s.-2010 /tables/10shrtbl08.xls. See also Hemenway, *Private Guns, Public Health,* p. 3.

8. Ketcham, *The Anti-Federalist Papers,* p. 202.

9. Chris W. Cox, executive director, NRA-ILA, letter to NRA members, February 8, 2010.

10. Barry Goldwater, "Why Gun Control Laws Don't Work," *Reader's Digest,* December 1975.

11. "Deaths: Final Data for 2007," CDC, and Hemenway, *Private Guns, Public Health,* p. 108.

12. McGinty, "The Rich, the Famous, the Armed."

13. "Ex-Marine Arrested on Gun Charge Had Poor Record, Manhattan Prosecutor Says," *New York Times,* February 29, 2012; "Ex-Marine from Indiana Takes Deal on Gun Charge," *New York Times,* March 21, 2012.

14. Report of Jeffrey Fagan, http://ccrjustice.org/files/Expert_Report_JeffreyFagan.pdf; "Street Stops by the Police Hit a New High," *New York Times,* February 23, 2011; "A Few Blocks, Four Years, 52,000 Police Stops," *New York Times,* July 12, 2010.

15. "Police Street Stops Hit a Record, Rising 14%," *New York Times,* February 15, 2012; "Taking On Police Tactic, Critics Hit Racial Divide," *New York Times,* March 23, 2012.

16. "At Council Hearing, Kelly Fights Back on Stop-and-Frisk Tactics," *New York Times,* March 16, 2012; "Police and Mayor Back Plan to Curtail Marijuana Arrests," *New York Times,* June 5, 2012.

17. James D. Wright, "Ten Essential Observations on Guns in America," *Society,* vol. 32, no. 3 (March–April 1995).

18. Interview with Jumaane Williams, New York City, January 25, 2011.

19. "City Officer Pleads Guilty in Gun-Smuggling Case," *New York Times,* February 7, 2012; "Three Former Officers Plead Guilty in Gun-Smuggling Case," *New York Times,* February 27, 2012.

20. Brian A. Monahan and Tod W. Burke, "Project Exile: Combating Gun Violence in America—Statistical Data Included," *FBI Law Enforcement Bulletin,* October 2001.

21. Edwin E. Hamilton, "Prelude to Project Safe Neighborhoods: The Richmond, Virginia Experience," *Police Foundation Reports,* January 2004.

22. "The Homicide That Didn't Happen," *Chicago Tribune,* February 9, 2011.

23. See Alex Kotlowitz, "Blocking the Transmission of Violence," *New York Times Magazine,* May 4, 2008.

24. NPR, March 27, 2011.

25. Data cited by Caroline Wolf Harlow, in Bureau of Justice Statistics Special Report, "Firearms Use by Offenders," November 2001.

26. Anthony A. Braga, David M. Kennedy, Anne M. Piel, and Elin J. Waring, "Reducing Gun Violence: The Boston Gun Project's Operation Ceasefire," U.S. Department of Justice, Office of Justice Programs, National Institute of Justice, 2001, pp. 28, 43, 27, 19.

27. See www.atf.gov/statistics/download/trace-data/2009/2009 -trace-data-new-york-nyc.pdf.

28. "Four Officers Are Shot in Brooklyn; Assailant Is Critically Wounded," *New York Times*, April 8, 2012.

29. See www.gunshowundercover.org/video, AZ Illegal Sale #1.

30. Garen J. Wintemute, Anthony A. Braga, and David M. Kennedy, "Private Party Gun Sales, Regulation, and Public Safety," *New England Journal of Medicine*, June 30, 2010.

31. California, Colorado, Connecticut, Hawaii, Illinois, Iowa, Maryland, Massachusetts, Michigan, Nebraska, New Jersey, New York, North Carolina, Oregon, Pennsylvania, and Rhode Island.

32. Colorado, Illinois, New York, and Oregon.

33. U.S. Department of Justice, Bureau of Justice Statistics, "Survey of State Procedures Related to Firearm Sales, 2005," table 6, p. 77, updated by "Trace the Guns: The Link Between Gun Laws and Interstate Trafficking," *Mayors Against Illegal Guns*, September 2010, p. 14.

34. David Olinger, "Hi-Point Maker Feels Mix of Pride, Pain," *Denver Post*, August 1, 1999, at http://www.extras.denverpost.com/news/shoto801a.htm.

35. David S. Fallis, "Virginia Gun Dealers: Small Number Supply Most Guns Tied to Crimes," *Washington Post*, October 25, 2010.

36. BuffaloNews.com, April 26, 2010, updated August 21, 2010. The lawsuit in State Supreme Court in Buffalo is *Daniel Williams and Edward Williams v. Beemiller, Inc., et al.* See www.bradycampaign.org/xshare/pdf /stateleg/williams-complaint7-28-2005.pdf, and www.buffalonews.com /city/article44977.ece.

CHAPTER 7

1. Michael Reagan, one of President Reagan's sons, wrote after the mid-2011 mass shooting in Norway by Anders Behring Breivik: "How long would the Norway gunman have lasted in Texas or any state where concealed-carry laws are on the books? I ran a survey while on a cruise: in Texas, 3 minutes; in Montana, 7 to 8 minutes; in Arizona, 2 minutes; and in Nevada, 3 to 5 minutes." The sixty-nine people who died, many

of them teenagers, were unarmed because of Norway's strict gun laws, Reagan wrote: "Had just one of them been armed, Breivik could have been stopped dead and lives would have been spared."

2. Marc Lacey, "Lawmakers Debate Effects of Weapons on Campus," *New York Times,* February 27, 2011.

3. Marc Lacey, "Governor Says No to Guns on Campus," *New York Times,* April 19, 2011.

4. *United States of America v. James Francis Barton, Jr.,* 09-2211, U.S. Court of Appeals for the Third Circuit, at www.ca3.uscourts.gov /opinarch/092211p.pdf.

5. Joseph Edward Olson, "The Minnesota Citizens' Personal Protection Act of 2003: History and Commentary," *Hamline Journal of Public Law and Policy,* vol. 25, no. 1 (Fall 2003).

6. Ibid., p. 39.

7. See, for the thesis, John R. Lott Jr., *More Guns, Less Crime: Understanding Crime and Gun Control Laws,* 2nd ed. (Chicago: University of Chicago Press, 2000); and for a thorough critique of the thesis, Tushnet, *Out of Range,* chap. 4, "Gun Control and Public Policy."

8. Olson, "Minnesota Citizens' Personal Protection Act," p. 28.

9. Ibid., pp. 50–51.

10. Ibid., pp. 68–71.

11. State of Minnesota, Department of Public Safety, Bureau of Criminal Apprehension, 2009 Permit to Carry Report, March 1, 2010.

12. Hemenway, *Private Guns, Public Health,* p. 281.

13. "Dayton Vetoes Gun Bill, Saying Residents Already Have Defense Rights," *StarTribune,* at www.startribune.com, March 6, 2012.

CHAPTER 8

1. Levinson, "The Embarrassing Second Amendment," 99 *Yale L.J.* 661 (1989).

2. Jackie Calmes, "Administration Invites N.R.A. to Meeting on Gun Policies, but It Declines," *New York Times,* March 15, 2011.

3. Winkler, *Gunfight,* pp. 63–74. As marksmen, despite the NRA's early efforts, Americans weren't much better by the time they went into World War I, according to Charles Winthrop Sawyer, a firearms and ammunition expert, who wrote in *Our Rifles,* a book published in 1920, that "American soldiers, as a body unskilled marksmen, fired about 7,000 shots for each casualty." "Now comes again the ancient propaganda, spread by a vicious

few, of international disarmament and everlasting peace," he lamented. "This pernicious doctrine, as old as nations themselves, and now proclaimed anew on the one hand by those who are educationally or mentally defective and on the other by seekers of gain who are knaves, is dangerous to all nations and especially menacing to the strength, the safety, and even the existence of our own United States." Creating "national expertness" with the rifle would ensure that the country remained strong during peace, Sawyer wrote. "In the days of our American ancestors the United States maintained its precarious existence only because every man was a user of arms in time of peace."

4. Cornell, *Well-Regulated Militia*, pp. 214–215.

5. Stephen Sanetti interview, Southport, CT, April 26, 2012.

6. Adam Winkler, HuffPost Politics, April 12, 2012.

7. "'Stand Your Ground' Bill Under New Scrutiny After Florida Killing," *Anchorage Daily News*, at www.adn.com/, March 27, 2012.

8. "Regulating Guns in America: An Evaluation and Comparative Analysis of Federal, State and Selected Local Gun Laws, at www.lcav .org/publications-briefs/reports_analyses/RegGuns.entire.report.pdf.

9. FBI letter, October 21, 2008, to Mayor Michael Bloomberg, at www.mayorsagainstillegalguns.org/downloads/pdf/FBI_NICS_Data _response.pdf.

10. "We believe that people adjudicated mentally incompetent should be prevented from buying guns. That's the law. But it can't be enforced because those records are often sealed. So we advocate that records of court-declared mental incompetents be unsealed and made available to the instant check system. Believe it or not, insanities like John Hinckley's would not prevent a gun purchase today because most mental records are invisible to the instant check system. Let's close the Hinckley loophole!" NRA Annual Meeting of Members, Denver, CO, 1999, from Wayne LaPierre Address to Members.

11. Michael Luo, "Some with Histories of Mental Illness Petition to Get Their Gun Rights Back," *New York Times,* July 3, 2011.

12. Michael Luo, "Felons Finding It Easy to Regain Gun Rights," *New York Times,* November 14, 2011.

13. Legal Community Against Violence, "Regulating Guns in America: An Evaluation and Comparative Analysis of Federal, State, and Selected Local Gun Laws," p. viii. San Francisco, CA, 2006. www.lcav.org.

14. Hemenway, *Private Guns, Public Health*, pp. 164–165.

15. Ed Connolly and Michael Luo, "States Struggle to Disarm People Who've Lost Right to Own Guns," *New York Times*, February 6, 2011.

16. Legal Community Against Violence, "Regulating Guns," p. xii.

17. Jeff Rossen, "Anyone Can Buy Guns, No Questions Asked," *Today*, MSNBC.com, February 9, 2012.

18. Evaluation and Inspections Division, Office of the Inspector General, Department of Justice, "Review of ATF's Project Gunrunner, November 2010," at www.justice.gov/oig/reports/ATF/e1101.pdf.

19. Gun Safety Foundation, "Selling Crime: A Handful of Gun Stores Fuel Criminals," January 2004, and Hemenway, *Private Guns, Public Health*, p. 143.

20. Fallis, "Virginia Gun Dealers," *Washington Post*, October 25, 2010.

21. Legal Community Against Violence, "Regulating Guns," pp. 145–154.

22. *Today*, NBC, March 3, 2000.

23. See www.projectchildsafe.org.

24. Legal Community Against Violence, "Regulating Guns," pp. 234–238.

25. 18 U.S.C. 922(z)(3).

26. Legal Community Against Violence, "Regulating Guns," pp. 221–228.

27. Hemenway, *Private Guns, Public Health*, p. 214.

28. Ibid., p. 94.

29. "Guns and Children: A Call for Great Adult Responsibility," cited in ibid., p. 149.

30. Connecticut, Massachusetts, Michigan, New Jersey, New York, Ohio, and Rhode Island.

31. Legal Community Against Violence, "Regulating Guns," pp. xiv–xv.

32. "Review of ATF's Project Gunrunner, November 2010."

33. Chris W. Cox, "Power Grab," *American Rifleman*, March 2011.

34. *CBS News*, February 23, 2011.

35. Chris W. Cox, "Border Battle Heats Up," *American Rifleman*, May 2011.

36. Sari Horwitz and James V. Grimaldi, "ATF's Oversight Limited in Face of Gun Lobby," *Washington Post*, October 26, 2010.

37. Office of the Inspector General, Department of Justice, "Inspections of Firearms Dealers by the Bureau of Alcohol, Tobacco, Firearms

and Explosives, Evaluation and Inspection Report I-2004-005," at www
.justice.gov/oig/reports/ATF/e0405/final.pdf.

38. John R. Hansen interview, Southport, CT, April 26, 2012; Stephen
Sanetti interview, Southport, CT, April 26, 2012.

39. Bob Lesmeister, "Group Petitions ATF over Rules Adopted Without Required Notice," *New Gun Week,* May 1, 2010.

40. ATF, "Study on the Importability of Certain Shotguns," January
2011.

41. NRA-ILA statement, January 28, 2011.

42. *Heller,* Opinion of the Court, p. 54.

43. *McDonald v. Chicago,* Opinion of Alito, J., p. 40.

44. Richard Feldman, "The NRA's Main Target? Its Members' Check-
books," *Washington Post,* December 16, 2007.

45. United Nations General Assembly Document A/63/334, August
26, 2008, "Towards an Arms Trade Treaty: Establishing Common International Standards for the Import, Export, and Transfer of Conventional
Arms," p. 14.

INDEX

Craig R. Whitney spent his entire professional career as a reporter, foreign correspondent, and editor at the *New York Times*, where he was assistant managing editor in charge of standards and ethics when he retired in 2009. He is the author most recently of *All the Stops*. He lives in New York City.

PublicAffairs is a publishing house founded in 1997. It is a tribute to the standards, values, and flair of three persons who have served as mentors to countless reporters, writers, editors, and book people of all kinds, including me.

I. F. STONE, proprietor of *I. F. Stone's Weekly*, combined a commitment to the First Amendment with entrepreneurial zeal and reporting skill and became one of the great independent journalists in American history. At the age of eighty, Izzy published *The Trial of Socrates*, which was a national bestseller. He wrote the book after he taught himself ancient Greek.

BENJAMIN C. BRADLEE was for nearly thirty years the charismatic editorial leader of *The Washington Post*. It was Ben who gave the *Post* the range and courage to pursue such historic issues as Watergate. He supported his reporters with a tenacity that made them fearless and it is no accident that so many became authors of influential, best-selling books.

ROBERT L. BERNSTEIN, the chief executive of Random House for more than a quarter century, guided one of the nation's premier publishing houses. Bob was personally responsible for many books of political dissent and argument that challenged tyranny around the globe. He is also the founder and longtime chair of Human Rights Watch, one of the most respected human rights organizations in the world.

• • •

For fifty years, the banner of Public Affairs Press was carried by its owner Morris B. Schnapper, who published Gandhi, Nasser, Toynbee, Truman, and about 1,500 other authors. In 1983, Schnapper was described by *The Washington Post* as "a redoubtable gadfly." His legacy will endure in the books to come.

Peter Osnos, *Founder and Editor-at-Large*